Praise for *Transforming Depression*

"What makes Rosen's work so alive is that he lets the material speak for itself. . . . The urgency of its subject matter transcends doctrinal differences of theory and goes straight for the jugular."
    —*Psychological Perspectives*

"Spellbinding. . . . This is an important book, one giving hope that sorrow can be transformed to joy and that the human spirit can soar again."
    —*Litchfield County Times*

"This sensitive, intelligent approach to depression opens new symbolic and practical meanings. Readers are inspired to see depression as a paradox of illness and transformation that demands a broader understanding than psychiatry has typically allowed. Useful and wise, this book will help those who suffer from depression and their caregivers."
    —Polly Young-Eisendrath, author of *You're Not What I Expected: Learning to Love the Opposite Sex*

"Rosen's approach to depression is sound, because it honors the natural movement of the soul in becoming depressed in the first place; because it does not cheat the self's demand that at least some part of the ego needs to die; and because it understands that a creative process is the way to accomplish this dying and yet preserve the life of the individual who must undergo this perilous transformation."
    —John Beebe, author of *Integrity in Depth*

"As clinical psychology seems increasingly dominated by pharmacological treatments, it is refreshing indeed to encounter a therapy that draws on the creative resources of the individual's own unconscious to guide the process of psychic renewal. For those who are depressed or who have a depressed family member, this book could be a lifesaver."
    —*Intuition* magazine

TRANSFORMING DEPRESSION

On The Hudson
Jung
BOOK SERIES

The Jung on the Hudson Book Series was instituted by the New York Center for Jungian Studies in 1997. This ongoing series is designed to present books that will be of interest to individuals of all fields, as well as mental health professionals, who are interested in exploring the relevance of the psychology and ideas of C. G. Jung to their personal lives and professional activities.

For more information about this series and the New York Center for Jungian Studies contact: Aryeh Maidenbaum, Ph.D., New York Center for Jungian Studies, 41 Park Avenue, Suite 1D, New York, NY 10016, telephone (212) 689-8238, fax (212) 889-7634.

For more information about becoming part of this series contact: Nicolas-Hays, P. O. Box 2039, York Beach, ME 03910-2039,

TRANSFORMING
DEPRESSION

Healing the Soul through Creativity

DAVID ROSEN, M.D.

NICOLAS-HAYS, INC.
York Beach, Maine

First published in 2002 by
NICOLAS-HAYS, INC.
P. O. Box 2039
York Beach, ME 03910-2039

Distributed to the trade by
Red Wheel/Weiser, LLC
P. O. Box 612
York Beach, ME 03910-0612
www.redwheelweiser.com

The following have given permission to use extended quotations from previously copyrighted
works: From Henry Miller: *The Colosus of Maroussi*, copyright © 1941 by Henry Miller,
reprinted by permission of New Directions Publishing Corporation; From "Modern Medicine
and the Healing Process," *Humane Medicine*, Volume 5, Autumn 1989, reprinted by permission
of the publisher; Poem #254 by Emily Dickinson from *The Complete Poems of Emily Dickinson*,
Little, Brown, and Company; From The Pharos, Volume 50, Number 3, copyright © 1987 by
Alpha Omega Alpha Honor Medical Society, reprinted by permission; From "Choruses from
'The Rock,'" from *Collected Poems 1909–1962* by T. S. Eliot. Copyright © 1963 by T. S. Eliot.
Reprinted by permission of Faber & Faber Ltd., London.

Library of Congress Cataloging-in-Publication Data Available on Request

Cover design by Sky *Peck* Design
Typeset in 10/12 Aldine 721

Printed in Canada

09 08 06 05 04 03 02
7 6 5 4 3 2 1

The paper used in this publication meets the minimum requirements of the
American National Standard for Information Sciences—Permanence of Paper
for Printed Library Materials Z39.48–1992 (R1997).

To my daughters, Sarah, Laura, and Rachel, who
have stood by me, encouraged me, and supported
my own anima development, creativity, and contact
with my soul. My dedication to the feminine is
natural since the *sui generis* Soul, the archetypal
feminine, is the only hope for humankind
individually and collectively.

"Choose Thou the darkness where
Our light must shine
Lighting the path, however dimly
To those who follow after."

—SANSKRIT PRAYER

"There is but one truly serious
philosophical problem and that
is suicide."

—CAMUS

"If we take people as they are,
we make them worse. If we treat
them as if they were what they
ought to be, we help them to
become what they are capable of
becoming."

—GOETHE

CONTENTS

PART I. BACKGROUND AND CONTEXT

PART II. AN INNOVATIVE WAY OF HEALING

PART III. FOUR TRANSFORMING JOURNEYS

PART IV. SPIRAL OF CHANGE: SYMBOLIC DEATH
AND NEW LIFE

ILLUSTRATIONS

COLOR PLATES (following page 158)

ACKNOWLEDGMENTS

I acknowledge with heartfelt thanks and gratitude: my parents, Barbara and Max Rosen, who taught me respect for ideas, revealed the creative process, demonstrated courage to communicate new beliefs and concepts, and by example showed me how to survive difficult times; my analysts, both Freudian and Jungian, who have been my healers and teachers: Fred Alston, John Perry, Kay Bradway, Paul Kugler, and James Aylward; my Jungian training analysts, who have been my teachers and healers: Donald Sandner, Daryl Sharp, Marion Woodman, Harry Wilmer, Joseph Wakefield, Julia Morgan, and Mary Eileen Dobson; my patients and students who have taught me more about education (knowledge through experience) and individuation (the healing process toward wholeness) than I could have ever imagined; my Jungian colleagues, for all their honest and helpful feedback (specifically I want to mention James Hall, Jan Bauer, Julia McAfee, and Jane Wheelwright); and my friend, Peter Rutter, who suggested, in the first place, that I submit my manuscript to Jeremy P. Tarcher.

I want to thank Jay Laengrich, a former student of mine, for research work. An important thanks is due Hadley Smith, artist, designer, psychologist, and friend, for her valuable input regarding what illustrations to include in the text. Hadley's help went way beyond my initial request. She reviewed the text and made significant comments and suggestions. Arnold Vedlitz, Luis Cifuentes, Maria-Cristina Garcia, Ann Gardner, Laura Torbet, and Joel Weishaus deserve special mention. Each graciously functioned as reader and critic. Mary Lenn Dixon and Faith

Short, too, served as readers and editorial consultants. I am also grateful to Nancy Rosen, my sister, who is also an editor, for feedback regarding specific sections of the book. I want to recognize Jane Blaffer Owen for her sensitive reading of the text and for providing time and space for me to write at historic New Harmony, Indiana. In addition, I want to thank Vicky Newman (for her early editorial help with the cases), Chrissie Battocletti, Louis Lucko, Jo Lynn Ross, Amy Hunnicutt, and Jody Trenckmann for clerical and editorial work; they often went beyond the call of duty. Jody, listed last, actually did the most.

I want to single out Jack Maguire for his invaluable assistance. Jack's expertise in the area of dreams, his editorial and writing skills, helped to make this volume much more understandable.

I want to acknowledge and thank David Stanford, my editor at Penguin, and Ned Leavitt, my agent, for being midwives to the birth of the first paperback edition. In addition, I express my heartfelt gratitude to Betty Lundsted for the rebirth of this Nicolas-Hays paperback edition.

The case illustrations in Chapters 6, 7, 8, and 9 involve spontaneous productions from the unconscious of each patient. These are manifestations of the therapeutic technique called active imagination described and discussed in Chapter 5. I want to express my sincere thanks to these individuals for agreeing to share their healing images and their clinical histories. Their identifying features and stories have been changed to preserve their anonymity.

Finally, I owe a debt of gratitude to Frank N. McMillan and his family (Mabel, Frank III, Molly, and Andrew) for their generous support of my creative pursuits in analytical psychology.

PROLOGUE

"After all, it is no more surprising to
be born twice than to be born once."

—Voltaire

This is a book about transforming depression and discovering a meaningful alternative to suicide. It grew out of painful personal experience, followed by many years of study and practice as doctor, psychiatrist, and psychoanalyst. Twenty-five years ago, when the reality of suicide arose, I did not recognize the psychological crisis that had the potential to either creatively improve or destroy my life. Nor did I connect my personal crisis to ancient and universal, or archetypal, patterns related to death.

A Personal Account

My interest in overcoming depression and suicidal impulses owes a great deal to several profoundly unsettling events in my youth and early adulthood. These are not unusual events; rather, they are so common as to be virtually archetypal, and so are worth reviewing.

My first serious encounter with depression occurred when I was fifteen. Finished with my sophomore year at Central High School in Springfield, Missouri, I had landed my first real job, making milk shakes at McDonald's. I was looking forward to a uniquely grand summer of money, fun, and freedom—a summer that began with the release of Elvis Presley's "It's Now or Never."

Suddenly, that splendid vision of summer was shattered. One day my mother said, "Pack up! We're going to spend the weekend with your grandmother." That weekend turned into two weeks. From my grandmother's place in Kansas City, we moved to Nevada, where my mother divorced my father. So much for my grand summer. Cut off from my home, my father, and my friends, I felt as if I were dying. But I did not feel hopeless; and herein lay the key to my psychological survival.

In retrospect, I understand that I was suffering from a reactive depression to my parents' divorce and my dislocation from home.[1] As a result, I went through a natural, albeit unconscious, grieving process. In the short term, this process enabled me to mourn the losses I had just endured and to adapt to my new situation. In the long term, it primed me to deal with future crises.

The first of these crises occurred two years later. By that time my mother, brother, three sisters, and I had settled south of San Francisco near Santa Cruz, California. My father had refused to help my mother financially, hoping to force her to return to him, so we were living primitively by comparison to our previous lifestyle: apple crates for cupboards, legs on doors with cushions on the tops for couches, and sleeping mats on the floor for beds. My mother worked far away from home, and I worked after school, often not getting home until nine or ten o'clock at night. In my loneliness, my new friend Dan and his family were an invaluable source of support. Dan's father Milt, in particular, helped me to shoulder my burdens and maintain a positive outlook toward life. Never angry or discouraged, Milt acted as a surrogate father: he accepted me, listened to me, and cared for me. I practically lived with Dan and his family.

The summer after I graduated from high school, I traveled to Missouri to visit relatives and friends. When I returned, my mother had shocking news: Milt had put a shotgun to his head and killed himself. Initially, I could only cry "No!" over and over again. When I asked "Why?" Mother answered, "I don't know. No one does." From my vantage point, Milt had everything: a wonderful family and home, and a good job that he liked. I thought to myself that if Milt could commit suicide, anyone could. Even, possibly, I could.

This awareness was a turning point in my thoughts about suicide. Although I had no other basis for imagining that I was capable of suicide, and despite the fact that the thought of committing suicide repelled me, I had made a vitally important acknowledgment: No one is immune from an inclination toward suicide. Conversely, it may be impossible to detect that inclination in someone else, even if you are quite close to that person.

A few years later, I had additional evidence of this. Sam was a friend who grew up with me in Springfield, who attended the University of California at Berkeley while I was there, and who moved back to Missouri to enter a graduate program in creative writing at the same time that I started medical school at the University of Missouri. Having known him most of his life, I felt my impression of his personality was pretty accurate. For the most part, he was outgoing, adventuresome, loving, funny, and happy. On occasion, however, he was depressed and withdrawn. Since he was a poet, it seemed appropriate that he should exhibit such an intriguingly contradictory blend of characteristics. No matter how far down his spirits sank, it seemed inevitable that they would rise again.

One glorious sunny day in October, Sam brought his customary jug of wine over to my house, and we sat in the grass beneath a tree talking about the troubles he was having with his wife. He wanted to leave her, but he hesitated because of the effect it might have on their young daughter. Adding to his despondency was the fact that he couldn't get more of his poetry published. I was used to functioning as a sounding board for his complaints—and this may have been the problem: Sounding boards don't really listen. Besides, I was preoccupied with medical school and my own marital problems. Sam said he felt like ending his life; but in my understandable desire to get him off this track, I simply responded, "Oh, things aren't *that* bad. They'll get better. Don't worry!"

Sam went home, picked up a kitchen knife, undressed, got into the bathtub, stabbed himself seven times in the stomach, and cut his left wrist all around to the bone. His wife found him and rushed him to the hospital, in time for surgeons to save his life. Nevertheless, it was apparent to everyone who knew him that his soul was gone. Neither his doctors nor his friends could bring it back. He hanged himself six months later.[2]

This painful history, in which I'd been so intimately involved, left me with a legacy of questions that clamored for answers. How could Sam have so betrayed his muse, along with all of us who loved him? How could I have missed realizing that he really did mean to commit suicide? How could I have stopped him? How could anyone or anything have stopped him?

Wrenching as these encounters with depression and suicide had been—the break-up of my childhood home, the shocking loss of

Milt, and the less surprising but even more searing loss of Sam—they were not as unbearable as the circumstances surrounding the end of my first marriage, which unfolded not long after I entered medical school. The enormous demands imposed upon my time and energy by the end of the first year in medical school strained our relationship to the limit. My wife, an actress, wanted to go away alone during the summer break, to perform summer-stock repertoire at a theater on Hilton Head Island in South Carolina. Unfortunately (or fortunately), I insisted on accompanying her.

One night, as I sat waiting for her in a bar, she walked in with her leading man. Ignoring me, she went on to demonstrate that her romantic involvement with this man did not stop when the acting did. As I watched the two of them, afraid of what might happen if I vented the rage I was feeling, I ran out of the bar, jumped into my car and sped wildly through the narrow and winding island roads. I envisioned crashing into an embankment, or going off a bridge, thinking death would be far better than the pain I was living through.

Then something very unusual happened. I spun the car into a field, stopped it, got out, and began running through the moonlit, junglelike terrain. As I ran, I could see myself from above, disappearing and reappearing beneath the trees. The quality of the vision, and with it my state of mind, became clearer and clearer—until finally, I heard a voice say, "Leave!" Later I came to realize that this inner voice issued from what has been termed the "Real Self."[3] The uncanny sensation from this experience remains my only out-of-body experience, which I now understand as one that is beyond ego.[4] Through this extravagant act of physical expression, I had unwittingly found my soul and spiritual center, and my Self had found me. My self-preservation instinct took command of my fate.

I left Hilton Head immediately, knowing and accepting that my marriage was finished. But the fact that I had been rescued did not mean my conscious mind was spared feelings of despair, helplessness, and worthlessness. I drove to New York City and consulted a psychiatrist, who was also a family friend. I found myself saying words to him that echoed words I had heard from Sam. "I'm a failure," I blurted out. "It's hopeless. Why live?"

His reply was simple and wise, and it has shaped my response to many setbacks ever since. "You are not a failure," he said. "You failed at a marriage."

What I Learned from My Experience

The strangeness surrounding this traumatic episode left an indelible impression on my life and on my practice as physician, psychiatrist, and analyst. I came to realize that my spontaneous out-of-body-ego experience was an example of what I now call *egocide,* the letting-go of a hurt and hurting dominant ego-image or identity. The suffix *-cide* means kill. However, egocide is a symbolic killing of the ego that is experienced as ego death: a sacrifice of the ego to the Self, a higher principle. Egocide is the core strategy for transforming depression, and the heart and soul of this book. In my case, it was the ego-image I had of myself as a husband that was sacrificed. When I released that image, I found I could surrender to a higher power within myself—the Self. [5]

From this powerful incident, I learned to appreciate that egocide represents an antidote to suicide, a way out of depression by affirming life instead of rejecting it. But egocide does not necessarily work like a switch, changing a sad person instantly to a happy one. A person who has experienced egocide still has to go through a grieving process for the ego-image that has been left behind, as I did after driving away from South Carolina. Nevertheless, the ability to let go and surrender does represent a transcendence over the limitations imposed by the previous dominant ego-image, and it does clear the way for an eventual transformation of one's ego and self-identity. (I am using ego to represent an awareness of one's conscious identity, and self to represent the person's unique personal being and expressions of self-esteem and self-realization.)

By the time I finished medical school, I had two significant leads from personal experience as to how one commits egocide. Creatively redirecting my despair on Hilton Head Island by racing through treacherous territory, I had, quite literally, risen above my suicidal ego-image as a rejected husband. Also, during my undergraduate and medical school years, painting had helped me to capture and vanquish depressive states. I was nineteen when I first learned this lesson as an undergraduate at the University of California at Berkeley. It did not come to me, however, in the classroom. Immersed in a period of deep depression, waiting for it to pass, I was inexplicably moved to paint my first emotional landscape—a spontaneous, free-style rendering of what I felt to be my state of mind at the time (see

Plate I). Much to my wonder, this single activity completely dis-
pelled my melancholic mood.

Only years later, when I read A. Lommel's *Shamanism: The Beginnings of Art*, did I fully appreciate why I had been able to paint
myself out of my depression. From the beginning of human history
to the present day, shamans have functioned as healers in tribal
societies, assuming a multifaceted role that is analogous to the combined roles of a medical doctor, a psychotherapist or analyst, and a
religious leader in our modern world. A shaman becomes a shaman
by facing a personal, life-threatening illness (usually severe depression) and overcoming it, using creative activities such as drawing,
crafting art objects, chanting poetry, or journeying (an intense, almost trancelike form of visualization) to do so. After self-ordination
and tribal acceptance, the shaman uses his or her creative talents to
assist others in dealing with their physical and emotional problems.
Thus, the value of what I had done by instinct to transform my own
depressed mood was confirmed by history. Today I see it confirmed
again and again in the lives of patients in psychotherapy and analysis.

Ahead of me, as a medical school graduate, lay the pursuit on a
professional level of further knowledge about depression and suicide.[6] Appropriately, one of the earliest and most important destina-
tions in that pursuit turned out to be the Golden Gate Bridge.

More Clues: What Survivors of Suicide Say

Aside from being a singularly handsome structure in its own right,
the Golden Gate Bridge has exceptional symbolic beauty as a pas-
sageway between city and country, harbor and ocean, sea and sky.
It is little wonder, therefore, that the Golden Gate Bridge is the place
of choice for people planning their own leaps from life to death. Since
the bridge opened in 1937, it is estimated that over two thousand
individuals have jumped to their deaths, making it a suicide shrine.[7]
Jumping is almost invariably fatal: The distance from rail to water is
about 255 feet; a jumper hits the water at about 75 miles per hour.
Nevertheless, one percent of the people who jump do survive.

As a resident in psychiatry at the University of California Medical
Center in San Francisco, I was interested in finding out what it was
like to confront and survive such a grandly staged and apparently
certain suicide attempt. This interest was sparked by reading a front-

page newspaper account of a survivor of a leap off the Golden Gate Bridge. I decided to formulate a research study and interview this person and other such survivors. When I discovered that there were only eight known survivors still living, I expanded my field of possible interviewees to include survivors of jumps from the San Francisco–Oakland Bay Bridge, which is also an imposing platform for committing suicide and offers the same low odds of survival. Initially, I was able to set up interviews with six of the eight Golden Gate Bridge survivors and one of the two San Francisco–Oakland Bay Bridge survivors. Later, I interviewed three more survivors of jumps off the Golden Gate Bridge.

In addition to gaining insights from these survivors that might be useful in detecting and preventing possible suicides, I was hoping to gather information that would help in treating people who go through the types of partial or symbolic deaths I have already mentioned, such as loss, failure, rejection, depression, or any psychological subjugation to a negative ego-image. Specifically, I wanted to refine my egocide theory and make it more therapeutically useful. For these purposes, I especially wanted answers to these two questions: (1) How have the survivors subsequently handled such an upsetting traumatic event—an experience so close to death? (2) What have been the long-term effects of such events on their lives?

The message I received from the interviewees was clearer and more significant than I had expected. The ten survivors gave varying reasons for jumping, but there was a common core feeling of aloneness, alienation, depression, rejection, worthlessness, and hopelessness. Although the ten had widely divergent views of religion before attempting suicide, they all admitted to feelings of spiritual transcendence after they had leaped.

The words of one of the two survivors who remembers actually hitting the water are particularly meaningful:

At first everything was black, then gray-brown, then light. It opened my mind—like waking up. It was very restful. When I came up above the water, I realized I was alive. I felt reborn. I was treading water and singing—I was happy and it was a joyous occasion. It affirmed my belief that there is a higher spiritual world. I experienced a transcendence—in that moment I was refilled with new hope and purpose of being alive.[8]

Surviving his suicide attempt gave another individual an entirely new and self-empowering identification with our culture's most prominent archetype of death transcendence, Jesus Christ:

> Before I jumped I was an agnostic—no real belief in God. After the jump I became fully Christian; I believed in God and Jesus Christ. Christ became a living reality for me [Later, in the hospital, he felt that Christ and his disciples were gathered around him]. It is still going on. I'm now in a period of painful growth—of being reborn.

A different survivor who described herself as being a devout Christian and regular churchgoer before her suicide attempt came through her jump with an even stronger faith:

> I felt chosen because I didn't die; I said this in front of the congregation. I was thankful. I cried in front of them. I wanted to help others. I pointed out how sovereign and powerful God is and how little we are, and that it's not up to us. I was pure and cleaner inside. I thought somehow I was helping others in the spiritual realm [and] others were helped by my testimony.

Yet one more survivor expressed his spiritual transcendence and transformation in more ecumenical terms:

> It's beyond most people's comprehension. I appreciate the miracle of life—like watching a bird fly—everything is more meaningful when you come close to losing it. I experienced a feeling of unity with all things and a oneness with all people. After my psychic rebirth I also feel for everyone's pain. Surviving confirmed my belief and purpose in my life. Everything was clear and bright—I became aware of my relationship with my creator.

By surviving self-chosen-death leaps, all ten of my interviewees wound up committing *symbolic suicide*—what I have termed *egocide*—instead of actual suicide.[9] In retrospect, they each realized that they had planned their jump in a confused and demoralized state, during which they had inappropriately defined their whole being in terms of a specific failing or negative ego or self-image. Even more

noteworthy, they each recommended that suicide barriers be con-
structed on both bridges. In every case, I interpret this plea as a
projection of an inner barrier against suicide: Contrary to most survivors of very serious suicide attempts, who are at much greater risk
for subsequent suicide, none of the ten survivors whom I interviewed had gone on to suicide.

What I learned from the bridge-jump survivors has become an
integral part of my own healing journey and of the healing journeys
I lead my patients to undertake: People can overcome depression and
suicidal impulses through egocide. In part, what I have learned from
these healing journeys has now evolved into this book.[10]

In developing my egocide and transformation theory, some of my
most important teachers have been these survivors. These ten individuals, who set out to commit suicide but survived, found out that
they had somehow cleared the way for psychic regeneration. In
surviving, they had symbolically killed their previous negative ego-
identities. Each of these individuals transcended the split between
inner death and life forces, between the negative ego and the Self.
Through the act of surviving their depressive and suicidal states,
they had transformed themselves. Their experiences became the
basis of a new paradigm for me and for my patients.

A Commonsense Model of Egocide and Transformation

Expressed as simply as possible, my theory of egocide and transformation presents a Bad News/Good News scenario of psychological development. The Bad News is that we all occasionally become
depressed: We fail, lose, or fall. For some individuals, depression can
reach a point where they feel completely worthless. In this dark
abyss, the person experiences a loss of soul and spirit: Hope's flame
is sputtering out. Suicide seems like the only solution. However, the
Good News is that only a part of the ego has to die (or be killed). This
Symbolic Death (or egocide) can usher in a positive psychic transformation, or New Life.

To reiterate, the model of egocide and transformation involves
four aspects: Bad News, Good News, Symbolic Death, and New
Life. The Bad News is a state of demoralization, a negative turn
leading to despair, or depression caused by a precipitating failure,
such as loss of a job. This is on an ego (I, me) level. The Bad News,

which involves loss, is based on rejection and is experienced as a wounding of the ego. If we can endure and persist, the untoward is followed by Good News. The Good News is that after the fall, we are able to pick ourselves up. We may need a helping hand, support, encouragement, and therapy, but we *can* get back up. There is ascent after descent; there is joy after despair; there is success after failure. Based on this Good News, the ego again feels that it is in control. The person then has an enhanced self-image.

People spend most of their lives on an ego level. However, when there is a major fall, a life crisis of some kind, there is a confrontation with death. At this time, we tend to become severely depressed, if not suicidal, and experience a feeling of losing our soul. Stuck in hopelessness, we become preoccupied with ending our life. Alcoholics Anonymous maintains that a person must hit *rock bottom*, hardly able to function, before major change occurs. In such an instance of extreme dejection, the ego can turn on itself in its last desperate act of control. The only recourse the ego feels it has left to master the situation of ultimate failure is to commit suicide. It is a conscious ego act.[11]

Therefore, in that fateful moment, if the person can transcend the inner struggle between death and life and gain insight and understanding, he or she can choose egocide and transformation, preserving the self and relationships with significant others. Anyone can talk and analyze a tragic situation to *death,* and go through a loss of that negative dominant ego-image, which has led to this confrontation with the cessation of life.

To reach the point of suicide, the negative ego colludes with the shadow—one's darkest repressed side.[12] The way to survive involves both egocide (killing the negative ego) and shadowcide (killing the negative shadow). In sum, this is killing the *false self.* This Symbolic Death leads to a further and greater fall, which actually feels like death. It is like entering an eternal void. This is a frightening transitional phase characterized by a death-rebirth struggle. When the ego is fragmented, the person feels lost. But when the individual contacts the center of the psyche, the Self (Supreme Being), it leads to a reorganization and reconstitution of the ego, which is now secondary to a higher principle. This is the emergence of the *true self* (genuine being).

The final phase involves New Life, based on the person surviving (suffering through) a death-rebirth experience. The individual feels reborn and morale is restored. I will now illustrate what I mean by utilizing the experiences of two well-known people, one who commits suicide and the other who commits egocide and undergoes transformation. The tragedy of the first case, as with all suicides, is that it could have been prevented.

Elvis Presley and Betty Ford

Elvis Presley, the individual in the first case, embodied the Icarus syndrome. He was flying high and got too close to the sun; after his wax wings melted, he crashed into the sea and drowned. He had become inflated (emotionally and physically) and remained stuck in the *king* state. Elvis was a creative but self-destructive *king*. The Bad News was that his drug abuse increased and he became severely addicted. After his divorce, he spiraled down. Occasionally he had an ascent based on uppers and his natural talent. However, he could not get out of the quagmire and kept spiraling down further into an abyss of no return. The Bad News got worse and he eventually committed suicide by a multiple drug overdose.[13] His negative ego colluded with his negative shadow, and drug taking became an acute form of self-destruction. If Elvis had gone through a Symbolic Death experience (committed egocide) and transformed himself, eliminating the drugs and his suicidal complex, he could have rejuvenated himself and been alive today, possibly with an intact family.

I want to mention another similar human predicament, but one whose outcome was survival. The individual is Betty Ford, a person admired by many.[14] Ironically, the Betty Ford Clinic could have been the very place where Elvis Presley went for help. Betty, unlike Elvis, was able to admit that she was depressed and self-destructive. She was able to let her suicidal complex die; rather than it killing her, she killed it. The Bad News was that she was addicted to alcohol, which could have taken her down an ever-increasing Bad News path to death. The Good News, on an ego level, was that she was able to transcend and gain insight into her situation and to make a choice to go through Symbolic Death, or egocide, and transformation. Based on contact with a higher power, the Self, her New Life involved a humble secondary ego position, in which she knew that she was not ultimately in control; she surrendered to this higher force. With restored morale, Betty Ford continued to pursue her own healing and the healing of others (altruistic service), which is characteristic of individuation (the process toward wholeness).

The Jungian Humanistic Perspective

Throughout the book, my psychological perspective is Jungian. Carl Jung focuses on major aspects of the psyche, which are repressed or unconscious during the time an individual is establishing his or her ego-identity (*ego* being the center of consciousness). Jung defines these aspects as: the *anima* (contrasexual female principle) in a man or the *animus* (contrasexual male principle) in a woman; the *persona* (the masks one wears, which are tied to social roles); the *shadow* (the dark, unknown, unconscious aspects of one's psyche); and the *Self* (the center and totality of one's being). In the Jungian paradigm, these aspects must be brought into the light of consciousness in the second half of a person's life, if that person is to become individuated. Basically, individuation is a process toward achieving psychic wholeness that involves the Symbolic Death of the previous, dominating ego-identity and the emergence of a newly reconstructed *ego-Self* identity.

It is Jung's dynamic theory of psychological death and rebirth that most directly informs my concept of egocide. Implicit in Jung's theory is a strong spiritual element similar to the one I detected in the psychological death-and-rebirth histories of the bridge-jump survivors. Unlike Freud, who thought that the spiritual dimension of life was neurotic or an illusion, Jung believed that the spirit was integrally related to healing and to becoming fully human.

According to Jung, the means by which a person spiritually transcends and transforms a limiting ego-identity is by delving deeper into the psyche and going beyond one's own *personal unconscious* into the *collective unconscious.* Jung postulated that just as each individual human embryo replicates the physical and biological evolution of the species as it unfolds, so each individual human psyche reflects the entire mental and psychological experience of the species. He found evidence of this collective unconscious in the pervasiveness of the same symbols, myths, and motifs in widely separated human cultures throughout history. Jung called these symbols, myths, and motifs manifestations of archetypes, and he considered it critically important to take the archetypal dimension into account during the course of any therapy aimed at restoring the health of the individual psyche.

In working with people's depressed or suicidal feelings, I have found that a patient's recognition and recasting of archetypes through creative expression (by specific acts or artistic productions) is an essential part of the *transformation* process. For example, if a patient is psychologically disturbed by an internal conflict with his or her father, that conflict can never be completely resolved by focusing attention exclusively on the personal father. To effect an engagement of the healing process, the patient must come to terms with the patriarchal archetype in his or her psyche, the collective unconscious record of images associated with all fathers that is influencing his or her reactions to the personal father in all sorts of potentially self-destructive ways.

Jung encouraged his patients to confront these images through a technique he called *active imagination,* a kind of free-flowing, non-goal-oriented creative meditation. The patients I discuss in Chapters 6–9 have confronted these images in a similar fashion through drawing, painting, writing (poetry and prose), ceramics, and dance.

This book has a natural affinity with Jungian psychology because death and rebirth themes are central to its healing philosophy and analytical therapy. Like the phoenix rising from the ashes, out of the forces of destruction emerge creative powers that contribute to the fulfillment of one's personal myth in conjunction with self-healing.

Egocide represents the creative process by which an individual symbolically confronts and destroys a negative, life-threatening identity, in order for a more positive, life-affirming identity to emerge. *Transforming Depression* recounts how this process has worked successfully in the context of analytical psychotherapy, even for people suffering so severely from depression that they were repeatedly in danger of committing suicide.

The Promise of This Book

This book tells the in-depth stories of two women and two men who have very different journeys but who all opt for the difficult but transforming path of egocide. These individuals were chosen because I felt many people would be able to relate to their stories.

Issues of depression, despair, meaninglessness, hopelessness, and
suicide are endemic in our society, and the cases involve these and
other pressing concerns, such as child sexual abuse, abandonment,
problems with alcohol, and adoption. *Transforming Depression* tracks
the metamorphosis of their meaninglessness, hopelessness, and demoralization into meaning, hope, and the morale-enhancing unfolding of their personal myths. It reflects the courage to be. These
individuals have committed egocide, shedding their depressive and
suicidal complexes, and transformed themselves in the process.
Their experiences serve as paths to guide others to do the same.
Betty Ford did this, too, and countless others have benefited. The
same choice was there for Elvis Presley; however, he was blinded by
a dark delusion that he was the *king*. Inside he must have known that
he was not. In order to have killed himself, he must have felt utterly
false, alone, worthless, and hopeless.

This book was written to offer people, from all walks of life, an
alternative to depression and suicide, via the alternate path of egocide and transformation: an arduous journey encompassing Symbolic
Death and New Life.

This volume is also about self-healing. I know from experience that even the most depressed or suicidal people can choose to
transcend and transform their self-punishing and self-destructive
impulses. Transcendence—rising above conflicting forces—is a necessary step in the transformation process. The value of transcendence is that one can rise above the battle and get an overview. It is
a mirror image of understanding, which I view as standing humbly
under a difficult issue in order to see it clearly. The drawback of
transcendence is that it can lead to aloofness, inflation, and isolation.
Transcendence is a step, not a place to get stuck! The next step,
which is essential for real change, is to transform. Transformation
results from a union of opposites and leads to something new: a
creative change.

This book can help you deal with Bad News, wait for the Good
News, and facilitate Symbolic Death and New Life through egocide
and transformation. For the patients I have treated over the past
seventeen years and those I continue to treat, it has consistently
produced qualitative, life enhancing change. The concept of egocide
and transformation will strengthen those who are struggling with
depression and self-destructive urges, as well as those who are helping others deal with these problems.

How This Book Is Organized

In the first three chapters, I focus on understanding depression, knowing suicide, and how we recognize and treat these conditions. For the knowledgeable reader, Part I (Background and Context) may be read quickly as a thought-provoking review. However, for the novice, it provides critical background information and a context for the rest of the book.

Part II (An Innovative Way of Healing Depression) heralds an innovative way of healing depression, disillusionment, and demoralization. Chapter 4 concerns this new therapeutic approach—egocide and transformation—and focuses on both individual and group therapies. In Chapter 5, the spotlight is on the pregnant technique of active imagination, which uses healing symbols as archetypes of creative transformation.

Part III (Four Transforming Journeys—Chapters 6–9) concerns in-depth cases from my practice (two depressed and two suicidal patients), which illustrate egocide and transformation. In Chapter 6, the reader will learn how dreams and active imagination help Rebecca recall and heal incest. Chapter 7 shows how Gary, a lost, adopted *puer,* contacts his biological parents, grows up, and finds his lost soul. Chapter 8 reveals how egocide and transformation reverses the suicidal inclination of Sharon, a very disturbed but gifted graduate student, who then embarks on a path to become a wounded healer. Chapter 9 shows how Paul, a melancholic and suicidal professional, slowly but surely commits egocide and transforms his depression and himself in the process.

Part IV (Spiral of Change: Symbolic Death and New Life) includes Chapter 10, which discusses crisis points and how egocide can help. For example, it is proposed that an emphasis on egocide would decrease teen suicide—the most tragic outcome to the early life crisis of adolescence. This final chapter also applies the egocide and transformation paradigm to our world, which grows smaller and smaller every day. The Epilogue reveals how meaning results from egocide and transformation.

The Beacon of Egocide and Transformation

I envision egocide as a process of illumination, of shining light on troublesome, hidden mysteries. This book is written as a guide for suffering individuals who are attempting to survive dark nights of the soul, for their loved ones who are providing needed support, and for therapists who are working with such tormented clients. It is about seeing into the darkness, discovering one's personal, soul-nourishing myth, and then living that myth fully and with joy. My greatest hope is that this new therapeutic approach ultimately will contribute to fewer cases of unproductive depression and unnecessary suicide, and to more occurrences of egocide and transformation.

In addition, this book is also about human survival. Beyond serving as a therapeutic model for severely depressed and suicidal individuals, the concept of egocide and transformation has relevance for persons who are not severely depressed or suicidal but who nevertheless experience sadness, depression, and demoralization, and feel the need for psychic regeneration. It also has pertinence for the Whole Human Family.

Egocide and transformation is timely because we now have the potential to commit mass suicide, and the issue for each of us, as individuals, is more closely connected to our world. The conscious destruction of our world, what I term *omnicide,* can be prevented. Ours is an exciting time to live in because we have the opportunity to abolish war and self-destruction. If we can transcend and transform the issues involved in hurting or killing ourselves, then there is sustaining hope for each of us, our families, our communities, our nations, and our world.

PART I

BACKGROUND AND CONTEXT

CHAPTER 1
Understanding Depression
and the Quest for Meaning

"Where there is sorrow, there is holy ground."

—Oscar Wilde

THEORISTS in psychology and psychiatry can be divided into two groups: the lumpers and the splitters. In classifying depression, lumpers strive to fit all possible forms of depression (which, in common parlance, would include sadness, moodiness, grief, suicidal despair, and so forth) under one umbrella. Splitters, on the other hand, endeavor to draw precise, significant distinctions between all possible forms of depression. These differences aside, both lumpers and splitters tend to define depression in negative terms, as a disorder or disease (or, in the case of splitters, as a multitude of disorders or diseases) characterized by a self-punishing loss of emotional and physical vitality.

I will take a middle ground, incorporating the most significant insights into depression offered by both lumpers and splitters. I will also depart from them both, viewing depression as a favorable affect and linking it to the quest for meaning. I believe that depression can help a person adjust to a new reality, and therefore can have a positive value.

Imagine aboriginal men and women forced to take shelter during the day in a dark cave, to escape a predator, bad weather, or an earthquake. Maybe they are hungry, cold, and fearful, but at least they are safer than they would be outside, and their withdrawal from the light of day has given them a chance to regain their equilibrium. Depression is analogous to seeking sanctuary in a cave. For the human psyche, depression is a natural reaction to a disruptive situation, and though it is unpleasant in many ways, it is essential if the psyche is to adapt to, and live through, that situation.

Or think of depression as a dark underground, where seeds from dying plants can germinate. If the soil of depression is nurtured properly, the result will be New Life for the psyche—in other words, psychic rebirth. This type of organic growth occurs naturally within us during our emotionally stormy adolescent years, when our psyche goes through the Symbolic but painful Death of the parent-dominated ego as a prelude to the birth of its own, young adult ego.

Although my view of depression as a positive state is atypical, it does have other proponents. In ancient times, Plato (arguably the first important splitter in Western thought) divided mental illness, and therefore depression (as one of its principal forms), into two main categories. One of them, disease, is indeed negative. But the other, divine gift, is decidedly positive and consists of four subcategories, each with its own special inspirational value: prophetic, religious, poetic, and erotic.[1]

In modern times, a very prominent advocate of depression as a positive force has been Carl Jung, who went through his own agonizing but transforming depression after his break with Freud in 1913, and experienced a psychological renewal similar to the death-and-rebirth experience of the adolescent.[2]

More recently, Arthur Schmale has argued for the adaptive role depression can play in the human psyche.[3] He states that "the [depressive] reaction, unpleasant as it may be when it is personally experienced, has adaptive significance for growth, reality testing, and even survival." In Schmale's theory, which he attributes to George Engel,[4] depression operates as a biological conservation-withdrawal mechanism that can be found not only in plants and single-celled organisms but also in more highly evolved animals, including primates and humans. This mechanism serves to protect the individual "by means of withdrawal and inactivity when stimuli become excessive and cannot be actively avoided." At the onset of withdrawal and inactivity, the mechanism allows for rest periods (such as sleep or hibernation) that may be either gradual or sudden. Another very recent book by Emmy Gut focuses on the adaptive role of depression and how unproductive moods can be made productive.[5]

I, too, see depression as potentially helpful. When an individual's psychological conservation-withdrawal mechanism is operating, the person is in a state of adaptive depression—a temporary period of inactivity like the period of incubation before a creative idea emerges. This is not a pathological reaction, but a natural, perhaps essential process, much like Anthony Storr's concept of solitude as a necessary state for active imagination and the reviving of mental health.[6] Depression becomes pathological only when the individual remains locked in this state of inactivity, instead of progressing beyond it.

Unfortunately, the prevailing trend in Western civilization has been to view all forms of depression as somehow shameful, with the exception of a reasonable period of grief after a major loss, especially the death of a loved one. To an outside observer, depression doesn't seem productive at all; on the contrary, the depressed person appears to be giving up, abandoning his or her soul to a dark abyss. Historically the Roman Catholic Church considered sadness and sorrow as symptoms of *tristitia*, one of the cardinal sins. In the secular world industry, optimism, and self-control have always been cardinal virtues. Thus, depressed people, subtly pressured by their culture to think of themselves as sick and possibly even evil, don't give themselves time and space to understand their depression so that they can recognize it for what it truly is. They're too ashamed or concerned with denying it, hiding it, or bemoaning it.

I'm not claiming that depression is all positive. I'm simply saying that depression has both positive and negative features, and that people who are depressed often must learn to understand the true nature of depression in order to complete their journeys back to health. To paraphrase Ecclesiastes, there is a time for darkness, depression, sleep, and withdrawal, and a time for lightness, joy, activity, and engagement. What is truly negative is to remain for long periods of time at one extreme or the other (manic-depressives, technically sufferers of bipolar disease, wind up experiencing the worst of both worlds in this manner).

Above all, I am suggesting that depression is an archetype—an affectual predisposition, as old as life itself, that expresses itself in biological, psychological, social, and existential/spiritual ways. As with any archetype, it has both a dark side and a light side. In this respect, depression resembles the Chinese principal of yin/yang, an archetype of all existence as a balance of opposites (Figure 1-1). The dark (yin) and the light (yang) function together to make a whole. Within each is a little of the other; they can't be separated by drawing a straight line.

FIGURE 1-1
Yin/Yang

How I Conceptualize Depression

I sympathize with lumpers and view depression as one basic entity. Objectively, it manifests itself through the persona as a *mood*. Subjectively, it may or may not be felt as an *emotion* and, on a deeper level, it takes the form of a felt or unfelt *affect*.

An affect refers to the deepest or archetypal level of the psyche. When an individual has an explosive outpouring of feeling, be it rage, anger, or grief, it is because the person has been touched at the core of his or her being. The result is a psychic eruption of affect—like a volcano spewing red-hot lava.

One level closer to the surface is the actual emotion related to the affect. It is a subjective state of feeling, in contrast to an archetypal affect or predisposition toward emotion. In any given situation, individuals may or may not consciously recognize the emotion they are experiencing; and even if they do, they may or may not express that emotion.

Mood is the uppermost level in which a feeling manifests itself and the first level of feeling an outside observer notices. Sometimes an individual exhibits a lack of congruity among affect, emotion, and mood. There is a depressive disorder known as *masked depression*, in which the individual manifests an untrue or false self, suggesting an affect that is not authentic. For example, a person may put on a persona of happiness and contentment; but behind that smiling face may be emotions and affects of depression and rage. What eventually happens in such cases is that the mask develops cracks and the true emotions and affects become evident, both to outside observers and eventually to the person harboring them. The false self has serious implications in regard to suicide.

Normally, depressed affects, emotions, and moods may cast gloom on a person's psyche for a few hours, a few days, or even a few months; but they do not indicate that the person has a mental disorder, nor do they interfere with his or her ability to lead a normal life. They are transient by nature and pass without causing major problems. However, when a person's depression is accompanied by more disruptive symptoms, such as severe despair that continues relatively unabated for a year or more and compromises his or her ability to function, then the depression is considered abnormal (or, strictly speaking, pathological).

The single entity of depression forms a continuum from normal to abnormal. On the extreme, normal end of the continuum are the temporary experiences of sadness, grief, and bereavement that don't impair one's ability to function—what most people would experience due to a mild disappointment or a real, important loss. At the other end of the continuum are the more lasting and impairing types of clinical depression, such as neurotic and psychotic depression.[7]

The Restoration of Morale

One characteristic common to all cases of depression, regardless of the particular symptoms or classification, is a loss of morale. In practice, morale makes itself known in a person's day-to-day morality, sense of purpose, and loyalties. Psychologically, if a depressed person's morale can be restored, then his or her chances of recovery are enormously improved.

Loss of morale is generally associated with a collapse of a person's spirit, will, or courage. In defining a state of demoralization as one of the universal characteristics of depression, Jerome Frank describes demoralized individuals as follows:

[They are] conscious of having failed to meet their own expectations or those of others, or of being unable to cope with some pressing problem. They feel powerless to change the situation or themselves. In severe cases they fear that they cannot even control their own feelings, giving rise to the fear of going crazy, which is so characteristic of those seeking psychotherapeutic help. Their life space is . . . constricted both in time and space. Thus, they cling to a small round of habitual activities, avoiding novelty and challenge, and are reluctant to make long-term plans. It is as if psychologically they are cowering in a spatio-temporal corner.[8]

Demoralized individuals feel that they can neither cope with nor extricate themselves from difficult life situations. Such a feeling generally stems from environmental stresses as well as from vulnerabilities built into the individual's psyche. Psychotherapy can be very effective in helping an individual overcome such demoralizing conditions as learned helplessness, existential despair, and hopelessness.

Like Frank, I think that demoralization is one of the major reasons why most people enter into psychotherapy. The restoration of morale involves a patient's quest for meaning: a life-regenerating meaning that can be the basis for new confidence in one's self and in the future.

Understanding Depression: A Holistic Approach

Let me reiterate that I am more of a lumper than a splitter in my view of depression and suicide. Yet to understand any single case, I believe that it is necessary to split the factors (biological, psychological, social, and existential/spiritual) before recombining them into a single system. If we separate a single factor group from all the others and say that it contains "the truth" about depression or suicide, that is exactly where, when, how, and why we get into trouble. Because I firmly believe that all factor groups must be considered in coming to a comprehensive understanding of depression or suicide, my approach to every case is a holistic approach, or what some might call a systems approach.[9] Before considering the whole system, however, let's look at the various factor groups: (1) biological, (2) psychological, (3) sociological, and (4) existential/spiritual.

Biological Factors

Biochemical compounds are clearly implicated in the etiology of depression. Depression is associated with low concentrations of certain monoamine neurotransmitters in the brain or with abnormalities in the reception of these neurotransmitters into individual neurons.[10]

Psychoneuroendocrinology (PNE) demonstrates that the monoamine neurotransmitters also regulate the secretion of hormones from the pituitary gland, along with the secretion of peptides from the hypothalamus. The adrenal and thyroid systems are two common endocrine systems that, when imbalanced, often lead to depression.[11]

Psychoneuroimmunology (PNI) studies the combined influence of psychological and neurological events on an individual's immune system.[12] A recent PNI study indicating that a person's psychological state of mind can influence his or her general health was included in Norman Cousins' book concerning the biology of hope.[13] It involved two groups of patients with malignant melanoma. One group—the control group—was given the standard medical treatment for this condition. The other group received the same treatment plus psychosocial enhancement, administered by a team called the Society of Challengers, which featured group support, therapy, and specific help in overcoming feelings marked by loss of control, helplessness, and hopelessness. We can assume that humor was a part of the psychosocial enhancement, since Cousins, a member of the Society of Challengers, was well known for having successfully treated his own life-threatening illness by keeping himself laughing (for example, by watching Marx Brothers movies).[14] Measurements of all subjects' mood states, personality adjustment to illness, quality of life, and immune-cell function were made at the beginning of the study and at six-week, six-month, and one-year intervals. These measurements indicated that psychosocial enhancement was correlated with significant decreases in tension, anxiety, depression, and dejection and significant increases in personality adjustment to illness, quality of life, and positive immune system changes.

Genetic studies (adoption, twin, and family) suggest that depression is inherited. This is particularly true with bipolar disorder or manic-depressive illness.[15]

Psychological Factors

Freudian views are important as a beginning. In early psychoanalytic theory, depression is attributed to a blockage of libido. This theory claims that when people give up their sexual desires without being gratified, they feel unwanted and unloved, with subsequent self-reproach and self-degradation.[16]

Sigmund Freud's classic work in this area, *Mourning and Melancholia*, contrasts normal bereavement with pathological depression.[17] According to Freud, a person can experience a depression equal to, or possibly more severe than, bereavement even though a loved one is still alive and healthy. This melancholia, as Freud calls it, can result from a loved one's being lost to an individual as an object of love or gratification. The individual feels anger toward the lost love object; but because that anger cannot be vented on the love object, it turns against the individual's own ego. This depressive backlash effect can be made even worse due to guilt feelings (from the superego) for harboring anger in the first place. Freud characterized melancholia as "a profoundly painful dejection, cessation of interest in the outside world, loss of capacity to love, inhibition of all activity, and a lowering of self-regard sometimes to an extreme delusional degree." Normal mourning or grieving yields the same symptoms, except that there is no significant lowering of self-regard.

Heinz Kohut maintains that without idealized love objects, an individual develops either an "empty depression" based on a lack of self-esteem and energy, or a "guilt depression," based on a self-rejection.[18]

Carl Jung, like other early psychoanalysts, saw depression as blocked libido—an "I am stuck" feeling—resulting in a loss of energy and enjoyment. However, he also saw it, radically different, as a regression into a symbolic "womb" associated with an unconscious state described as "psychic death," which was often accompanied by "loss of soul." To Jung, such a slide into depressive depths represented an involuntary introversion on the part of the individual, facilitating a "relapse into the past" for the purpose of integrating the activated aspects of the past into consciousness and into the present.[19]

Jung also wrote about regression to the *prima materia* (i.e., the collective unconscious) where "the danger is great," and the individual "hangs between annihilation and new life," but where he or she also finds the "maternal vessel of rebirth." He states further: "If this *prima materia* can be assimilated by the conscious mind it will bring about a reactivation and reorganization of its contents." In addition, Jung envisioned the sacrifice of the hero or heroine identity as a "renunciation of egohood" and repossession of one's lost soul.

Jung's interpreters take different stances when it comes to articulating the specific value of depression. Odajnyk, for example, states: "Only those depressions are useful and healing in which the ego stays intact but willing to compromise with the pressing drives and the needs of the unconscious."[20] This sounds more like a Freudian or neo-Freudian view. In contrast, I maintain that the ego must symbolically die in severe depression for meaningful change and healing to occur. Steinberg's thinking is more in line with my point of view. Utilizing a redemption model, he sees successful analysis of severely depressed individuals as involving a death of the negative parental introjects (which the depressed person tends to project onto others) and the rebirth of a "newly organized ego [that] represents a greater approximation to and reflection of the Self."[21] Later, Steinberg outlines Jung's view of depression as carrying the potential of transformation through a death-rebirth experience and describes this transformative depression as purposive and creative.[22] Steinberg sees psychotic depression as existing on a continuum with other forms of depression and maintains, as do I, that the more severe the depression, the more compounded it is with self-reproach and repressed aggression turned against the self. (And, I would add, toward the negative ego-identity that needs to symbolically die.)

Behavioral approaches use learning theory and functional analyses for their conceptual bases. Behavioral theories of depression identify specific and particular behaviors as necessary for the onset and maintenance of depressive symptoms.[23] For example, behaviorists maintain that depression is caused by a loss of positive or increased negative reinforcement in the person's environment.[24]

In contrast, the cognitive approach to depression, as offered by Aaron Beck, holds that it is not external events that lead to depression but an individual's internal representations of those events.[25] Essentially, Beck assumes that negatively distorted thinking patterns (ideas and images) are the root cause of depressive symptomology. In other words, people are predisposed to depression by faulty internal information-processing systems, which appraise losses in a destructive manner. The result is the generation of inappropriately negative attitudes that have a harmful influence on how these people subsequently judge themselves, the world, and the future.

Although the behavioral/cognitive approaches are limited, they are important and powerful. After all, no therapy is worth its salt unless there are cognitive and behavioral changes. However, the affective component which is equally vital emerges most clearly in interpersonal relationships.

Theories centering around the interpersonal aspects leading to depression stress the contribution made by an individual's unsatisfactory relationships and disturbed social roles, both as a child and as an adult.[26] John Bowlby has eloquently revealed the special developmental importance of an individual's affectual bonding with the mother—or an early parental surrogate—in avoiding depression later in life.[27] The rationale is that the latent memory of this early intimacy serves to offset any subsequent feelings of worthlessness and hopelessness that might predispose the individual to become depressed. Without such maternal bonding, the individual is likely to form weak social bonds when he or she matures, and weak social bonds increase the chances for depression.

Social Factors

Several investigations have reported that depression may be brought on by high levels of stress. Such stress comes as the result of life events that significantly alter a person's social matrix, such as a change in job status, economic situation, or living conditions. An event of this nature (known as a social stressor) demands a considerable amount of psychological adjustment on the part of the individual, and a failure to adjust can invite depression.

Studies have shown that depressed patients have almost three times as many social stressors during the six-month period prior to the onset of their depression than normal controls do.[28] Such findings help explain the predominance of major depression among women, separated or divorced people, and adolescents, since these groups are more vulnerable to high levels of stress than other groups.[29]

However, despite the undeniable contribution of social stressors to depression, it cannot be assumed that these stressors in themselves are either necessary or sufficient causes of depression. Instead, they may act upon an already existing predisposition to depression, such as an individual's lack of personal resources (e.g., money, close family ties, physical health) to withstand a crisis.

To date, not enough research has been done in this area, probably for two reasons: (1) There are no objective criteria for establishing whether a depressed person's existing lack of personal resources is the cause or the effect of his or her depressive illness; and (2) The functional distinction between a depressed individual's personal resources and the stressful life events that he or she has experienced is often blurry. Similar difficulties impede research into whether certain socially disadvantaged individuals, such as the homeless, the poverty-stricken, the unemployed, and oppressed minorities, suffer depression because the social structure to which they belong deprives them of specific roles, valued identities, and control over their own destinies.[30]

Existential/Spiritual Factors

Engel, a physician and theorist whom I greatly respect, has challenged the medical profession to expand its technological, disease-focused model to a more illness-oriented, patient-centered, biopsychosocial model.[31] In my opinion, however, he does not go far enough. Like Jung, I feel that in addition to biological, psychological, and social factors, which I have already discussed, the issue of the patient's soul must be addressed. Indeed, I consider soul the central element in any healing process: physical, mental, or societal.

I define the soul as:

> that enlightening spirit or life-giving force which gives rise to those stabilizing, integrating powers that make a being whole and a person fully human. Such persons can find meaning and purpose in life and can feel [and experience] optimism, sensitivity, receptivity, empathy, and creativity. The soul is the seat of one's emotional moral nature—of one's feelings and love (Eros)—in contrast to mind and intellect, which are the seat of thinking and reason (Logos).[32]

My premise for insisting that the soul be considered in any healing effort is perhaps best expressed by the nineteenth-century existentialist Friedrich Nietzsche: "[The person] who has a *why* to live can bear with almost any *how.*" The same philosophy is embraced by Viktor Frankl's school of logotherapy, which "focuses on the meaning of human existence as well as on the individual's search for such a meaning."[33] Frankl developed his psychology of meaning while he was an inmate at Auschwitz and other Nazi concentration camps during the Holocaust. He discovered that the search for meaning is a primary motivation for the actions of human beings and that virtually any amount of suffering can be endured if the sufferer is able to find meaning in it.

In Frankl's psychological approach, depression results from existential frustration. A person becomes existentially frustrated when he or she fails to find meaning in life and in suffering (Frankl describes the consequence of this failure as a loss of the "will to meaning"). Therefore, to Frankl, it is not stress or tension that produces depression but the inability to find meaning for the stress or tension. Indeed, he does not consider stress and tension as major problems in terms of depression:

> What man actually needs is not a tensionless state but rather the striving and struggling for a worthwhile goal, a freely chosen task. What he needs is not the discharge of tension at all cost but the call of potential meaning waiting to be fulfilled by him.

The depressed individual experiences a feeling of total meaninglessness and inner emptiness, a condition that Frankl calls the "existential vacuum."

Jung's view is similar.[34] He maintains that "the psyche needs to know the meaning of its existence." Referring to Lao-tzu, he reveals how significant the quest for meaning is by characterizing the Tao (roughly speaking, "life force") as "meaning" or "purpose." Given this allusion, it is interesting to note that, in the philosophy of Taoism, a precondition for finding meaning or acquiring spirituality is an internal emptiness—an available, potentially sacred space, which sounds a lot like Frankl's existential vacuum.

Abraham Maslow's description of a "sense of meaningfulness" as an after-effect of a peak experience offers yet another close approximation to Frankl's theory about the importance of meaning to a person's psychic health. Maslow states that a human being needs "values, philosophy of life, a religion or religion surrogate to live by and understand by, in the sense that he or she needs sunlight, calcium or love."[35]

Jung's psychology maintains that a person's progress toward wholeness (individuation) involves the development of meaning in his or her life and contact with a higher force or Supreme Being (the Self). This theory is comparable to what Maslow calls self-actualization. Maslow claims that for people to be self-actualized, they must have values which correlate with meaning and spirituality. If they don't, they will develop what he terms "value-illnesses," which "result from valuelessness and are called variously anhedonia, anomie, apathy, amorality, hopelessness, and cynicism." It is no contradiction of Maslow to add depression and demoralization to this list.

My approach to overcoming depression also pays tribute to the importance of finding meaning in one's life and in one's suffering. I help my patients do this through creative expression and artistic productions. It's an ancient idea: Plato, for example, commented on the powerful healing connection between music and the spirit: "Musical rhythm and harmony find their way into the inward places of the soul." But it's also an idea that has a multitude of supporters today. Recently, one of the most widely read advocates of this idea has been Robert Fulghum.[36] When asked once if he ever experienced a kind of "midwinter spiritual rot" or depression, he responded, "Listen, I get lows it takes extension ladders to get out of!" He explained that whenever he wants to pull himself out of his depressive spells, he listens to Beethoven's Ninth Symphony.

A Holistic Approach to Understanding Depression

Let's construct a couple of cases of depression to illustrate how all these factor groups we've looked at can interrelate. Let's assume, for example, that a man loses his job (social factor). Since his job took up most of his time and energy, he now feels that his life has lost its direction and purpose (existential/spiritual factor). Subsequently, he succumbs to feelings of depression (psychological factor), which make him neglect his health to the point where he no longer has as much energy as he used to have (biological factor).

For our second scenario, let's suppose that a young woman invests too much importance in what her parents think about her (psychological factor). She is forever depressed because she feels she can never live up to their expectations. Because of her depression and continual worrying, her immune system weakens, causing her to suffer from chronic infections (biological factor). When she's sick, life seems meaningless (existential/spiritual factor); and this attitude alienates her friends (social factor).

Where depression begins in either scenario is difficult, if not impossible, to pinpoint: It may well have its roots in earlier events. What is certain in both scenarios, however, is that all four of the cited factors feed, and feed upon, the individual's depressed state of being. It's only logical, since these same four factor groups represent principal and inseparable components of human life in general.

Conversely, depression can be overcome only by positive developments in terms of all four factor groups. In the first vignette, for example, if the man takes better care of his physical health (biological factor) and seeks therapy (psychological factor), life may seem more worth living (existential/spiritual factor), which may give him the added incentive he needs to land another job (social factor). The woman in the second illustration may decide to listen to her friends' constructive advice (social factor) and, as a result, may not concentrate so hard on pleasing her parents (psychological factor). This may lead to less depression and worrying and fewer infections (biological factor). Given her improved health, she may no longer find life quite so meaningless (existential/spiritual factor). Again, in each scenario, it's impossible to say exactly at what point depression may cease to exist as an unmistakable condition. All the factors cited would make a contribution.

While it's fairly easy to trace my holistic systems model of depression in these scenarios, real life cases are seldom so clear-cut and accommodating. As a therapist or as an observer of an actual person's depression, one may be able to see that all four factors are involved, but the interconnections among these factors are inevitably much more complicated, mysterious, and resistant to change than any hypothetical scenario can indicate.

To illustrate this point, let me describe two real-life situations that I experienced as a psychiatric consultant in a hospital.[37] In each situation, I witnessed relatively entrenched cases of depression for only a brief period of time. Nevertheless, it was evident to me that these cases could be most effectively understood in the context of a systems model.

The first case involved Ed, an ex-professional golfer, who was dying from a malignant melanoma that had spread throughout his body. Out of pride, Ed had sacrificed his financial savings to pay his medical bills so that he wouldn't have to rely on his family, friends, or welfare for help. When I saw Ed, I could tell that he was profoundly depressed in biological, psychological, social, and spiritual terms. Therefore, I utilized the following antidepressants: medication, psychotherapy, social services, and spiritual support. The result was a noticeable improvement in Ed's depressive symptoms that enabled him to die in peace and with dignity.

The second predicament concerned Eleanor, a widow in her mid-fifties, who had been diagnosed with ovarian cancer. When I made my initial visit to Eleanor's darkened hospital room, her son and two daughters were gathered around her bed, so I sensed right away that she had a lot of family support. After introducing myself and explaining that I was there to evaluate her depression, Eleanor started crying and said to me, angrily, "So you're the psych doctor I told them I didn't need to see. I am not crazy!" She wiped her tears away and continued, "Yes, I am depressed, but who wouldn't be?" She paused again and then said in a loud voice, "I am not a mental case! Wouldn't you be depressed if they took your home away in order to pay your medical bills?"

What could I do for this woman? I acknowledged her feelings by responding, "Yes, I would be depressed." I tried to intervene with social services, to no avail. I also offered psychological and spiritual support, which she declined. Eleanor was not suffering from what could be scientifically classified as a clinical depression; so, at her request, I did not return, although I left her with an open-ended offer of my assistance.

To be honest, this situation left me feeling helpless. Clinically or not, the woman *was* depressed, and a definite element contributing to her depression was the lack of reasonably affordable health care in the United States (she would not have experienced the same problem in Canada or in the United Kingdom, for example). But this particular social factor in her depression was not operating in isolation. It was aggravating her physical illness by decreasing her immune response (biological factor). This worsening of her health, in turn, was adding to her family's worries—a predicament that was causing her to experience even greater stress (psychological and social factors). Thus, the patient was progressing more and more deeply into a valueless nightmare challenging the meaning of life (existential/spiritual factor).

The Meaning and Purpose of Depression

Intervention to reverse depression can take place at any point in the holistic systems model. In the above case, the social factor seems to be the one to change but, since it is a societal issue, the solution will be a political one. In general, however, I believe that the most powerful healing emotion is what Jerome Frank calls *expectant faith,* and therefore the factor group that holds the most promise for initiating a reversal of depression is the existential/spiritual factor group. Let me share with you another clinical case that illuminates this point.[38]

Marian's body was ravaged with cancer. Beginning in her lungs, the cancer had invaded her spine and had caused weakness in her legs and severe pain in her back. While in the hospital, she became paraplegic. After many tests and X rays, her doctors concluded that nothing could be done to reverse the process.

I first learned of Marian's case when one of her doctors requested a psychiatric consultation. I asked this doctor two questions: "What is the patient's problem?" and "How can I help?"

The doctor replied, "She's depressed. She can't accept the fact that she'll never walk again, and that we can't do anything to cure her. Anyway, she needs someone to talk to."

Immediately I wondered why this doctor couldn't talk with his own patient. What got in the way of his accepting her, listening to her, and establishing a healing partnership with her? Was he overworked? Did he feel helpless because he couldn't cure her physically?

When I met Marian, her initial concern was, "Am I crazy?" I reassured her that she was not going out of her mind and then explained my role—to discuss any problems she might have in adjusting to her present condition. After a long pause, she asked, "Why do I wake up crying in the night?"

Clearly, I thought, she had much to cry about—her spreading cancer, her back pain, and the loss of function in her legs. But she was, in fact, already managing to deal with these problems rather successfully, thanks to her religious faith. She kept a Bible and other spiritual books on her bedstand, and she confided to me that God had told her that one day she would walk again. What seemed to be troubling her more was the feeling that she was a burden to her family. She had always taken care of them, and now she was having difficulty being on the receiving end of their care, although they had demonstrated that they were eager to give her as much help as they could.

Recognizing the healing power that the patient drew from her spiritual beliefs, I replied to her concern about depending on her family with a verse from the Bible (something that is not my standard practice): "Whatever one soweth, that shall one also reap." Marian's reaction was a smile so broad and transforming that I knew she had found a peaceful resolution to her problem.

Afterwards, I recreated the conversation for her doctor. Most likely he realized that he could have done what he had asked me to do: Accept the patient, listen to her, and be empathic. To help him work through his feelings, I discussed from my own perspective the helplessness of not being able to offer a cure to someone who is ill, emphasized how difficult it is to take care of someone who isn't going to recover, and acknowledged that it was appropriate for him to ask for assistance by calling me in on the case. I also agreed to continue to see the patient until her discharge from the hospital. In subsequent interviews, she said she often thought about dying and was not afraid. I came to appreciate that her interpretation of God's promise that she would walk again meant once she was in heaven.

What does it say about modern medicine when physicians feel compelled to ask psychiatrists to talk with, and listen to, their patients? It suggests that physicians subscribe to a very narrow biomedical model in their approach to illness. Following this model, they typically use terms of pathology to describe their patient's emotions—ignoring the fact that emotions have a positive as well as a negative therapeutic value. Marian's doctor, for example, described her conviction that she would walk again as "delusional" and "a denial of her illness." In reality, however, her conviction indicated that she had a large reservoir of *expectant faith* waiting to be tapped.

In arguing that joy, inspiration, and hope are healing agents in cases of depression, Verena Kast cites Bloch, a German psychologist, who maintains that hope can be learned.[39] It seems to Kast—and me—that what Bloch is really saying is that human beings have an innate propensity to search for light (metaphorically speaking) in any darkness. At times, a depressed individual may, indeed, feel that the darkness of depression will never end. However, if he or she persists in cultivating this innate propensity, the light of hope will eventually and inevitably shine forth, illuminating his or her entire world—biological, psychological, sociological, and existential/spiritual—with new meaning.

Now that we have ventured through the land of depression with its vast and varied terrain, it is apparent that it is a surround not only of suffering and despair but of great value and meaning. However, there is the underworld of Hades with its cancer—a potentially malignant depression with its life-threatening component: *suicide*. In the next chapter, we will look at that realm, its risks, and how it embodies the seeds of creative transformation.

CHAPTER 2

Knowing Suicide and Its Creative Potential

"The passion for destruction is also a creative passion."
—MICHAEL BAKUNIN

SUICIDE is a very unusual act and a uniquely human problem. Etymologically, the English word *suicide* is taken from Latin and means killing of the self. However, the German equivalent *Selbstmord*, which translates as self-murder, is more to the point. Suicide, after all, is premeditated murder where enigmatically the murderer and the victim are the same person. What makes it even more abhorrent is that it completely goes against the most basic natural law—the law of self-preservation. Only humans, apparently, are capable of performing such an act. Thus Camus says, "There is but one truly serious philosophical problem, and that is suicide"; and thus Shakespeare (through Hamlet) phrases the central question of human existence as "To be, or not to be."

Throughout history, most societies have tried to forestall any individual inclination toward suicide by declaring it taboo, attaching a stigma to it, or by drawing strict distinctions between justifiable and unjustifiable suicide situations.[1] Some of the earliest recorded societies portrayed suicide as forbidden because of two related beliefs: Suicides live miserably in the next world; the ghosts of suicides seek revenge by attempting to destroy others as they have destroyed themselves.[2] In more advanced ancient civilizations, such as Greece, attitudes toward suicide became somewhat more ambivalent.

Today the rate of suicide is much higher in the Western world than in the emerging nations of Africa and other developing countries. Though these latter societies generally look upon suicide as evil, most experts feel that the real factor behind the lower suicide rate is that individuals in these societies lack inwardly diverted ag-

gression based on guilt, self-reproach, or a sense of unworthiness.[3]
Havelock Ellis offers an interesting observation relating to this issue:

> The prevalence of suicide . . . without doubt is a test of height
> in civilization; it means that the population is winding up its
> nervous and intellectual system to the utmost point of tension
> and that sometimes it snaps.[4]

In the same spirit, I believe that an individual's suicide has its origins
not only in the conflicts and complexities within his or her own
psyche, but also in the conflicts and complexities within the society
that has shaped his or her experience.

Sociological Factors

All roads in contemporary thinking about the causes of suicide
lead to Emile Durkheim, whose classic work *Suicide* was originally
published in 1897.[5] Durkheim extends responsibility for a given
suicide from the individual to the society, making suicide not only a
personal moral issue but also a collective, human welfare issue.
Durkheim goes on to classify suicides into three basic categories:
egoistic, altruistic, and anomic.

Egoistic suicides occur when the individual is not properly integrated into society; that is, he or she is cut off, lonely, and not part
of a group. An example in twentieth-century America's highly mo-
bile society would be the isolated divorced person without family,
friends, or a long-standing community of neighbors.

Altruistic suicides occur when an individual is so absorbed in a
group (social, political, or religious) that he or she voluntarily sacrifices his or her life for its leader, its causes, or its values. The
Japanese kamikaze pilots of World War II fit this description.

Anomic suicides result from an individual's inability to cope with
sudden changes in his or her social situation. The suicides that
followed the New York Stock Exchange crash of 1929 exemplify this
kind of suicide.

Teen Suicide

In America today, teenagers are the group most at risk, and here suicide appears in both its egoistic and anomic forms. While suicide is the ninth leading cause of death in the population as a whole, it is the third leading cause of death among American teenagers (second among fifteen- to nineteen-year-olds).[6] Nearly half a million teenagers attempt suicide every year, and more than six thousand succeed, a suicide rate that is two and a half times higher than it was twenty years ago, and almost four times higher than it was thirty years ago. If we project the present rate evenly across the time span of one year, that means that a teenager tries to commit suicide every 1.1 seconds; and every 80 seconds one of these teenagers does, in fact, die. An estimated 53 percent of high school students have suicidal thoughts and 13 percent attempt suicide. During college, the situation gets even worse, with an estimated 65 percent having suicidal thoughts and 15 percent attempting suicide.

Why is suicide such a major problem among people who have so much of their lives ahead of them? What can we learn about suicide from investigating the reasons behind this tragic trend?

In my opinion, the intrinsic social vulnerability of young people—poised between being dependent children and independent adults—makes them so susceptible to thoughts and acts of suicide. The uncertainty that characterizes present-day American society also provides contexts for yielding to this susceptibility. In a sense, all suicidal people, regardless of their age, suffer similar problems concerning who they are and how they are going to live in society as they know it. But to see these problems in the life of a young person is to see them in their purest, most dramatic, and most revealing form.

Few images capture the agony and tragedy of adolescent suicide as poignantly as the photograph on the October 2, 1988, cover of *The New York Times Magazine,* which shows the face of April Savino, a teenage girl who committed suicide while the magazine was putting together its excellent article on homeless adolescents. She was a fifteen-year-old who had run away from divorced parents and had lived for four years in Grand Central Station. After the break-up of a significant relationship, she shot herself in the head on the steps of a nearby church. This is an idiosyncratic personal history that is nevertheless eerily symbolic of the whole problem of suicide in general, as well as of teenage suicide in particular: A potentially worthwhile life, receiving insufficient nurturing at home, and finding no real place or meaning outside the home, ends itself. The fact that such a young human being would wind up committing suicide on the steps of a church is an especially appalling symptom of a malignant value-illness spreading through our society.

One major factor contributing to this value-illness is the ever-present threat of global annihilation by means of nuclear weapons, a threat to which adults immersed in busy lives can easily grow callous, but which is palpable and menacing to most adolescent minds. Before the break-up of the Soviet Union, a study of U.S. and U.S.S.R. teenagers revealed that their primary worries centered around their parents (whether they would die or get divorced, which can be easily associated with the death of their personal family), and around the threat of nuclear war (which can be similarly associated with the death of the entire human family).[7]

Since the end of World War II, teenagers have had to come to their own understanding of the nuclear menace hanging over them. Facing this possibility for the first time as a fledgling adult, it must appear as if Freud's *thanatos,* or death instinct, were rampant among civilized nations, with the ongoing possibility that one suicidal individual, in the wrong place at the wrong time, could press a button and make the Earth itself go up in flames. Many teenagers who commit suicide may, in fact, be making the most profound statement that they can about this situation, which is "Why live in such a world?"

When an individual's child (parent-related) ego disintegrates, the newly emerging adolescent (adult-related) ego can make powerful contacts with the Self. It can also see the shadow—the dark side of the psyche—better than older individuals with adult ego defenses can. Native American tribes used to turn to adolescents for insights into the future, precisely because adolescents possess this double-edged visionary capacity.[8] Perhaps we should listen more carefully to what our suicidal adolescents are telling us.

In addition to the potential loss (literal or effectual) of parents, the threat of nuclear war, and pollution of the ecosystem, other issues lead more and more of today's youth to contemplate or commit suicide; almost all these issues arise from social or individual problems. Such factors include:

- break-up of an intimate relationship
- family discord
- fear of violence
- drug or alcohol problems
- serious physical or mental health problems
- lack of spiritual values
- lack of direction in life
- failure in school
- unwanted pregnancy (or conflict over abortion)
- stress of entering or leaving college

For more than two centuries experts have debated whether descriptions of suicide, real or fictional, might harm vulnerable people, and that debate is especially fierce when applied to impressionable adolescents. It all began in 1774, with the publication of Goethe's novel *The Sufferings of Young Werther.*[9] Werther, an intelligent and artistically inclined young man, tends to immerse himself in outrageous dreams, grandiose plans, unrealistic loves, and hopeless passions. Eventually he exhausts himself and is left feeling empty: "I suffer much," he says, "for I have lost what was the sole rapture of my life, that holy, animating force with which I created worlds all about me; it is gone!" As a result of this "loss of force," he kills himself with a bullet to the head, leaving behind a suicide note to one of his unrealistic loves. Young Werther's tragic fate, and the romantic manner in which it is expressed, immediately inspired a wave of imitative suicides.

The memory of that event has continued to haunt psychiatry, so much so that the American psychiatrist D. P. Phillips has called the influence of suggestion on suicide the "Werther effect."[10] Currently, these resultant epidemics of teen deaths are known as "copycat suicides." Today, the impact of television on suicide stirs up just as much debate as the impact of the written word used to. Phillips and Caratensen have reported that thirty-eight nationally televised news or feature stories about suicide from 1973 to 1979 adversely influenced suicide rates among American teenagers.[11] In another related project, Gould and Shaffer found similar results relating to the impact of suicide storylines in four fictional television movies.[12]

Psychological Factors: Non-Jungian Viewpoints

Freud postulated two basic drives in the human psyche: the sexual drive, which he called *libido*, and the aggressive drive, which he called *destrudo*. Suicide involves the aggressive drive turned inward in its most extreme (or murderous) self-destructive form.[13] If depression (anger directed against the self) conflates with the death instinct, then the individual is likely to commit suicide.

Karl Menninger refines Freud's concepts and posits three necessary components for a suicidal act to take place.[14] The first is the *wish to kill*, which represents the aggressive drive. The second is the *wish to be killed*, which reflects a strong emotion like murderous anger turned inward. The third is the *wish to die*, which represents the death instinct. Menninger maintained that all three of these components have to be present for an actual suicide to occur. He also said that there is *always a wish to be rescued*, and today this forms the basis for all suicide prevention and therapy.

Donald Winnicott believes that suicide relates to an ambivalence about death.[15] For some people, this ambivalence involves a simultaneous attraction-repulsion toward death as a state of being. For other people, this ambivalence takes the form of a feeling that one is already dead even though one is still physically alive. These individuals, he says, "spend their lives wondering whether to find a solution [to their feeling of 'deadness'] by suicide, that is, sending the body to death which has already happened to the psyche." Winnicott emphasizes that the individual who is profoundly depressed and contemplating suicide has very mixed emotions about death and about exploring what died long ago, that is, the *true self*.

In a nonpathological situation, the *false self* (what McAfee calls the persona or caretaker self[16]) is experienced simply as a sense of emptiness, inauthenticity, and meaninglessness. In a pathological situation, the individual thinks the false self is the real self, because the true self is completely hidden. Winnicott links this dilemma to suicide: If the conditions which will make it possible for the "true self" to come into its own cannot be found, "the clinical result is suicide."

Psychological Factors:
Jungian and Post-Jungian Viewpoints

Jung never directly addressed the topic of suicide in an essay, but his views are very clearly expressed in his letters.[17] He opposed suicide unequivocally as a crime against the Self. In a 1946 letter, he wrote:

> The idea of suicide, understandable as it is, does not seem commendable to me. We live in order to attain the greatest possible amount of spiritual development and self-awareness. As long as life is possible, even if only in a minimal degree, you should hang on to it, in order to scoop it up for the purpose of conscious development. To interrupt life before its time is to bring to a standstill an experiment which we have not set up. We have found ourselves in the midst of it and must carry it through to the end.

Later, in 1951, he wrote about suicide to a severely depressed American woman:

> The goal of life is the realization of the Self. If you kill yourself you abolish that will of the Self that guides you through life to that eventual goal . . . You ought to realize that suicide is murder, since after suicide there remains a corpse exactly as with any ordinary murder. Only it is yourself that has been killed.

And finally, in 1955, this reference to suicide occurs in a letter he wrote to a sick, elderly woman in England:

> If your case were my own, I don't know what could happen to me, but I am rather certain that I would not plan a suicide ahead. I should rather hang on as long as I can stand my fate . . . as long as it is humanly possible. . . . Therefore, I cannot advise you to commit suicide for so-called reasonable considerations.

Bruno Klopfer, a Jungian analyst, takes a more developed anti-suicide position that is very much in line with my concept of ego-cide.[18] He infers, before Jung's letters were published, that based on Jung's essay "The Soul and Death," Jung would be opposed to suicide. In summarizing the Jungian perspective on suicide, Klopfer states: "[It] emphasizes another aspect of death, which rarely comes to the conscious awareness of persons with suicidal tendencies: namely, the longing for spiritual rebirth. The principle of dying and being reborn belongs to the essence of the unfolding life process." Klopfer adds: "Death in this connection is clearly conceived as the death of the ego that has lost contact with the Self and thus with the meaning of life. The ego has to return to the womb of the [Great Mother] to reestablish this contact and to be reborn with a new meaning for life."

Discussing this journey of the ego, Klopfer is careful to point out how perilous, as well as miraculous, it can be: There is "always the danger of [it] ending in destruction rather than in rebirth . . . [but] if the patient is made aware of this danger and is helped to face it by the analyst, the suicidal crisis can be transformed into a profoundly healing and life-giving experience."

Jane Wheelwright, another Jungian analyst, has a perspective similar to that of Klopfer.[19] She offers these thoughts on the link between depression and suicide ideation:

> I have come to suspect . . . that our periods of depression, which are like small deaths, can be used in a sense, as practice for our exit. . . . It is a misinterpretation of this process which, more often than not, leads people into suicide. The downward pull and immobilization that accompany deep depression are mistaken for sensations of physical death rather than of the psychic death which, as a matter of course, precedes psychic rebirth. Suicidal people often fail to recognize that it is nature's demand for a change in attitude or an increase in self-awareness which brings on the depressed state. They do not realize that to bring about a change in their lives, they have to experience despair and to face the black night of their tunnelled state of mind in order to come out into the light of change. It does seem that nature, however, intends for certain people to bow out, and these have no alternative. They will have too little will to tolerate the non-understandable. Their egos are overpowered and

lost, and they are helpless to save themselves. But those who are willing to at least make the effort of coping with their suicidal feelings stand a good chance of coming out ahead.

James Hillman, in his book *Suicide and the Soul,* takes quite a different approach—one that is uniquely his own. [20] He regards suicide as a rational deed to be understood and accepted, and recommends that analysts maintain "dispassionate scientific objectivity" toward the action. I disagree with his perspective, which creates serious problems in clinical treatment. Whereas Hillman criticizes physicians and psychiatrists for not being able to treat the issue of suicide with detached objectivity, I maintain that they and other healers need to evaluate suicide subjectively as well as objectively. My own philosophy is that in order to heal oneself and others, a premium must be placed on life. Hillman even calls into question the maxim "Where there is life, there is hope." He claims that this is a maxim for the physician, not the analyst, but it seems to me that this maxim applies to all healers. He further claims, "The hope which the patient presents is part of the pathology itself," a statement I find to be contradictory to the key part that hope plays in healing.

In his three-volume discourse on psychoanalytic treatment, Thomas French deals extensively with hope as the activating force of the ego's integrative function and as a prime mover in the healing process. [21]

Menninger cites a study of suicide in which the researchers found that "when hope disappears through the loss of opportunities to reach life's goals, destructive drives previously subordinated to other goals become discharged . . . against the self." [22] This study has been corroborated by Aaron Beck and his co-workers, who have shown that hopelessness has the highest correlation with subsequent suicidal behavior. [23]

Hillman's call for viewing a suicidal person with "dispassionate scientific objectivity" could tap into "countertransference hate," which could precipitate a suicide. [24] Depressed and suicidal patients, being hypersensitive and vulnerable, could perceive dispassionate neutrality as rejection and abandonment. Clinically, such a development would be disastrous. Hillman distances himself from countless therapists and analysts when he derides suicide prevention activities and involuntary hospitalization for acutely suicidal patients. The contrary but usual clinical, ethical, and legal position is that clearly distraught people ought to be protected against grave suicidal impulses. Repeatedly I have seen that the hospital can be the very womblike sanctuary where egocide and transformation can occur, thus preventing actual suicide.

In her recent book, *The Creative Leap,* Verena Kast addresses the issue of suicide.[25] This is a thoughtful and balanced contribution to the literature by a Jungian analyst. On the subjective side, she stresses the importance of the therapist's attitude toward suicide and death itself. Kast's caring compassion for and understanding of suicidal patients is tempered by the factual reality of suicide. As she notes, it does happen despite all of our efforts to prevent and avert such a tragedy.

I take issue with Kast only on one point. She maintains that we do not know if suicide is existentially good or bad and adds that a suicide might be the proper end result of an individuation process. I question this point of view except in very rare cases. Hitler is one such example. However, I see this kind of case as the exception that proves the rule. As per the Hindu perspective, suicide is essentially bad karma and fundamentally out of step with nature.

Derek Humphry, founder of The Hemlock Society, takes a contrasting view: Suicide is good karma, particularly for those people with terminal illnesses.[26] In his book, *Final Exit,* Humphry outlines ways to kill yourself alone or assisted by friends, relatives, and doctors. I know there are exceptions, such as understandable cases of passive euthanasia, but as a rule I maintain, as does Jung in his letters, that this type of ego-planned self-murder goes against nature's way.

Physician mercy killing and assisted suicide, cases of active euthanasia, are especially troubling, since they are contrary to the professional precept "Do no harm," from the Oath of Hippocrates. Mercy killing is not a new practice: In 1939 Sigmund Freud had his internist, Max Schur, inject him with two lethal doses of morphine.[27] At the time of his death, the world was told it was of natural causes. However, the truth was hidden for thirty years and only revealed by Schur posthumously. The founder of psychoanalysis took the call to death literally, rather than symbolically.

In the summer of 1990, American newspapers and magazines were full of stories about how Janet Adkins, a fifty-four-year-old woman who had been diagnosed with Alzheimer's disease, used a suicide machine furnished by Dr. Jack Kevorkian to give herself a lethal dose of potassium chloride.[28] This puts the physician on the side of killing, not healing; it's no wonder that Dr. Kevorkian is called "Dr. Death." Sadly, today this practice is more common and seems to be more accepted.[29]

Archetypal and Mythic Perspectives

As a Jungian, I also have to consider suicide from a much more instinctual perspective. Is there an archetype for suicide? In other words, is there a predisposition to murder oneself built into the human species: an ancient behavioral pattern or drive that is latent and unconscious (at least, for most individuals), but that can be detected in our myths and artistic creations?

Although there is plenty of evidence to support the existence of a death instinct in the human psyche, there is little evidence to support the existence of a suicide instinct. Although we know that individuals and groups can choose to kill themselves, this could easily be based upon a suicide complex with the archetype of death at its core. This is very different from an innate tendency to self-destruction, which would be related to a suicide archetype. In fact, with a few historical exceptions, there seems to be a suicide taboo in the human psyche that parallels the incest taboo.[30] Because it is all-important for a society to preserve and maintain itself, it is just as contrary to everyone's best interests for an individual to turn aggression inward toward the self as it is for an individual to turn it outward toward another member of the community. Aggressive energy is much better vented in hunting game for food, competing in sport, carrying out debate, or transformed in creative expression.

Besides human history, however, in our search for a suicide archetype, we have to look at human creative expression, and there is no other mode as fruitful to examine for this purpose than the fairy tale or folk tale. Marie-Louise von Franz argues that "fairy tales are the purest and simplest expression of collective unconscious psychic processes."[31] In a compact and compelling format, a fairy tale shares with myth the ability to reflect basic archetypes that are embedded in human culture.

After years of reading fairy tales, I have found only a few (such as "Rumpelstiltskin") that incorporate suicide into their storyline. This lack of attention to suicide should be encouraging to us as a species, because it implies that there is not a natural propensity to suicide at the archetypal core of the human psyche. Nevertheless, the fact that the suicide motif occurs at all in fairy tales means that suicide is an important and enduring dilemma of the human condition. In other words, while suicide may not be an archetypal issue in the human psyche, it can be a very significant issue (expressed as a suicidal complex) in an individual's response to the particular life he or she is living.

Marie-Louise von Franz maintains that there is a *symbolic suicide* motif in many fairy tales; and, as I've learned through personal communication with her, she agrees with my concept of egocide. According to von Franz, the hero or heroine in fairy tales almost always goes through an ego-sacrifice, which leads to transformation and rebirth. The Self and the shadow (as a positive creative force controlling the negative destructive force) both contribute to this symbolic ego death. While she has no trouble with my term egocide, she prefers the term *ego-sacrifice*. She also feels that a killing of the shadow, shadowcide, can occur, but that the danger that such a process might lead to an actual suicide is great.

Myths deal with suicide far more often than fairy tales do. Von Franz attributes this trend to the fact that myths are more closely related to specific cultures and, therefore, reflect more often the circumstances under which certain cultures allowed suicide. The ancient Chinese and Japanese cultures, for example, produced a plethora of myths justifying situational suicide, as did the ancient Roman and Irish cultures, although suicide-related myths from the latter two cultures were, in effect, suppressed by the Roman Catholic Church.

Greek mythology, however, is probably the richest and most prolific source of myths containing the suicide motif; which is understandable, since suicide was permitted in ancient Greece if one could argue a convincing case for it. Suicide is most often depicted as an appropriate action when an individual has violated a social taboo, is suffering from a hopeless love, is unable to tolerate the grievous death of a loved one, or is faced with an unavoidable loss of honor. For example, Jocasta, Oedipus's mother, hangs herself when she discovers that she has unknowingly married—and had children by—her son, thus committing incest.

From an archetypal and mythic perspective, suicide is a definite possibility for individuals who are unable to envision any way out of seemingly unbearable negative situations. But this seems to be based on a suicide complex, not on a suicide archetype.

Creativity and Suicidal States

Shiva, the Hindu deity, does a dance of creative rebirth out of destructive death energy all the while stepping on the ego (symbolized as a dwarf). Similarly, I have found that involving patients in creative expression after the destructive act of egocide parallels the healing process of transformation.

In an intriguing essay entitled "Creative Suicidal Crises," Norman Tabachnick proposes something akin to egocide and transformation for severely depressed and suicidal individuals.[32] He posits that a suicidelike state signals a potential movement of the individual away from a self-destructive mode of being (often manifested as a suicidal crisis and/or an untenable lifestyle) into a new, more rewarding mode of being. He comments: "There are groups of artistic creative efforts which are accompanied by suicidelike states." What Tabachnick calls suicidelike states, I call egocidal states. The tragedy occurs when this distinction is not understood, and the affected individual becomes confused and does, actually, commit suicide.

Tabachnick points out, as others do, that a suicidal urge on the part of a creative artist is especially complicated in its significance. Such an urge has, in his words, "meanings other than being a precursor to the *act* of suicide. One meaning may be . . . I am tired of life or some aspects of it as I presently experience it—I want to leave what I now have [or am]." What the creative person really needs in such a situation is a Symbolic Death (an egocide of the self-destructive ego-identity) followed by a creative rebirth. Again, the tragedy occurs when such a person, like poets Sylvia Plath and Anne Sexton, gambles with death and loses, confusing symbolic need with literal reality.

Other famous twentieth-century writers who are known to have suffered from severe depression and who eventually committed suicide include Jack London, Virginia Woolf, Hart Crane, Ernest Hemingway, Yukio Mishima, Yasunari Kawabata, John Berryman, Primo Levi and, most recently, Jerzy Kozinski, to name a few. Many

artists who have almost taken their own lives testify—directly or
indirectly—to the distinction between egocide and suicide. After
trying unsuccessfully to kill himself, A. Alvarez concluded, "Life
itself is the only argument against suicide. I'm a great believer in
growing up, and I think I grew up by the suicide attempt. It killed
off the adolescent."[33] From my point of view, what Alvarez did
succeed in doing by attempting suicide was to commit egocide, the
killing off of an immature and self-destructive ego-identity. In this
respect, his failed suicide experience had a healing effect, much like
the failed suicide experiences of the people who survived jumping off
the Golden Gate and San Francisco–Oakland Bay bridges.

Like Alvarez, American novelist William Styron came close to
ending his life; but, in his own words, he found his way "through the
darkness back to the light."[34] He describes a "second self," a murderous, evil shadow part of his psyche, that was planning his death.
This Dr. Jekyll/Mr. Hyde battle became consciously dangerous after
he stopped drinking. His depression worsened and he suffered immense physical pain, insomnia, hopelessness and, at times, deadly
horror. He sought relief and release by planning his death. Fortunately, he was saved from suicide by music. A soaring passage from
Brahms's "Alto Rhapsody" suddenly "pierced [his] heart," and he
entered a psychiatric hospital. Later he realized that this piece of
music evoked memories of his mother, who died when he was thirteen years old.

It is noteworthy how Styron characterizes his recovery in the
psychiatric hospital: "I'm convinced I should have been in the hospital weeks before. For, in fact, the hospital was my salvation." There
he engaged in art therapy, which he found valuable, describing his
first sculpture as "a horrid little green skull with bared teeth" that
seemed to be a replica of the depression he was beginning to overcome. He was also helped during this period by what he calls "a
religious devotion to persuade one of life's worth." This devotion
was first expressed to him by his loved ones, primarily his wife, and
then experienced by himself.[35]

Styron understood, in retrospect, that "seclusion and time" were
"the real healers." He also came to appreciate that "depression is not
the soul's annihilation." That is, since depression can and does end,
there is no need to end one's life. However, he could not grasp this
while he was in the worst throes of his depression, a situation which
he relates to the beginning of Dante's *Inferno:*

In the middle of the journey of our life
I found myself in a dark wood,
For I had lost the right path.

In discussing this passage, Styron says:

One can be sure that these words have been more than once employed to conjure the ravages of melancholia, but their somber foreboding has often overshadowed the last lines of the best-known part of that poem, with their evocation of hope. For those who have dwelt in depression's dark wood, and known its inexplicable agony, their return from the abyss is not unlike the ascent of the poet, trudging upward and upward out of hell's black depths and at last emerging into what he saw as "the shining world." There, whoever has been restored to health has almost always been restored to the capacity for serenity and joy, and this may be indemnity enough for having endured the despair beyond despair.

At the close of this chapter we realize that hope is the essence of finding a healing option to suicide. In the next chapter, we will concentrate on recognizing and treating depressed and suicidal individuals within a holistic systems model.

CHAPTER 3

Recognizing and Treating
Depressed and Suicidal People

"Healing is a lifelong process."
—ROSEMARY GORDON

In the popular imagination, to treat a person's illness successfully, whether that illness is physical or psychological, means to cure that person. I question this notion. As I tell my students, "Only hams are cured!" In my opinion, to treat a person's illness successfully means to effect a healing process in that person, which is related to integrity.[1] Both heal and holy come from the Old English word *haelen*, "to make whole."

Jungian analytical psychology, in particular, rarely promises to cure an underlying condition that is causing psychological problems. Instead it aims at promoting a person's individuation, which is an ongoing journey toward wholeness. Whereas the idea of finding a cure implies taking reductionistic, narrowly focused approaches to treatment, the idea of actuating a healing process implies taking a multidimensional holistic approach to treatment.

Perhaps the most prevalent misconception about the treatment of depressed and suicidal persons is that most of them can be "cured" by medication alone. There is no question that antidepressant medications help. In repeated double-blind scientific studies (i.e., with neither the administrators nor the subjects knowing who got medication and who got a placebo until afterwards), 60 to 70 percent of the severely depressed patients who improved were taking tricyclic medications.[2] However, these figures also mean that the other 30 to 40 percent of these patients responded favorably to placebos. In other words, they improved with *no* pharmaceutical agent.[3]

If we could determine why and how so many individuals respond favorably to placebos, our treatment of depressed and suicidal people would be greatly advanced. Among other things, doctors wouldn't feel compelled to rely so heavily on antidepressant medications to provide relief for their depressed and suicidal patients. If this placebo puzzle were solved, we would probably be tempted to agree with Oliver Wendell Holmes that we would be better off if all medications were dumped in the sea. Only then would we realize that the most powerful medicine of all, and the most likely source of the placebo effect, is what Jerome Frank calls "expectant faith"[4] and what others call hope.

Recognizing Depression and Suicidal Risk

Of course, the first step in treating any condition is recognizing that it exists. In terms of the depression continuum, let's examine the two principal varieties of normal depression beyond mild sadness: uncomplicated grief and uncomplicated bereavement.

Recognizing Normal Depression

Uncomplicated grief is precipitated by separation and loss and manifests as depressed mood. However natural and normal grief may be, it is still a difficult, distressing, and painful emotion.[5]

Uncomplicated bereavement is a somewhat more focused and intense form of uncomplicated grief and is a person's natural response to the death of a loved one. Typically it's a depressive experience that lasts no longer than six months. This does not mean that the person suffering the loss ceases to feel sad about it; rather, it means that the period during which bereavement dominates his or her emotional life has run its course.[6]

Recognizing Abnormal Depression

The abnormal part of the continuum can be roughly divided into two categories: minor depression (i.e., neurotic depression or dysthymia) and major depression (i.e., psychotic depression or melancholia). In both types of abnormal depression, the individual suffers depressive symptoms (such as depressed mood, disinterest or lack of pleasure in life, loss of appetite and weight loss, insomnia, fatigue or loss of energy, sense of worthlessness and guilt, difficulty with thinking or concentrating, and thoughts of death and suicide). Sometimes depressed people cannot function socially or carry on a productive life. Major depression is considerably more serious and extreme: The patient often is completely unable to cope with normal life and may suffer from hallucinations or delusions.

The most important clinical distinction among all the various forms of abnormal depression is between unipolar mood disorder and bipolar mood disorder (also known as manic-depressive illness). The former consists of purely depressive symptoms (such as major or psychotic depression), whereas the latter consists of a continuous alternation between manic and depressive symptoms.[7] Unipolar mood disorder is anywhere from 10 to 20 times more common than bipolar mood disorder.

In Hippocrates' humoral theory, melancholia (literally black bile in Greek, and one of the four humors) was associated with the cold, dry autumn months of increasing darkness.[8] Hippocrates' theory held sway for over a millennium. Although it seems absurd today as a serious medical doctrine, we still pay it homage in the way we talk—and, therefore, think—about depression. In English and most other European languages, to be depressed is to be cold, dark, morose, and in bad humor, to lose one's sense of humor. It is noteworthy that another depressive condition, Seasonal Affective Disorder (SAD), tends to overwhelm certain people in autumn and winter, and it appears to be caused by a deprivation of sunlight.[9]

The role of alcohol in depression is an important one. The chicken-and-egg debate over the relationship between alcohol and depression is long-standing, because so many depressed people are also heavy drinkers. Some believe that chronic overconsumption of alcohol leads to depression; others maintain that depression leads to chronic overconsumption of alcohol.[10] I think that both are true: Alcoholism can lead to depression, and depression can lead to alcoholism. I also think that in an alcohol-related depression, as in most cases of depression, spiritual/existential factors offer the greatest potential for change.

In response to a letter from William ("Bill") Wilson, one of the co-founders of Alcoholics Anonymous, Jung stated that he had told a client, Roland H., that his situation was hopeless unless he "could become the subject of a spiritual or religious experience." Jung's prescription matches his theory about why his client became an alcoholic in the first place: "His craving for alcohol was the equivalent on a low level of the spiritual thirst of our being for wholeness, expressed in medieval language: the union with God."[11]

Recognizing Suicide Risks

One out of six clinically depressed persons eventually commits suicide. Three out of five entertain thoughts about suicide, indicating that suicide is more than just a possibility in a case of depression—it's a serious risk. Failed suicide attempts, suicidal gestures, or suicidal threats of any type should always be taken as cries for help that involve gambles with death. This is especially true if the individual has a prior history of attempting or considering suicide. Not all depressives, however, have suicidal thoughts; nor do all who entertain such thoughts do so in a serious way, or ever actually attempt suicide. Also, not all suicide attempters suffer from clinical depression, although most do; many are diagnosed with various forms of personality disorder, schizophrenia, anxiety disorder, and organic conditions.

The general risk of suicide in the U.S. is 1 per 10,000. Low risk would be 1 per 1,000. Moderate risk would be 1 per 100 (e.g., for a person with a history of a previous suicide attempt—which is 100 times the risk for someone in the general population). High risk would be 1 per 10 (e.g., for a person with a history of a previous suicide attempt which was also either medically or psychiatrically serious).[12]

According to Beck, hopelessness is the best predictor of suicide, and the next best predictor is the presence of depression.[13] How, then, are we to instill hope in individuals who feel hopeless, or who are on the path to feeling hopeless? The answer to this question, and the thesis of this book, is that such hope can result from egocide and creative transformation of the self.

Self-Assessment of Suicide Risk

An individual who wants to know whether to seek help can do a self-assessment. A high suicide risk is related to affirmative answers to four questions:

1. Do you feel that your world is narrowing and you are more alone and alienated than ever before?
2. Do you feel unable to express anger toward others and increasingly blame yourself for everything that goes wrong?
3. Do you feel hopeless?
4. Do you think of dying and of ways to kill yourself?

Extending the Assessment of Suicidal Risk to Friends and Family

To help in your assessment of risk to self or significant others, it is important to know that the basic risk factors for suicide are:

1. suicidal thoughts;
2. terminal behavior (e.g., giving away valuable possessions and acting as if one is not going to be around much longer);
3. detailed suicide plan with a lethal method at hand;
4. presence of psychosis (especially featuring delusions that involve suicidal thoughts);
5. presence of an organic brain disorder such as acute intoxication or chronic disease, especially one which affects the brain, e.g., AIDS (which could lead to poor judgment and impulsiveness);
6. severe loss or threat of loss (e.g., death of, or final separation from, a loved one; loss of a job; or the advent of a serious illness);
7. a history of alcohol or drug abuse;
8. family history of suicide.

Someone who suspects suicidal intentions in a friend or relative should take the following five steps:[14]

1. Take the time to accept the distraught person and listen to what he or she has to say.
2. Begin your inquiry with sensitive, open-ended questions related to depression and hopelessness.
3. If the person admits to depression and hopelessness, ask if he or she has thoughts of dying or ending his or her life.

4. If the individual has thoughts about suicide, ask if he or she has any plans or means to carry out these thoughts.
5. If the person admits to having a suicide plan and the means to carry it out, ask, "What is stopping you?"

Assessing suicidal risk will affect a decision as to whether inpatient or outpatient treatment is indicated. Now let's deal with this thorny issue.

Do You or Someone You Love
Need Hospital Treatment?

Whether or not someone should be hospitalized is essentially a judgment call, one of the hardest decisions in the treatment of a depressed and suicidal person. Forming a collaborative partnership with a doctor is the best course to follow. Sometimes severely depressed or suicidal people may even have to be hospitalized against their will, rendering the decision all the more difficult. Once you know what is best, be assertive and persistent.

In order to generate some guidelines, let's assume that we're talking about individuals who already have attempted suicide by overdosing on drugs.[15]

As a rule of thumb, if such a person is not psychotic or severely depressed, does not suffer from severe insomnia, is not acutely suicidal at the time, has good social support, is hopeful about the future, and has a stable relationship with his or her doctor, then I would suggest outpatient treatment (see Table 3-1). In contrast, if the

TABLE 3-1
CHOOSING THE BEST TREATMENT FOR YOURSELF
AND YOUR LOVED ONES

Inpatient	*Outpatient*
Psychotic (delusional)	Non-psychotic
Severe depression	No severe depression
Severe insomnia	No severe insomnia
Acutely suicidal	Not acutely suicidal
Hopeless	Hopeful
No family or support system	Family or support system
Lack of stable relationship with doctor	Stable relationship with doctor

depressed person is unable to function, delusional or hallucinating, acutely suicidal, suffering from severe depression with unyielding insomnia, with little or no social support, hopeless about the future, and without a stable relationship with a doctor, then I would suggest hospitalization, even if the person is unwilling to cooperate.

Unfortunately, it is all too easy to err on the side of not hospitalizing a suicidal patient. In a study of people who committed suicide by overdose, 91 percent had been in recent contact with a physician, nearly all of whom were primary-care doctors: family practitioners and internists.[16] Over half of these individuals died by overdose from recent prescriptions for a lethal amount of sedative hypnotics or tricyclic antidepressants; 80 percent had a history of suicide threats or attempts, but only in 40 percent of the cases was the doctor aware of this history. Altogether, there was substantial evidence of depressive illness in 73 percent of the patients, yet this diagnosis was made in only 50 percent of the cases. Among those cases in which it was made, very few were actually treated. If they were treated, it usually did not involve adequate therapy.

To help remedy this, primary-care physicians ought to evaluate every individual who seems sad and depressed for a clinical diagnosis of depression. It should be standard practice to ask depressed patients whether they've ever considered or attempted suicide—especially if the person is an alcoholic (or an abuser of other drugs). Persistent insomnia should be recognized as a serious sign of clinical depression. A physician should not routinely write potentially lethal prescriptions for sleeping pills and tricyclic antidepressants for severe depression.

The best situation to be in, when dealing with depression, is a healing relationship with a doctor. It seems to me that in any therapy, the patient's needs (expressed and at times unexpressed) ought to determine all formal and informal aspects of treatment. In terms of biological needs, for example, the patient who is clinically depressed and shows signs that he or she would benefit from antidepressants should receive this treatment. In terms of psychological needs, there is a very wide range of possible therapeutic approaches, and the patient and therapist ought to take advantage of such a range by being selective and integrative. The same is true for social and existential needs. The patient and the therapist need to ask, "What's best in this situation?" The answer might be, for example, biological, psychological, social, and existential treatments, all four, or facets of each.

More than anything else, depressed individuals need caring concern and human responsiveness. My point of view is to stay focused on maintaining a strong doctor-patient relationship. I maintain that all measures necessary must be taken to keep a person from committing suicide, while at the same time providing a real human bond. In this way the depressed or suicidal person can develop new options and hope for the future. As Mendel states:

> Human contact is the key to suicide prevention. . . . Spending time with the patient, offering a relationship based on demonstrative reliability, and nondemand do prevent suicide.[17]

In my judgment, one of the most clinically significant aspects of a depressive illness is the patient's conviction that his or her depression will never remit. It is critical that both patient and doctor be careful not to concentrate on the darkness of the tunnel, but rather on the light ahead. That light is hope, faith, and love (the three intangibles of healing).[18] Mintz suggests that *hope* may provide "suicide antibodies."[19]

Next we will survey various treatments (biological, psychological, social, and existential/spiritual), and then illustrate a holistic approach with the case of an AIDS patient who was severely depressed and suicidal.

Biological Treatment

Within the biological realm of treatment there are the following approaches: somatic, pharmacologic, phototherapy, and diet.

Somatic Therapy

The most prevalent somatic (physical) approach to treating depressive and suicidal states is based, colloquially speaking, on shocking those states out of a patient's mind.[20] However, for many, electroconvulsive therapy (ECT) is a controversial approach. Why are so many repulsed by the notion of shocking the brain? We seem to have much less revulsion about shocking the heart electrically to convert potentially lethal arrhythmias back into normal rhythm. Perhaps it's because we're more inured in general to interfering with the body (heart) than we are to meddling with the mind (brain). Witness the strong impact of Ken Kesey's book *One Flew Over the Cuckoo's Nest,* and of the popular movie based on that book: ECT (also known as electroshock treatment) was presented as a barbaric type of punishment.

There is no denying that ECT has been abused by doctors in the past, as have all medical, surgical, and psychiatric treatments; this possibility is always present. Some critics of ECT are specifically concerned that it can cause long-term memory loss or brain damage. However, most studies reveal that it does not. Probably the most convincing argument to allay this fear is to compare ECT patients with individuals who have epilepsy. The latter suffer similar grand mal seizures, and yet these seizures do not result in long-term memory loss or brain damage. ECT is primarily used today when patients fail to respond to antidepressant drugs. Despite its scandalous reputation, ECT remains an effective therapy for psychotic depression, at times more effective than antidepressant drugs.[21]

Pharmacologic Interventions

The pharmacologic treatment of depression has primarily consisted of monoamine oxidase (MAO) inhibitors and tricyclic antidepressant drugs, and these treatments are effective. However, antidepressants have a slow onset of action (up to two to three weeks), can produce innumerable adverse side effects (dry mouth, blurred vision, drowsiness, cardiac arrhythmias, dizziness, urinary retention, constipation, impotence, and tardive dyskensia—a problematic neurological disorder), and can be taken in lethal overdoses, which makes them especially dangerous for suicidal individuals.

MAO inhibitors were initially viewed as a panacea for depression in medical and psychiatric circles. However, it was soon discovered that they can have some dangerous side effects, the main one being hypertensive crisis. Patients on MAO inhibitors must avoid foods containing tyramine (such as certain cheeses, wine, beer, and pickles), or risk suffering a hypertensive crisis. Additional possible side effects of MAO inhibitors include negative skin reactions, constipation, and impotence. Nevertheless, this medication is effective and safe when used carefully.

Several more effective antidepressants recently have been introduced, which are safer, have greater specificity, and have fewer adverse side effects. They consist of heterocyclics, triazoloben-zodiazepines, triazolopyridine derivatives, serotonin reuptake inhibitors, and various other compounds.[22]

Lithium carbonate was first used to treat depression in ancient Greek and Roman times, when immersion in mineral springs now known to contain large quantities of this compound was practiced. In 1949, John Cade, an Australian psychiatrist, rediscovered lithium carbonate's therapeutic value in tempering mania. It can facilitate a complete turnaround to health in the manic patient, whereas before its use, 23 percent of manics died after being admitted to a hospital in an acute manic condition. The condition of mania is reversed once the blood level of lithium reaches a therapeutic level. Lithium carbonate has also been demonstrated to be very beneficial in moderating cases of bipolar (manic-depressive) illness, increasing the periods between episodes of mania and depression and decreasing the length and severity of those episodes. This is important because 15 to 20 percent of bipolar disorder sufferers commit suicide if their symptoms continue without relief.[23] However, lithium carbonate can cause toxic side effects in patients with thyroid and kidney problems. It is also risky for patients with heart conditions. Nonetheless, it has been shown to be safe when precautions are followed and patients have their blood levels monitored carefully.

Critical to the use of all antidepressants is realizing that they are only adjuncts to psychosocial and existential/spiritual approaches. For the patient and the physician, treating depression and suicidal inclinations only with medication is a potentially dangerous and narrow path to follow. In our addiction-prone society, people could quickly become dependent on such medication and ignore other, potentially more effective treatment options. As Franz Kafka states in his story *The Country Doctor,* "To write prescriptions is easy, but to come to an understanding of people is hard."

Phototherapy

Seasonal Affective Disorder (SAD) symptoms occur during the fall and winter, and exposure to full-spectrum light (the light closest to sunlight) for several hours a day relieves these symptoms.[24]

Now I want to share a personal note about SAD. My depressive spells tend to occur in the winter. When I lived in Rochester, New York, where the winters are long, gray, and bleak, my winter-time melancholic episodes were exceptionally intense. Now that I live in Texas, where there is far more sunlight and short winters, I am much less depressed.

In 1973, long before SAD became the popular medical/psychiatric entity that it is today, I clipped a news item from the February 28 issue of the *Medical Tribune* with the headline: "Depressed Danes to Get Trips to Sunny Spain." The source of this report, ironically, was Elsinore, Denmark—the setting for Shakespeare's *Hamlet*! The article states:

> On the proposition that climate works wonders on the psyche, relays of 100 neurotic and depressed Danes will soon be getting generous doses of sunny Spain. Montebello, a day and weekend care center here and in Hillerod, started construction last year of a hundred-bed hospital in the little Spanish town of Benalmadena near Torremolinos. Denmark is dark and damp much of the year, and it is hoped that the change of climate will help accelerate recovery from milder mental disorders.

This news item makes me wonder if the concerned Danish psychiatrists and administrators were depressed themselves and wanted Spanish holidays as well. It also makes me wonder if the desire for more sunlight in the winter could create a new, health-related growth industry for Texas, perhaps in cooperation with Mexico.

On a more serious note, it seems to me that SAD does overlap with melancholia and other depressive conditions. One of the ways to test this hypothesis would be to carry out large-scale treatment programs in state mental hospitals using phototherapy with depressed patients. It would also be interesting to have some data on what actually happened to those depressed Danes.

Diet Therapy

Another comparatively simple approach to depression involves dietary control. In a recent study, caffeine and refined sucrose (white sugar) were eliminated from the diet of depressed patients, resulting in an amelioration of depressive symptoms that was still in effect at a three-month followup. It was also found in a double-blind study that depression came back two and a half times as often when refined sucrose was reintroduced into the diet than when caffeine was.[25]

Psychological Treatment

Psychological treatments include the following psychotherapeutic approaches: behavioral, cognitive, interpersonal, and psychoanalytic. Seldom are depressed or suicidal patients given biological treatments alone. Although many advances have been made in somatic and pharmacologic treatments, usually some form of psychotherapy is utilized in conjunction with it. In fact, in treating depressed and suicidal patients, psychotherapy is frequently the most important mode of treatment, and often it can be effective whether or not it is accompanied by antidepressant medication.

It is important to keep in mind Jerome Frank's maxim about psychotherapy: It is likely to succeed if there is a match between what the patient wants and what the therapist has to offer.[26] That is why knowledge of, and experience with, many approaches is helpful.

Behavioral and Cognitive Therapies

Behavioral therapy shapes antidepressant behavior by positively reinforcing behaviors that are not associated with depression, and by negatively reinforcing depressive symptoms.[27]

Cognitive therapy attempts to influence positive change in what a patient thinks as distinct from how the person behaves, the belief being that behavior is determined by one's thoughts. The aim of cognitive therapy is to orient the patient toward recognizing and correcting faulty patterns of cognition and the behaviors which accompany them.[28]

Interpersonal Therapy (IPT)

The IPT approach to depression holds that the manifestations and possible causes of a patient's depression lie within his or her primary social group. Therefore IPT focuses on the patient's current interpersonal relationships and on the patient's relationship with his or her extended social environment.[29]

Short- and Long-Term Psychoanalytic Therapy

The goal of brief, time-limited psychoanalytic therapy is to effect a change in the personality of the patient, improving such psychological constructs as trust, intimacy, coping, and grieving. However, as it works *directly* on a patient's defenses and resistances, short-term psychoanalytic therapy may be anxiety-provoking.[30]

Although the classical psychoanalytical approach is theoretically the same as the short-term psychoanalytical approach, one difference is the length of treatment; it does not follow a set time line and can last for several years. Another difference is the emphasis on transference rather than on defenses and resistances. Finally, the analyst or therapist in the classical approach is largely passive and encourages free association, as opposed to the more active role of the short-term therapist and the discouragement of free-association techniques.

The Adlerian point of view holds that all individuals need a sense of security and control over their environments, and that each person has a different idea of what security and control are and how they may be obtained. Adlerian psychoanalytic therapy is aimed first at helping the depressed or suicidal patient to realize and understand his or her unacceptable behavior, and then to take responsibility for it. The individual is made aware of his or her potential for change and is guided and supported in making constructive changes.[31]

Another Psychological Approach

Edwin Shneidman sees each case of suicide involving the following aspects: neuroanatomical, biochemical, psychological, social, spiritual, and philosophical.[32] I, too, think that a systems approach is the best one to take in considering such a multifaceted enigma as suicide. Shneidman's opinion is that in order to prevent suicide, something needs to be done for the suicidal individual. He suggests decreasing the pain, reducing the stress, eradicating the sense that there is no way out, and helping the individual realize that there are other options. This approach facilitates the transformation of hopelessness into hope—something most people want from therapy. The following vignette of Shneidman's illustrates this clearly:

> A young woman in college believed she had only two alternatives: either be a virgin or be dead. Unfortunately, she was

pregnant and because this did not fit into her "either/or" perspective, the only option she could see for herself was suicide. She even bought a gun.

Fortunately, Shneidman's therapy intervened to keep her from using it. He worked with her to create an entirely new list of options: abortion, giving the child up for adoption, or keeping the child. In other words, he helped her to see that there were, in fact, other choices she could make. Also, he was very clear about his own philosophical position—that he could not condone suicide because it was not a possibility for *life*. In essence, he was rekindling the patient's inner flame of hope.

Social Treatment

The two primary forms of social treatment are family and group therapies. The emphasis up to this point has been on the individual and on a one-to-one relationship between the doctor and patient (or therapist and client). There also exists a growing utilization of therapies that take place in groups, with individuals coming together to help each other work out their problems. Such therapies exist not only for depressive and suicidal states, but also for many associated problems like alcohol and substance abuse.

Family Therapy

The therapist, the patient, and the patient's family members are all involved in this therapeutic approach, which aims at treating the depressed or suicidal individual and combines ideas from psychology and sociology. The psychological goal in this context is for the patient to achieve some kind of inner peace, while the sociological goal is for the patient to achieve harmony with his or her outer environment.[33]

Group Therapy with Suicide Attempters

As part of a research project, I was co-leader of three different groups of suicide attempters in the following settings: general hospital, community health center, and university medical center.[34]

These therapy groups with high-risk subjects had a positive impact on preventing future suicides, which demonstrates that group therapy with suicidal individuals in a homogeneous composition can be efficacious. Over time, many of the patients became assistant therapists, which makes these groups similar to the Alcoholics Anonymous model.

Alcoholics Anonymous (AA) and Narcotics Anonymous (NA)

For alcoholics and narcotics abusers, AA and NA can offer invaluable group support in breaking both addictive and depressive patterns. AA and NA are alike in almost every way except for the specific addictions they treat. Each one is designed to be a self-help support group. The addiction is perceived as a disease, so the biological aspect of the member's problem is emphasized. But the treatment of the addiction requires a change deeper than a mere physical one, that is, a change on a psychosocial and spiritual level as well. The spiritual element is at the center of AA and NA,[35] just as it is with egocide and transformation.

Existential Treatment

According to van Deurzen-Smith, the aim of existential therapy is to help a depressed and suicidal person reflect upon life and develop reasons to live. It involves two basic assumptions: 1) human nature is intrinsically flexible, and 2) life makes sense and one's attitude toward life creates meaning.[36]

From an existential perspective, life is seen as a quest for meaning, so that problems can be dealt with in light of that meaning. Viktor Frankl's logotherapy, based on existentialist thought, considers depression to be the result of an "extended frustration," or of a lack of the "will to meaning"; that is, the striving to find a purpose in life.[37]

Treating Depression: A Case in Point

Above all, I think that it is important to view all possible treatments for depressive and suicidal states in a holistic way, and to draw from as many different modalities of therapy as appropriate in treating any depressive or suicidal person. In other words, the patient as individual, not a particular therapeutic approach, ought to guide the therapy.

For a severely depressed and suicidal person, thoughts of meaninglessness approach hopelessness. He or she is cut off from many values, and has little or no spirit or energy for living a full life. Instead, the despairing soul merely exists. Let me share with you the story of a patient that illustrates how various biological, psychological, social, and existential factors can combine to depress and demoralize even a very resourceful person, and how such depression and demoralization can be effectively treated.[38]

In January 1982, Michael returned from San Francisco to his hometown of Rochester, New York, to attend his mother's funeral. She had died of breast cancer. He had been extremely close to his mother, and losing her was letting go of the one constant support that he had had for all of his thirty-seven years. He did not get along with his father, but they were cordial at the funeral. Seeing his father again, however, brought back an especially painful memory: His father had forced him to leave home after discovering that he was homosexual, fifteen years earlier.

After the funeral, Michael was glad to get back to San Francisco. He had no idea that his mother's death was to herald the worst year of his life. In the spring of 1982, he quit his job and founded a consulting firm, which got off to a good start. But in the late summer, paradoxically, he felt depressed and experienced increasing fatigue and arthralgia. In the fall, he set up a new home with a partner in hopes of settling down, but the relationship did not work out. All through November he sank deeper and deeper into depression, developing a fever, night sweats, and diarrhea. He had not improved by Christmas, when he visited his father. His father suggested that he move back to Rochester to recover; indicative of how bad he felt, Michael agreed. It seemed as if his father were reaching out to him because he was an only child and now, after the death of his mother, his father's only immediate relative.

When he returned to San Francisco to arrange for his move to Rochester, Michael's condition rapidly deteriorated. In addition to worsening diarrhea and night sweats, he developed a persistent cough. By the time he flew back to Rochester, in late March 1983, he had lost thirty-eight pounds. A few days after his arrival, he was so ill that his father took him to Strong Memorial Hospital Emergency Department, where he was admitted to the ICU with labored respirations and a fever of 104°F. While he was there, Michael overheard doctors talking about the possibility that he had AIDS. Like everyone else at the time, he equated AIDS with death.

In the ICU, after his condition was stabilized, a lung biopsy revealed that he had pneumocystis carinii pneumonia, a key indicator of AIDS. After hearing this news, he began to talk about being a dead man. He felt helpless and hopeless. He thought about suicide, and how he would kill himself once he was transferred to a medical floor. A medical student assigned to him was an empathic and patient listener, and she managed to elicit his suicidal thoughts. Michael told me later that he felt this student genuinely cared about him. Emboldened by this feeling, he asked her, "Is it crazy to think that I could live, that I could survive AIDS?" She indicated that it wasn't, but that he might still benefit from a psychiatric consultation.

It was in this context that I first met Michael. Outside his room there was a sign outlining precautions similar to those for patients with infectious hepatitis. After putting on a gown, gloves, and mask, I entered the room, introduced myself, and shook his hand. I could tell immediately that this human contact was reassuring to him. I told him I knew very little about his case, but I had heard that he was depressed. I sat down and listened as he recounted the history I have summarized here. He asked me, as he had asked the medical student, "Is it crazy to think that I could survive this deadly disease?" I thought for a minute, and then said, "No, it's not crazy." From that moment on, he gave up his preoccupation with suicide as a way out.

What had happened? Michael had been offered hope—first by the medical student and then by me. This hope turned out to be powerful medicine. Specifically, he latched on to the hope that he might be the first case, or one of the first cases, to survive AIDS. He reasoned that most malignant forms of cancer were originally thought to be nontreatable and noncurable, but for many of these cancers treatments had eventually been found. He also drew hope from reading about unexplained spontaneous remission of some supposedly untreatable cancers. I acknowledged that there were such cases but cautioned that they were very rare. My goal was not to get him all fired up with possibilities but to keep alive the small flame of hope that had been ignited with the assistance of the medical student. I continued to see him during his hospitalization, then for eight months as an outpatient on a weekly or biweekly basis.

As time went on, Michael suffered several complications of AIDS. Pneumocystis pneumonia came and went again. He exhibited disseminated herpes and cytomegalovirus and started complaining of left lower leg numbness and foot drop. In addition he developed Kaposi's sarcoma, a cancer which greatly increased his risk for early mortality. From the AIDS hotline in New York City and the Center for Communicable Diseases I learned that patients with his constellation of problems lived an average of four to six months. I did not tell him this for obvious reasons.

Michael's hope and desire to live helped him overcome his physical problems temporarily. His health actually began improving. He arranged to have his father and a friend complete his move to Rochester. After his nearly two-month hospital stay, he moved into his own apartment. Miraculously, he operated a consulting business out of his own apartment for four months, even though both his primary physician and I advised him to wait for a while before starting back to work. Prior to his discharge I had actually thought that he might never have the physical, mental, and emotional strength to work again, but there was no stopping him. When I met with him as an outpatient, Michael talked about his will to live, his pride in his work, and his desire to write a book on "the theory of knowledge." We also talked about death and dying, but he would never discuss these issues in depth or at length.

About four and a half months into Michael's outpatient therapy, there was a significant turning point. He initiated a handshake when he came in—something he didn't routinely do. When I inquired about the handshake, he said that he was hurt by his father's refusal to shake hands with him. When he had learned that his son had AIDS, his father's homophobia had resurfaced in a heightened way. Because he was afraid he might catch the disease, despite all the evidence to the contrary, he rarely visited Michael in the hospital and he was glad when Michael moved out of his house.

Now that he was estranged from his father and removed from his friends in San Francisco, Michael faced a serious lack of social support. Fortunately, we were able to arrange home visits and contact with sympathetic volunteers through AIDS/Rochester, Inc., and he found these arrangements helpful. He also had a dedicated friend who stood by him and provided immense comfort and day-to-day assistance.

Nevertheless, the continued rejection by his father took an enormous toll on Michael. His physical condition began to wane, but he continued to work. Six and a half months into therapy he started missing appointments. When I would call him later, he would say that he forgot or had been too tired to come. He was also humiliated by the fact that he had to go on Medicaid, since his insurance had run out and he was now uninsurable. There was also a long delay in social security disability relief. At one point, he became so outraged that he called the U.S. Secretary of Health and Human Services directly to complain. Amazingly, Michael got through, and his voice joined the many that eventually changed federal policy and expedited disability payments for AIDS patients throughout the country.

I saw Michael again in early December 1983. He was emaciated and extremely weak, and the limp in his left leg had worsened. Again, he was depressed and demoralized; and yet he refused to take antidepressant medication, which had been his position throughout the whole course of his treatment. Michael's way was to do it on his own, indicating that he still had some inner resources to fight against despair.

In January 1984, Michael stopped coming for outpatient therapy. I checked in with him by phone several times, but eventually he did not return my phone calls—or my letters. I last saw him during a hospitalization in June 1984. Michael was glad to see me, but he looked gravely ill and seemed despondent. His Kaposi's lesions were not responding to radiation, and he was weaker than ever. He felt that his doctors were giving up on him and he talked about dying. In September he was admitted once more, and he died suddenly the first night of this final hospitalization.

I share this account of Michael as a testament to his courage and will to live even though he was suffering from a devastating disease. Several times he looked right into the face of death and said, "Not yet!" The fact that he survived a year past his anticipated time of death remains an inspiration in the face of the darkness that surrounds this catastrophic disease of AIDS. My hunch is that his strong will to live—supported first by an exemplary medical student, then by numerous physician specialists, nurses, social workers, AIDS/

Rochester, Inc. volunteers, and his friend—extended his life and made it more meaningful. Michael's story underscores the fact that the power of *hope* is available to everyone: It is an internally generated medicine that taps into the archetype of the healer within.

The Greek myth of Pandora beautifully symbolizes the fact that hope is the best and last resort in dealing with problems of human existence. After Pandora had opened her box and released all the horrible things into the world, including ghastly creatures of despair and monsters of violence, out came Hope, in the form of a bird. The bird is an ancient archetypal symbol of the spirit; and the human spirit's capacity to hope is what most needs to come out of a holistic approach to treating depressed and suicidal individuals.

> "Hope is the thing with feathers
> That perches in the soul,
> And sings the tune without the words,
> And never stops at all."
>
> —EMILY DICKINSON

Hope and Self-Love

Most psychological theorists believe that if we are accepted by our mother and/or father, or by a parental surrogate, in the first two years of our life, then we have a fundamental, biologically rooted sense of self-acceptance on which we can rely ever afterward. This sense of self-acceptance is very much like what Kay Toolery calls an "affective reserve of hope and self-love"—something that protects life and that can be therapeutically augmented. Within each person there is "an inner, untouchable cache of warmth and richness; a personal, unloseable, unspendable treasure; an emotional insulation against psychological chill or shock. This is an *affective* reserve. It has nothing to do with those harder, colder, more rational structures that well-developed ego skills erect against despair or breakdown."[39]

In developing her affective reserve theory, Toolery observes that in suicidal adolescents the biggest problem seems to be not self-hatred or guilt but "a deficiency disease, a lack of love for their lives and a lack of hope." I would extend this characterization to adults and the elderly as well as adolescents. In an increasingly depersonalized era of automation and computerization, it is more and more difficult to find meaning in life and, therefore, to find nourishment for hope and self-love.

Toolery goes on to say that we can make all the difference for these severely depressed youths (or, as I would have it, demoralized people in general) by emphasizing that "this too shall pass," and by facilitating their quest for a golden key that will unlock the "treasured mythology of the Self." She emphasizes that the individual (particularly the young person) is prone to suicidal depression if he or she has not internalized a symbolic amulet or talisman which the individual connects to his or her large Self (beyond the ego)—a special coin, stone, shell, or image. In terms of therapy for depression in particular, I interpret this premise as meaning that a person's depression cannot be resolved until that person finds and reconnects with his or her lost soul, so that the candle of hope can be relit.

Crying and Laughing

Now I will focus on the value of tears and humor in treating severe depression. Crying is a built-in way of allowing grief and sadness to flow from our psyches, and laughing (as Norman Cousins rediscovered) is a built-in way of allowing hope and happiness to enter. Often, the two processes blend together. If you do too much laughing, you may start shedding tears; and if you weep excessively, you can easily wind up laughing. In the healing process, crying and laughing both act to relieve tension and to restore balance.

Of the two processes, laughter tends to be the less appreciated, and yet it can often do more good. President Abraham Lincoln knew this when he said: "With the fearful strain that is on me night and day, if I did not laugh I should die."

Arthur Koestler has noted that laughter provides "relief from stress [that] is always pleasurable, regardless whether it was caused by hunger, sex, anger, or anxiety."[40] He further notes something very important to the thesis of this book: "Laughter prevents the satisfaction of biological drives, it makes a [person] equally incapable of killing or copulating; it deflates anger, apprehension, and [ego] pride." In other words, when laughing we cannot do harm to our-selves or others. It's especially difficult to imagine killing oneself while laughing, when the ego *is* deflated, which is somewhat similar to what goes on in egocide and transformation.

In our healing journeys, creating opportunities to laugh and cry keeps us from developing rigid attitudes about ourselves and our situations. It temporarily breaks up defensive walls and even gives us a taste of death—an interruption from our normal patterns of breathing, observing, thinking, and responding—so that we can re-create ourselves and our situations afterward. In this respect, crying and laughing are self-transcending activities that can be dra-matically helpful in treating our depressions. They can lead to what Koestler calls *creative regeneration*—the goal of all successful psycho-therapeutic endeavors.

Creativity and Healing

In guiding my patients to orchestrate egocides instead of suicides, I have found that it helps immensely to involve them in creative expression and specific works of art therapy (based on active imagi-nation). This outer activity parallels the inner psychic resynthesis of the fragmented parts of the ego, after being guided by the anima (soul) and animus (spirit) to contact the Self, which is the healing aftermath of egocide. Indeed, creative products of active imagination often stimulate that resynthesis to occur. The next part of this book, "An Innovative Way of Healing Depression," concerns these very issues.

PART II

AN INNOVATIVE WAY OF HEALING

CHAPTER 4

Egocide and Transformation:
A New Therapeutic Approach

*"In the act of sacrifice . . . the ego decides
against itself . . . [and] subordinates itself
to a higher authority which is . . . the
principle of individuation or the Self.*

—MARIE-LOUISE VON FRANZ

Now I want to present a novel approach to treating depressed persons and those who want to kill themselves. It involves egocide, transcendence, and transformation. The method I advocate for treating depressed and suicidal patients differs from the other approaches I have described, although it works in harmony with any one or more of them. I call this approach *egocide and transformation*.

Let me simplify matters for a moment and refer to it more colloquially as a Commonsense Model (see Table 4-1). The Bad News is that every depressed person, even while under the care of a therapist, is bound to go through periods of failing, falling, and losing, which will lead to grief, despair, and, possibly, suicidal thoughts. The Good News is that only a part of the depressed person—the aspect of the ego involved with the Bad News—has to die or be killed symbolically. Then the person can develop a new ego-identity and self-concept that will lead to fresh chances to succeed. In other words, the person goes through a Symbolic Death, which I term egocide. This process feels like dying, so it sets in motion a kind of mourning process. However, once the mourning for the lost dominant ego-identity is complete, the person experiences New Life, an existence that is more promising than the one left behind. I call this rebirth a transformation.

Let's look at some well-known examples of people who made this kind of healing journey through dark nights of their souls. Each example illustrates that an individual must first endure depression in order to transcend it and transform his or her life. After this healing,

TABLE 4-1
COMMONSENSE MODEL OF
EGOCIDE AND TRANSFORMATION

Bad News	In a period of failing, falling or losing, the depressed individual experiences such grief or despair that the person wants to die, i.e., commit suicide.
Good News	The depressed person does not have to die totally; only part of the individual's psyche has to die or be symbolically killed off.
Symbolic Death	Letting go of or killing off the destructive part of the psyche, the dominant ego-image or negative identity, through egocide.
New Life	Egocide makes possible a psychic transformation and a new ego-Self axis evolves, allowing for one's full potential to develop and one's personal myth to be affirmed.

each of these individuals made vital contributions to bettering the lives of others.

Abraham Lincoln suffered from recurrent bouts of severe depression, no doubt resulting from the death of his mother at an early age and the harsh treatment at the hands of his father. When he was twenty-nine years old, he became morbidly depressed after the death of his beloved fiancée, Ann Rutledge. He wandered the Illinois river banks confused and grief-stricken. His friends thought he might be suicidal, so they removed his knives and razors and kept watch over his activities. At the age of thirty-two, Lincoln began experiencing deep depressive spells, as he describes in a letter to his law partner, John Stuart:

> If what I feel were equally distributed to the whole human family, there would not be one cheerful face on earth. Whether I shall ever be better, I cannot tell; I awfully forbode I shall not. To remain as I am is impossible. I must die or be better.[1]

Karl Menninger, in his book *The Vital Balance,* offers another telling account of Lincoln's depression:

On his wedding day all preparations were in order and the guests assembled, but Lincoln didn't appear. He was found in his room in deep dejection, obsessed with ideas of unworthiness, hopelessness, and guilt. Prior to his illness, Lincoln was an honest but undistinguished lawyer whose failures were more conspicuous than his successes. This was when he was considered well—before his mental illness made its appearance. What he became and achieved after his illness is part of our great national heritage.[2]

In 1821, the English philosopher John Stuart Mill, then only twenty years old, became morbidly depressed. Apparently, he couldn't escape thinking that he would never be happy, even if he were to obtain everything he desired. Eventually, however, he was able to push himself beyond this state, by some means that were apparently not clear even to himself. In his *Autobiography*, Mill states:

> The experiences of this period . . . led me to adopt a theory of life, very unlike that on which I had before acted, and having much in common with what at that time I certainly had never heard of, the anti-self-consciousness theory of Carlyle. I never, indeed, wavered in the conviction that happiness is the test of all rules of conduct, and the end of life. But I now thought that this end was only to be attained by not making it a direct end. Those only are happy (I thought) who have their minds fixed on some object other than their own happiness; on the happiness of others, on the improvement of mankind, even on some art or pursuit, followed not as a means, but as itself an ideal end. Aiming thus at something else, they find happiness by the way.[3]

Another meaningful example of a person overcoming depression is William James, the founder of both American psychology and American philosophy. At the age of twenty-five, James dropped out of medical school because he was severely depressed and was entertaining suicidal thoughts. Cameron, his biographer, writes:

> He awoke every morning with a horrible dread. For months he was unable to go into the dark alone . . . he wondered how other

people could live so unconscious of the pit of insecurity beneath the surface of life. . . .

The world owes a great deal to those personal misfortunes. James was thrown heavily upon his own resources; his incapacities and frustrations at such a time gave him an intense and intimate appreciation of the deepest philosophical and religious problems; his illness clearly developed and deepened the bed in which the stream of his philosophic life was to flow.[4]

Menninger suggests that by transcending their illnesses, these three individuals became what he terms *weller than well.* They were able to enter into the darkness and commit egocide rather than suicide; afterward, they were able to transform their identities. Each of them was involved in a journey toward wholeness that was related to a cycle of living and symbolically dying, and living again, which is the antithesis to the ego's ultimate claim to control, i.e., suicide.

Whatever impels a person to seek death, there is virtually always a better alternative than killing oneself. Sometimes the temptation to commit suicide can be strong and even comforting. Nietzsche, for example, said: "The thought of suicide is a great consolation: By means of it, one gets successfully through many a bad night." However, thoughts of suicide, under certain conditions, may be dangerous to entertain. I propose a different maxim: Contemplate egocide, a humbling but healing act of creative transformation; by means of it, one goes through a Symbolic Death, and on to New Life.

From Suicide to Egocide

A prime catalyst in the development of my egocide and transformation theory was my research involving survivors of jumps off the Golden Gate and San Francisco–Oakland Bay bridges. What most impressed me about the survivors was that not one individual in this high-risk group went on to commit suicide; indeed, each survivor went through a transcendent experience after his or her suicide attempt. I struggled with the problem of what to call the self-chosen close encounter with death that these individuals had undergone. I settled on the term egocide because this symbolic death-rebirth experience changed their lives so much that their whole view of themselves (their ego-identity) changed dramatically. From this start, I developed a new Jungian-oriented analytical approach to the psychotherapy of depressed and suicidal patients.

Enoch Calloway, who supervised this research, had a major influence on my thoughts about these survivors of suicide. When I came back from my first interview with a survivor, I told Calloway that my interviewee had gone through what seemed to be a religious experience. It sounded very mystical to me because this person felt that he was somehow linked to God, and that this link was why he had survived. Having just completed my psychiatric residency, I could have easily diagnosed this person as a schizophrenic, paranoid type, with religious delusions of grandeur. However, Calloway urged me not to dismiss what this survivor was saying, and not to categorize him so glibly.

Calloway suggested that I write everything down, organize the data, and only then see what patterns emerged. He also urged me to read *The Varieties of Religious Experience* by William James, who had studied religious experiences scientifically, documenting all the data he could obtain and then discerning patterns.[5] This book conveyed an important and meaningful message to me: Value the subjective; it is as real as the objective.

With Calloway's encouragement, I began to think and write about what I termed *egocide*.[6] The survivors of suicide had really meant to annihilate themselves. However, what they did instead was to destroy (or sacrifice) their egos. Their conscious ego identities died— that is, they symbolically killed their former perspectives of themselves and of life. However, what Jung calls the Self was not destroyed.

Clarifying Jungian Concepts

The type of experience I've just delineated has significant implications for therapeutic work with depressed and suicidal patients. As a first step toward making these implications clear, let me review some of the concepts involved in Jungian psychology and, therefore, in my theory of egocide and transformation (see Figure 4-1). For those who do not know Jungian psychology, this section is essential; for those who do, it will serve as a helpful review.

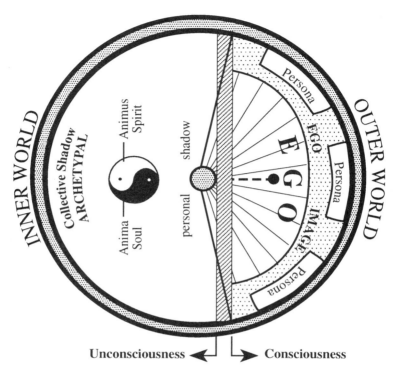

FIGURE 4-1
Structure of the Psyche à la Jung. Ego is the Center of Consciousness.
Self is the Center and Totality of the Psyche.

Ego and Shadow: Conscious and Unconscious

The ego, as Jung defines it, exists only in a conscious state and, therefore, differs from the ego as Freud defines it. In the Freudian model, the ego is both conscious and unconscious. In the Jungian model, according to Jung himself:

> We understand the ego as the complex factor to which all conscious contents are related. It forms, as it were, the center of the field of consciousness.[7]

Jung describes the ego as resting on the unconscious, and being influenced by subliminal and retrievable memories as well as by intrusions of the shadow.

The personal shadow is that which is repressed, unknown, and often evil about oneself. It is typically projected onto other people and usually represented as same-sexed figures in dreams. James Hall calls the shadow: "that 'dark' alter ego." He adds: "Although the shadow seems unacceptable to one's present ego-image, it often contains unrecognized positive qualities needed for further individuation."[8]

The shadow also has been described as having negative and positive poles.[9] Whereas the negative pole contains the culturally undesirable attributes that have been repressed (e.g., primitive, lustful, aggressive, hateful, envious, murderous, and anti-social qualities), the positive pole contains idealized traits that also have been repressed (e.g., heroic, visionary, spiritual, vital, noble, and refined qualities).

Erich Neumann defines shadow as

> The unknown side of the personality, and that it normally encounters the ego, the center and representative of the light side and of consciousness, in the form of a dark, uncanny figure of evil—to confront whom is always a fateful experience for the individual.[10]

He continues,

> At first, the figure of shadow is experienced externally as an alien and an enemy, but in the course of its progressive realization in consciousness it is introjected and recognized as a component of one's own personality. Yet when the personal shadow has been assimilated, the archetypal shadow (in the form of the Devil or Adversary) still remains potent in the psyche.

Ego, self, and Self: I, personal being, and Supreme Being

The ego, as the center of consciousness, is concerned with personal image and identity and therefore the self, which means that it is involved with life on a day-to-day basis. As such, the ego and self are subordinate to the Self, of which they are a part.

Jung envisioned the Self as the center and totality of the psyche, encompassing both the conscious and the unconscious. He further viewed the Self in a spiritual way: "Unity and totality stand at the highest point on the scale of objective values because their symbols can no longer be distinguished from the *Imago Dei* [Image of God]."[11] In addition, the Self is an archetypal image of the Creator: "The ego stands to the Self as the moved to the mover."[12]

The ego tends to dominate the first half of one's life and is connected to one's identity, ambitions, and accomplishments. Often at mid-life a crisis occurs, which leads to a potential transition from an egocentric life to a life where the ego has a new position subordinate to the Self.[13] The second half of life is characterized by the development of an "ego-Self axis."[14] Whatever one calls it, the change constitutes a paradigm shift on an individual level, comparable in significance to the paradigm shift that took place on a socio-historical level around the year 1600, when the Ptolemaic concept of the sun circling the earth was replaced by the Copernican concept of the earth circling the sun.

In the Freudian psychological model the ego, like Ptolemy's earth, is firmly in the center. The essential message is "I, the ego, am in charge here." I call this the General Alexander Haig Syndrome. When President Ronald Reagan was shot by a would-be assassin, Alexander Haig, Reagan's Secretary of State at the time, appeared on television claiming, "I'm in control. I'm in charge." Like Haig in this situation, the ego may think of itself as being in control and having the power to command, but that is not necessarily the case. I concur with the Jungian view that the ego, like Copernicus's earth, is *not* in the center; rather, the Self is. This fact becomes painfully manifest for those who undergo a major life crisis, clearly threatening the ego in those who suffer severe depression, and potentially transformative for those who commit egocide.

Ego and Ego-Image: The I and Its Portrait

The ego (I or me) is a complex (a grouping of related experiential images held together by a shared feeling tone) with an archetypal core (the Self). In discussing the development of an ego-identity, Hall introduces the term ego-image and characterizes it as follows: "What is 'healthy' for one dominant ego-image at a particular stage of life may be decidedly unhealthy for the nascent ego-image of the next stage of life.''[15] In other words, while the inner being based on the ego and its connection to the Self remains essentially the same, one's portrait (ego-image) is constantly changing. This, Hall maintains, permits ''a clear distinction between the image of the ego and the ego itself, which in its basic form consists of a center of subjectivity based on the archetype of the Self.'' Important in relation to the concept of egocide is Hall's notion that:

> Whenever the present dominant ego-image is changing, the ego feels some threat of dissolution, even if the change is in the desired direction. The ego in process of change seems to move from one identity [dominant ego-image] toward another, usually more comprehensive, that is, the person is actually individuating.

Persona and Shadow: Dr. Jekyll and Mr. Hyde

The ego wears a mask, the persona, to assume a role in order to relate to, and interact with, the outer world. Usually the persona is opposite to the shadow. For example, a woman who is very sweet, super-kind, and overly cooperative on the surface might tend to have a sour, cruel, and manipulative shadow. An illustration from literature is Robert Louis Stevenson's famous Dr. Jekyll and Mr. Hyde doubling: a single individual with the persona of a saintlike doctor and the shadow of a devilish criminal. As these two examples imply, the persona often is a self-adopted role based on the norms, traditions, ideals, and values of the collective or culture.

Tragic problems can occur when an individual identifies too closely with his or her persona, that is, when the ego merges with the persona or social role. Problems can also occur if the persona is excessively developed so that the individual becomes rigid, insensitive to the surrounding world, or thick-skinned. The other, equally problematic extreme is an inadequate development of the persona, which can cause the person to become hypersensitive to the outside world, or thin-skinned. The healthy ego functions independently from the persona and knows that it can choose or not choose to identify with persona roles.

When an individual identifies too strongly with the collective self, this engenders a false self,[16] like the stereotype of the organization man or woman. Madison Avenue and the mass media help encourage such untrue ego- and self-images through promoting specific life-styles as desirable, by dictating what is normal vs. abnormal, and by directly or indirectly preaching the value of conformity (or a calculated and stylized non-conformity).

Anima and Animus: Yin and Yang

Just as the ego relates with the outer world via the persona and self, it relates with the inner world via the shadow and the contrasexual aspect of the psyche: the feminine in a man (*anima*, which means soul in Latin) and the masculine in a woman (*animus*, which means spirit in Latin). Jung states:

> The effect of anima and animus on the ego . . . is uncommonly strong and immediately fills the ego-personality with an unshakable feeling of rightness and righteousness. The cause of the effect is projected and appears to lie in objects and objective situations.[17]

Subsuming spirit in soul, Jung considers the animus and anima to be "soul images." He maintains: "The soul-complexes seem to belong to the ego and the loss of them appears 'pathological.' "[18] Loss of soul and the related loss of love, faith, and hope often lead to severe depression and suicide. Regaining soul while undergoing egocide and transformation is an effective antidote to depression and suicide.

Egocide and Shadowcide:
Symbolic Killing of Ego and Shadow

Why symbolically kill the disaffirming introjected parental ego and negative ego-image? In dreams and in the Jungian practice of active imagination (creative artistic expression of unconscious conflicts), the reason for such an act is usually clear. Marion Woodman gives an example of such a reasonable killing in a dream told to her by a young woman suffering from a crippling father complex.[19] "My brothers and I killed our father," she said, recounting her dream. "He was haunting us, terrorizing us. We pounded him with stones in the alleyway. We put his body in the car trunk and buried him in a field." Woodman, claiming that her patient's dream illustrates her transition into mature womanhood, states, "She must *symbolically kill* her father."

Jung also refers to the patient's need to "kill the symbolic representative of the unconscious . . . the Terrible Mother who devours and destroys."[20]

Egocide for the bridge-jump survivors represented an extreme case of symbolic suicide—a dramatic, real-life extension of a psychic dilemma analogous to the symbolic killing of the father in the dream of Woodman's patient. In the case of each attempted suicide the Self survived, while the problematic ego-image and identity, along with the negative pole of the shadow—which was adversely influencing the ego-image and identity—were destroyed.

One of my patients, Stephen, a middle-aged professional, came to see me after the only other males in his immediate family had destroyed themselves. His father had died from alcoholism and his brother had committed suicide. Stephen was also on a path toward sacrificing himself but, after a little more than two years of analytical therapy using my model, he committed egocide instead. The telling moment came in a dream in which he climbed up to a platform atop one of the towers of a suspension bridge. Then he jumped off. When he leaped, he left his former destructive ego-image and evil shadow identity behind. Upon awakening, he miraculously found himself alive, uninjured, and reborn, and his new identity was no longer dependent solely upon the ego. In the surrender of ego, the Self had been experienced and his new ego was secondary to this higher power.

Analytical therapy nearly always involves shadowcide. Initially the shadow is projected and then dealt with in problematic interpersonal relationships, including negative transference reactions. As the projections are withdrawn, shadow dreams of evil same-sexed figures are more common. For example, when I was dealing with my own negative shadow, I had dream confrontations with vicious male figures; at one point I killed a cruel male mafia leader, which is an example of shadowcide. At that time, my identity or dominant ego-image was associated with a self-harmful father complex. Shortly thereafter, I psychically murdered my father. This symbolic killing of my negative ego, shadow, and father complex cleared the way for transformation. Years later, I had a dream in which my deceased father came back from the realm of the dead and moved toward me, uncharacteristically smiling, then he embraced me. He had substance to him, but I knew that he was from the other side. This is an image of acceptance of my personal shadow and father complex (as well as my father) based on a psychic transformation.

Beyond the personal, and on a broader collective scale, we tend to project the archetypal shadow onto others. This is called scapegoating. An example would be Reagan's early characterization of the U.S.S.R. as an "evil empire." However, once he got to know Gorbachev personally, Reagan began to withdraw his shadow projection off of the land he led. When Reagan left office, he described the U.S.S.R. as a hospitable place and Gorbachev as his friend.

Another depiction of egocide and shadowcide is the case of Maureen that appears in June Singer's book *Boundaries of the Soul*.[21] Nineteen-year-old Maureen came to see Singer after being hospitalized for slashing her wrists. Her father was a successful businessman but a detached and often absentee father. When Maureen was three and a half years old, her mother was hospitalized for severe depression. Maureen described her as cold and unfeeling and said she hated her mother. She reported that her mother had told her, "You were born without trust."

It was obvious to Singer that Maureen had an extremely negative mother complex; furthermore, Maureen had "two figures in conflict within her": *a little girl* (a nuisance, screams when neglected, gives up and withdraws, refuses to grow up) and *a big girl* (motherlike, no feelings or emotions, cold, and hard). As Singer so aptly characterizes it, "Here was the whole story of herself and 'the other.' " The other is sometimes used to describe the shadow.

Singer encouraged Maureen to express herself through active imagination in art. In one session when Maureen was angry, she fingerpainted one figure running away from another figure. After staring at the images for a few seconds, she said sternly, "One of them will have to be killed." This is the essence of egocide. The importance of this breakthrough experience for Maureen (and, by association, the importance of egocide and transformation in general) is evidenced by Singer's commentary on Maureen's subsequent history:

> This marked the beginning of the most crucial period in the therapy. Maureen was testing me and she even went so far as to

make a gesture in the direction of another suicide attempt. She thought I would hospitalize her and thereby reject her as her mother had done. I did not. I asked her whether I could trust her to continue working on her problems and not give up. She said yes, and I did trust her. Gradually she began to trust me again, and this time it seemed that she was involved in therapy in a different way than she had been previously. The [art] had helped her to feel that she had some way of reaching the unconscious and looking into it. She did not have to close herself off from it any longer.

The last picture that Maureen made was of one seated figure: She was finally integrated and no longer split in two. Maureen had committed egocide and shadowcide and had gone through a death-rebirth experience—a transformation. Singer captures this dramatic change when she states, "From this point in analysis (after the last drawing), Maureen began to have dreams, and the spiral of individuation took another turn."

The adolescent wants and needs to psychically kill off and let go of his or her dominant ego-image and identity, which is tied up with parental introjects. Neumann, too, calls for the murder of parental figures on a symbolic level, as not only okay but necessary.[22] This experience would be egocide; ideally the adolescent would transform the parental image into his or her own ego-image and unique identity, and his or her own personal myth would begin to unfold (the individuation process).

Goethe extolled the adolescent experience and claimed that he repeatedly chose to go through self-generated adolescentlike crises (death-rebirth experiences) throughout his life. In other words, he was recommending periodic experiences of egocide and transformation or Symbolic Death and New Life. The killing energy is harnessed and undergoes metamorphosis; when the suicidal complex is transformed, the individual is changed. But every death experience, literal or symbolic, requires mourning.

Even though egocide is based on letting only a part of the ego die, it feels like total ego death, and one feels dead. Therefore, the person so afflicted needs to go through a mourning process for the lost ego-image and identity. Verena Kast and Elizabeth Harper Neeld both outline helpful schemas for grieving such losses.[23] [24]

I want to emphasize the importance of the mourning process in egocide, because a death experience has transpired even though it is symbolic in nature. As Kast notes:

> The dreadful despair must be accepted as such and must be regarded as appropriate to this particular life situation. In addition, the chaotic emotions, especially the anger, must be endured. This is made easier by an understanding that this emotional chaos represents the dismantling of the old patterns of relationship and the old habits and therefore also the creation of a new potential.

Over time, through the mourning process, the killed ego part becomes an accepted inner figure, a friendly ghost. The energy of the accepted Symbolic Death of the previous dominant ego-identity is transformed into New Life. One's new ego-image based on a deeper ego-Self connection leads to better relationships with others. In my egocide model, the painful death experience (Symbolic Death) is undeniably an evil of sorts, a kind of destruction (Bad News); but it is followed by creative reconstruction (Good News) and renewal (New Life). Beethoven's words are apt here: "I am patient, for I remember that every evil is attended with some good."

Mapping the Healing Journey

In mapping a territory it is wise to learn from those who have gone before. Just as I was taught by the bridge-leap survivors, analytical work with my patients has led to trail blazing through a wilderness of depression. Others have been there, too: Stanislav Grof traversed this difficult terrain with his patients and the trail they made is of comparable value.[25] Likewise, the anthropological study of Joseph Henderson and Maud Oakes outlines a similar pathway that is of a collective nature.[26]

Let me now provide a map which will help orient and guide us (see Table 4-2). The table is divided into three horizontal bands, representing three major stages, and four vertical columns. The first column presents symptoms and experiences people typically have during each stage of illness—or, from the perspective of my model, during each stage of egocide and transformation. The second and

Stages	Depressive & Suicidal States Symptoms & Experiences	Grof's Death-Rebirth Stages	Henderson & Oakes' Rites of Passage	Individual Analytical Psychotherapy
I	*Bad News* Depressed, suicidal, alone, alienated Negative ego and shadow identity related to loss and sense of failure Feels worthless, helpless, hopeless Indescribable suffering Hell: a no-exit situation Disorganized and disabled Unable to function *Symbolic Death*	Antagonism with mother (First stage of clinical delivery) ego death (A feeling of total annihilation and disintegration)	Rite of separation Disengagement (Symbolized as passing through a gate or door)	Resistance by patient and negative personal transference Acceptance and empathy by therapist/analyst Building trust and positive transference Regression in the service of positive ego Personal unconscious conflicts and complexes Through analysis, negative introjects die Death of the *false self* egocide and shadowcide
II	Feels numb, dead, anxious Confused, despondent, withdrawn Senses light at the end of the tunnel *Good News*	Synergism with mother (Second stage of clinical delivery) Death-Rebirth struggle	Rite of transition (Symbolized as immersion in waters of death and life)	Strong therapeutic alliance develops Archetypal positive and negative transference Regression in the service of the Self ego-Self axis Collective unconscious complexes
III	Less depressed and withdrawn Brighter and hopeful New directions, relationships, and creative acts Meaning in life *New Life*	Separation from mother (Third stage of clinical delivery) Death-Rebirth experience and Re-emergence into light	Rite of incorporation (Symbolized by mandalas and other creative expressions of integrated wholeness)	Regression in the service of the self Sees self and therapist/analyst realistically self-Self axis Rebirth of the *true self* Action and creative resolution Sense of wholeness and personal myth

third columns compare stages in the different yet similar models of Grof (*Death-Rebirth Stages,* second column) and Henderson and Oakes (*Rites of Passage,* third column). The fourth column describes what is occurring in analytical therapy during each stage.

In the first stage, you feel extremely depressed and suicidal. Whether or not you are alone in your personal life (often you are), you feel isolated and alienated. Usually you have suffered some Bad News, some loss that has triggered a feeling of helplessness, which frequently progresses to a feeling of hopelessness. Internally, your candle of hope is flickering. You feel like a failure and assume a negative ego-image and identity: The shadow takes over the ego, so that you feel worthless. Your persona is marred and you are unable to perform effectively. The false self is predominant, and you experience inauthenticity, emptiness, and meaninglessness. There is unbearable suffering, a living hell as many people describe it, and you feel disorganized, disabled, and incapable of working. Your ego is dying. This is the actual experience of egocide or Symbolic Death.

After I published my first article on the bridge-jump survivors, Stanislav Grof contacted me. He was intrigued by my empirical study, because he had made some of the same observations when he studied the use of LSD in psychotherapy with suicidal patients. He carried out this study with a series of suicidal patients for whom every other kind of therapeutic intervention had failed. Grof discovered that all of these patients went through what he called an ego death experience and none went on to commit suicide.

Grof outlines three Death-Rebirth Stages utilizing a model of clinical delivery. He describes the first stage of a patient's illness as *antagonism with mother* with ego death, accompanied by a feeling of total annihilation and disintegration. The patient then enters the second stage of illness and therapy, where his or her experience is archetypal, within the collective unconscious. During this second stage, which Grof calls *synergism with mother,* the patient grapples with the mother archetype, that which gives and takes back all life. Thus, the death-rebirth struggle is both positive and nurturing as well as negative and devouring. The third stage, *separation from mother,* involves the death-rebirth experience itself—an emergence from darkness into light that parallels the physical birth experience.

Henderson and Oakes' Rites of Passage likewise involves the collective unconscious. In studying a variety of human cultures, they discovered that similar symbolic death-rebirth experiences occur as rituals on a social level. Hence, they describe these experiences on a psychological level as initiation rites or rites of passage. These rites of passage also proceed in three stages. Disengagement, or the *rite of separation,* is the first stage. This rite is usually symbolized as passing through a gate or door and represents, roughly speaking, the individual's departure from an outmoded identity.[27] The second stage, *rite of transition,* is characterized as an immersion in the waters of life and death (water itself symbolizes the unconscious and the feminine). The third stage consists of a *rite of incorporation,* wherein creative activity leads to integrated wholeness.

Emotional Blueprint of the Healing Journey

At each stage of a depressive illness, there is a correspondingly different stage in the therapeutic analytical process (the fourth column of Table 4-2). During the first stage, you nearly always exhibit resistance and express a lot of negativity and rage. This behavior is an understandable test to see if your therapist can genuinely accept you and empathize with you. Be wary of a negative response (hateful rejection) by your therapist.[28] You can always leave your therapist and find one who is accepting and caring. Building trust with your therapist allows you to go through a constructive "regression in the service of the ego."[29] This regression is to be in the service of positive ego. Your therapist ought to point out and support every ego strength you have, emphasizing all your assets, capabilities, and talents, thus giving you a safe place to identify, confront, understand, and abandon ego deficits and liabilities.

Once your initial resistance has been overcome, conflicts related to the personal unconscious can be faced and resolved. In Stage I the primary task is to understand and work through complexes (conflicts) you have with your parents. Again, this is a time to acknowledge your strengths and capabilities and thereby reinforce your positive ego-image. Then, through the analytical process, negative introjects (negative mother and father complexes), i.e., disaffirming parts of the ego, are identified and killed off (or allowed to die)—in other words, talked or analyzed to death. This is the essence of what I term *egocide.* During the final part of the first stage, you actually feel as if you are dying. The dying negative ego-image and false self are pulling your healthy ego and identity into the sea of the unconscious to join them in Symbolic Death. To say the least, this is a very painful and difficult time in therapy.

During Stage II of your illness and therapy, you usually feel dead and are extremely dependent: a confirmation that your previous ego-identity is dead. You become anxious, confused, despondent, and withdrawn; there is synergism with your therapist, who becomes a mother surrogate. It is as if you are back in the womb and totally reliant on your mother. The strength of the positive transference and therapeutic alliance is critical at this stage. There is a "regression in the service of the Self."[30] You experience Good News and begin to see light at the end of the tunnel. Your reintegrated, reconstituted, and stronger ego, which includes more of the shadow and the contrasexual aspect of the psyche (anima or animus), helps you to contact your center, the Self, which encompasses all of consciousness and unconsciousness. During this stage the ego-Self axis develops, and it is at this point that you begin working with the collective unconscious complexes and archetypes. At the end of the second stage, you begin to feel hopeful and less depressed, which ushers in the next stage.

The third and final stage of your illness and therapy is characterized by separation from your therapist and a death-rebirth experience. You work on ending therapy, and the frequency of sessions decreases. You create expressions of integrated wholeness which represent a union of opposites [examples include: yin (female) and yang (male), and good and evil]. The way to transcend opposites is to integrate them. The Self, a union of opposites, often manifests itself in creative acts such as mandalas, which are found in all human cultures past and present. Rebirth or New Life is the culmination of the last stage which signals self-realization. It is in this closing phase that the *self-Self axis* develops,[31] and you feel that life has meaning and purpose. Action and resolution become apparent in your outer life, often in the form of creative productions and life changes (e.g., spontaneous healing images, changes in significant relationships and careers).

Controlling the process of egocide and transformation in the midst of a real-life crisis can be extremely difficult. Psychotherapy offers a container within which that process can be more effectively handled and, therefore, geared more toward *individuation*, Jung's term for the healing journey toward wholeness.[32] Carl Rogers postulates a similar concept and process in what he terms *self-realization,* which he describes "as a life-long process of realizing an individual's potentialities to become a fully functioning person . . . to be that self which one truly is."[33] Abraham Maslow's parallel view is that the ultimate value is the human spiritual need for *self-actualization,* in other words, you must be true to your own divine nature.[34] The psychotherapeutic relationship between you and your therapist creates a *temenos,* a sacred space, where such a transformation can take place in privacy and relative security.

Reflect on the paradigm of egocide and transformation, presented succinctly in Table 4-2: Lincoln, Mill, James, Styron, Alvarez, and the survivors of jumps off the Golden Gate Bridge were able to transcend their depressive and suicidal states and commit egocide and shadowcide (rather than suicide) and undergo a transformation of their conscious identities. They, like the four individuals I will discuss in Chapters 6–9, embodied Ecclesiastes' "A time to kill and a time to heal." What they symbolically killed was the negative ego and shadow, not the self (their unique personal being). They did not commit suicide from which there is *no* return, but rather their healing was based on Symbolic Death, reconnecting with the soul, and reorienting by the Self. They were involved in a journey toward wholeness that was and is related to living and dying naturally—the antithesis to suicide. Egocide, the Symbolic Death of the false self, leads to New Life and the rebirth of the true self.

A step-by-step progression from inner symbolic violence to inner healing (similar to egocide and transformation) is described by Marion Woodman, who introduces the concept of *psychic suicide* in her book *The Owl Was a Baker's Daughter.*[35] Psychic suicide (virtually identical to egocide), refers to the urgent necessity to confront and do away with denying parental complexes. "What the theologian considered sacrifice," Woodman states, "becomes in this context psychic murder."

In her second book, *Addiction to Perfection,* Woodman gives clinical examples of people who feel the need for "conscious sacrifice of ego demands (unconscious power), being cleansed of ego desire, being spiritually chaste."[36] To Woodman and these patients, "sacrificing ego demands is saying Yes to life." Woodman's cases, primarily female patients with anorexia nervosa, are in the process of overcoming severe depression and self-destructive behavior, and they are caught in negative mother and father complexes. As Woodman says, "The addiction to perfection is an addiction to unreality which leaves little room for the feminine."

Egocide: Helping Suicidal and Depressed Persons in Group Therapy

The egocide and transformation paradigm is very applicable to the group-therapy setting, which does a remarkably effective job of preventing suicide.[37] This kind of group could be characterized as a Suicide Attempters Anonymous group, but unlike Alcoholics Anonymous, it utilizes two co-therapists as co-leaders. Having co-led three of these groups in various settings, I know that Suicide Attempters Anonymous groups can function as extended families for these otherwise lonely and alienated individuals. Also, the stigma of suicide doesn't bother other group members, because they are all in the same boat—having gotten there with the same ticket (i.e., a suicide attempt). Even the co-leaders are somewhat like family members, sharing their personal feelings (but not their personal problems), so that they are more compassionate. The result for a group member is a sense of hope and belonging that forestalls hopelessness.

The course of development for a Suicide Attempters Anonymous group parallels the three stages that I have already outlined for individual therapy (see Table 4-2). The first stage can be characterized as resistance and building trust (getting to know one another); the second stage as a sharing and repeating of past behavior (catharsis and crisis); and the third stage as action and resolution (working through and socializing together). Each stage lasts approximately four to five months. Because of the open-ended nature of these groups, it is commonplace for old members to leave and new members to come in; but these partings actually help ongoing members to deal with the death-rebirth theme that is so much a part of the egocide and transformation model. The social aspects of the groups (dinners and parties) usually center around birthdays and holidays, which are very difficult times for these individuals.

A Suicide Attempters Anonymous group offers troubled, isolated, and severely depressed individuals unconditional acceptance. It's a framework within which group members can focus on understanding depression, can learn to feel worthy of love, and can risk expressing anger and other negative feelings without losing their self-esteem. The group offers concern and personal interaction that carry over into the members' lives outside the group and that help to promote healing. By serving as a surrogate family, the group underscores the fact that no human being need be alone. The hope and compassion generated in the group transcend the disaffirming aspects within the psyches of the individual members and eventually lead to transformation of their depression.

As an example, let us consider the story of Ellen, a middle-aged health professional who had long-standing, severe, and crippling depression. She had been orphaned early in life and had no known family. I first met her after her third serious suicide attempt. She had not responded to several high-dose trials of antidepressants, including tricyclics and MAO inhibitors, or to two full courses of ECT. Before she joined the group for suicide attempters that I was co-leading, she had just been in individual psychotherapy; but it had not proved beneficial.

For Ellen, the group became a new world—one that constructively challenged the destructive value system she had created for herself. During the first couple of months, she continued to obsess about death and ending her life. She lived alone on the twenty-third floor of a high-rise apartment building, and she often called me, the co-leader, and other group members, threatening to jump off her balcony. Her condition worsened, and I became concerned that she might commit suicide at any moment. With the support of the co-leader and her individual therapist, I tried to get her readmitted to a university-based psychiatric inpatient service. However, because she didn't want to submit herself to a stereotactic neurosurgical operation (which alters brain tracts thought to be involved in obsessions with death and suicide, and which the chief of the psychiatric service felt was the only viable procedure), she understandably refused to cooperate.

Finally, the group members got so frustrated and upset over Ellen's situation and attitude that they took action on their own, without the assistance of the co-leaders. They rented a truck and moved her out of her lonely and dangerous high-rise apartment, and into a ground-floor room in a residence club. Within a month Ellen seemed much less depressed. She reported to the group that she had met a slightly older man who lived at the residence club. This relationship developed into an intimate liaison, and gradually her chronic depressive symptoms and obsessive suicidal preoccupations gave way to joyful emotions and a zest for life. Love: What an alternative to brain surgery!

Ellen's recovery was a healing process both for herself and for those around her. It was based on loving, creative, and life-sustaining action by a family-like group of people with similar experiences who really cared. It was hope, faith, compassion, and love, the intangibles having to do with the soul, that were involved in her healing process.

In this kind of group therapy, the individual (ego and self) surrenders to and learns to trust the group (a higher power—in the round—like the Self). The group then facilitates positive ego reconstitution based on self- and (Self-) acceptance. Thus the group itself serves a transcendent function to assist members to transform themselves.

To be sure, the model for any group of this type is Alcoholics Anonymous (AA). Alcoholism is a chronic form of suicidal behavior, and joining AA involves a surrendering of ego. In the initial phase (step one), AA members admit that they are powerless over alcohol, and they yield to the group, which is—and represents—a power greater than themselves. As Jan Bauer describes it, this ego surrender is a "recognition that the ego alone cannot bring about [positive] change."[38]

Another feature of the AA program that parallels the suicide attempters' group experience is the use of veteran members to help novice members. People who have been through a hellish experience are uniquely effective in leading others still immersed in the same experience to see a way out. In the Suicide Attempters Anonymous groups I have co-led, long-term members (some of them in the groups for over three years) have become assistant therapists with excellent results. Together with the co-therapists, assistant therapists of this type can help facilitate the breakup of an individual's suicidal complex by analyzing it to death. Egocide, again, leads to transformation: symbolic death of the false self and the emergence of the true self, which is unconditionally accepted and nurtured.

The Dangers and Powers of Egocide

Egocide is not to be embraced lightly as a mode of therapy or life. It is a soul-wrenching process and must be pursued with immense respect for the dangers involved. The most serious of these dangers is suicide, which should always be regarded as an ever-present possibility. The agony of the first stage of therapy is so painful that in a moment of desperation, when severely depressed, you may want to act on a wish to escape into permanent sleep. To forestall this from happening, your psychic pain level needs to be monitored as carefully as possible. If you are unable to tolerate the pain of worsening melancholia, then admission to a hospital ought to be considered.[39] Styron declared that the hospital was his salvation, not his prison, as some (like James Hillman[40] and Thomas Szasz[41]) would have us believe. The protective confines of a womblike shelter can be just what the inner healer ordered!

Psychosis is another possible problematic outcome of egocide.[42] The term egocide literally means killing the ego; but in practice it actually refers to the symbolic death of a dominant ego-image and disaffirming identity. If, instead, your entire ego disintegrates, then you will be psychotic (i.e., without an ego). This eventuality is comparable to what happens to a small minority of people who take LSD: Their egos dissolve and they remain egoless psychotics. The threat or possibility of such an outcome during the egocidal process might require the use of anti-psychotic medication and, possibly, hospitalization.

The final egocide-related danger is regression to a former persona.[43] This regression does not lead to New Life, but rather to a former state of being, or old life, like a recently divorced person returning to his or her parents' home and staying there permanently. The divorced person regresses from a spouse persona to a dependent-child persona. Such a regression is a negative development with the person getting stuck in a former and superficial as well as inappropriate role and identity; that is, a false self.

Having warned about the dangers of egocide, let me end this chapter by praising its positive powers. Egocide is a vital step in transforming a depressed and suicidal individual into a life-affirming person. Edward Whitmont speaks of such a powerful transformation in his book, *The Symbolic Quest:*[44]

Only through critical times of suffering and despair can transformation occur; for when push comes to shove the individual's limitations are accepted, forcing the ego to renounce its centrality and thereby allowing the Self to emerge. Now a dialectic relationship between the Self and ego can engage so healing and wholeness may occur.

Agreeing with Goethe, I want to stress that egocide is a recurring process. Peter Mudd comments on "the ego's achieved capacity to die repeatedly an ongoing series of conscious voluntary psychological deaths in the service of individuation."[45] This statement seems to affirm that egocide is an ongoing and repetitious phenomenon.

Finally, I cite Oliver Wendell Holmes and say that the power of egocide and transformation can rescue lives, which may help to atone "For those who never sing/But die with all their music in them."

CHAPTER 5

Healing Images:
Symbols of Transformation

"Whatever else the unconscious may be, it is a natural phenomenon that produces symbols, and these symbols prove to be meaningful. The symbolic process is an experience in images and of images."

—CARL JUNG

THERE is a vast difference between egocide and suicide. After all, you do kill yourself in suicide, and you don't in egocide. Nevertheless, they are alike in a crucial way: The same intense anguish and pain is met along the path to either egocide or suicide. Saying that egocide is symbolic suicide does not make it any less challenging or forceful an act. The key to understanding this lies in an appreciation of the significant roles that symbols play within the human imagination and how they affect human lives and human culture.

Simply put, a symbol is an image that is infused with meaning—a meaning so profound and multidimensional that often we are unable to translate it into words. The American flag, for example, is a concrete image, something we can see and touch; but it also functions on a symbolic level, invested with, and evoking, all manner of feelings associated with a complex of things that are real and abstract, personal and collective: the U.S. government, anti-U.S. government demonstrations, the Olympics, freedom, liberty, gravesites, school-day pledges of allegiance, parades, home, Washington, D.C., patriotism, Betsy Ross, a man on the moon.

Symbols transcend logic. They inspire and motivate us in ways that reason can't, and, alternatively, they give us the power to grasp, identify, and control what reason can't. They both alter our experience and permit us to shape our experience. Speaking of the power of such symbols on a collective as well as a personal level, Erich Neumann states:

The images that burst forth in the [person] gripped by the depths, the song that is their expression in words, are the creative source of nearly all human culture; and an essential part of all religion, art, and customs sprang originally from this dark phenomenon of creative unity in the human soul. Primitive [people] regarded this creativity of the psyche as magic, and rightly so, for it transforms reality and will always do so.[1]

Jung describes depression as being connected to regression in its regenerative and enriching aspects and, almost as a prescription, he maintains that depression represents "the empty stillness which precedes creative work."[2]

Thus, egocide as symbolic suicide can and does stir the core of the person's psyche. The therapy by which an individual's egocide is made to lead to a positive transformation relies heavily on the evocation of healing symbols.

Elaborating Some Key Concepts

At this point, three important concepts associated with egocide and transformation deserve further clarification.

Archetypes

Archetypes are innate in the human psyche. They are ancient, affectively charged motifs and predispositions toward ideas, images, and patterns of behavior that are common to all human beings. More specifically, archetypes are intricate and fundamental parts of the collective unconscious, a concept that Jung postulated in clear distinction from the strictly personal unconscious of Freud's psychology. Paralleling Darwin's theory of physical evolution, Jung's theory of psychic evolution proposes that all of history is embedded within each individual psyche in the form of archetypes.

In many respects, archetypes manifest themselves in an individual's life somewhat as instincts do. As Jung states:

> Instinct is an essentially collective, i.e., universal and regularly occurring phenomenon, which has nothing to do with individuality. Archetypes have this in common with instincts and are likewise collective phenomena.[3]

In fact, instincts and archetypes intertwine in the human psyche. For example, a newborn baby has an instinct to suckle the mother's breast. This instinct is tied to an ancient predisposition of the off-spring to find the mother based on an archetype. We recognize this form of behavior as imprinting in animals,[4] but it takes on a more evolved form in humans, which leads to attachment behavior.[5] An essential part of an archetype (like the invisible atom) is the existence of *a priori* organizing factors, which are inborn modes of functioning that constitute, in their totality, human nature.[6]

Jung's use of the term *archetype* encompasses both positive and negative possibilities. For example, the mother archetype encompasses the kind and nurturing mother who feeds and caresses her child, and the wicked and terrible mother who rejects and neglects her child. Both of these associations exist for the child, regardless of that child's experience of the personal mother. This theme of opposites, which is the cornerstone of Jungian psychology, also applies to the Self, which is the timeless center and totality of the psyche. As such, the Self is the archetype of wholeness and eternity, symbolized by the circle or uroboros (the image of the snake biting its own tail—see Plate III), which has no beginning and no ending. The Self consists of an affirming higher force as well as a dark side, or shadow. The Self also represents androgyny in that it contains both contrasexual aspects of the psyche: the feminine (*anima* or soul), and the masculine (*animus* or spirit). In Taoism, a similar concept of the Self exists. It combines the ever-present principles of yin (the dark and feminine) and yang (the light and masculine). (See Figure 1-1).[7]

In Jungian psychology, the term Self is "an empirical concept . . . that expresses the unity of the personality as a whole . . . The supraordinate personality in contrast to the ego, which . . . is only the center of consciousness."[8] In other words, the Self is the central archetype in the human psyche—the innate healing force that is within every individual and the key to the self-realization process, individuation.

In addition to the Self archetype, there are numerous other archetypes that also factor into the individuation process. In Jung's words:

> The concept of the archetype . . . is derived from repeated observation that, for instance, the myths and fairy tales of world literature contain definite motifs which crop up everywhere.

We meet the same motifs in the fantasies, dreams, deliriums, and delusions of individuals living today. These typical images and associations are what I call archetypal ideas [and images]. The more vivid they are, the more they will be colored by particularly strong feeling-tones. . . . They impress, influence, and fascinate us. They have their origin in the archetype, which [like an atom] . . . is an irrepresentable, unconscious, pre-existent form that seems to be part of the inherited structure of the psyche and can therefore manifest itself spontaneously anywhere, at any time. Because of its instinctual nature, the archetype underlies the feeling-toned complexes and shares their autonomy. [The archetype] is also the psychic precondition of religious assertions and is responsible for the anthropomorphism of all God-images. [9]

Transformation

In the context of my egocide and transformation paradigm, transformation means to change the nature of our personality. Jung posits that the ego, or our conscious identity, is a complex that is based on our personal history and that has to do with our personal unconscious and introjected parental characteristics and conflicts. If we remain unaware of this and do nothing about it, we can evolve into a manifestation of our parents' wishes, and not of our true self. At the core of the transformation process is an archetypal death-rebirth experience. The Self is the force behind the sacrifice (Symbolic Death) of the dominant ego-image that is impeding individuation. [10] The Self, the archetype of all archetypes, represents a forward-striving function which, through the eruption of affect-laden archetypal images into consciousness, facilitates the process of transformation that can lead to the manifestation of our true self. We then can accept that we are here for a special purpose: to fulfill our own personal myth.

The most important archetype of transformation is the healing and centering Self archetype. It is commonly symbolized as a mandala (a balanced and harmonious nest of concentric circles and at times mixed with squares and triangles, used in meditation), sun wheel, or sacred circle. Neumann offers a particularly intriguing description of the Self archetype symbology:

The basic archetypal image of this creatively transformed reality of the world is the self-contained rolling wheel of eternity, every single point of which is a "turning point," that "often concludes with the beginning and starts with the end."[11]

Active Imagination

Albert Einstein viewed imagination as more important than information. Joseph Joubert considered imagination to be the eye of the soul. June Singer calls the Jungian process of active imagination "dreaming the dream onward."[12] In Jungian psychology, active imagination is a part-directed, part-conscious, meditative-like state that an individual uses to go deep into the unconscious and bring to light dreams or fantasies which, as Jung states, "want to become conscious."[13] The elaboration of these unconscious dreams and fantasies utilizes intuition, sensation, thinking, and feeling and results in a creative act of expression: painting, sculpting, writing, song-making, singing, or dancing. In effect, active imagination is a process of letting oneself go with the flow of the unconscious and then manifesting one's insights in an artistic form or product.

Anthony Storr recommends writing as one of the forms of active imagination especially effective in promoting healing.[14] He maintains:

> Putting things into words has the effect of giving reality to unformulated mental contents . . . [it] captures the ephemeral. It is [also] the means whereby we detach ourselves both from the world about us and from the inner world of our own emotions and thoughts. It is by means of words that we objectify, that we are enabled to stand back from our own experience and reflect upon it. Words about the self make possible a psychical distance from the self, and without distance, neither understanding, nor control, nor willed, deliberate change is possible.

Storr also touches upon the concept of creative psychotherapy involving drawing and painting:

> When patients find it difficult to describe what they are feeling in words, I sometimes suggest that they should draw or paint

their experience. Some will object that they cannot draw; but since it is not works of art for which one is asking, this does not matter. Paintings, partly through the use of color, are often vividly descriptive of a patient's mood, particularly as revealing an underlying depression which may not be manifest in the patient's talk or manner. Paintings are not only useful as revealing the present "state of affairs," but also have a therapeutic function in themselves. Some patients produce serial paintings which most interestingly record their emotional progress.

Healing and Archetypes of Transformation

While doctors and therapists may not be able to cure their patients completely, they can always help them by being involved in their healing processes. In fact, there seems to be an innate archetypal basis to the healing doctor-patient relationship which is transformative.[15] In native cultures, past and present, this relationship is between the shaman and the sick individual, the one who has lost his or her soul. Through the relationship with the healer and the experience of a symbolic death and rebirth, the ill person finds his or her soul again and is transformed, thus entering into a process of healing toward wholeness.

A central element in an individual's transformation involves the union of opposites. Prior to the occurrence of this union, the individual undergoes a radical experience of opposites. To describe this condition, Jung uses the term *enantiodromia* which means running counter to.[16] In the philosophy of Heraclitus, enantiodromia designates the play of opposites in the course of events—the view that everything that exists turns into its opposite. From a Jungian perspective, it means, for example, that to live fully we must confront death; to experience death fully we must be alive; to love we must know hate; and to do good we must know evil, especially our own shadow.

States of religious conversion involve archetypes of transformation. For example, being born again in a Christian context is associated with the archetypal symbol of the cross, with its unifying intersection. In the preconversion state, the person typically suffers severe depression and is often divided against himself or herself. He or she feels lost in an abyss of despair—preoccupied with death and, not uncommonly, suicide. It is at this point that conversion occurs. Then light and hope return, along with a new sense of self-esteem connected with integrative symbols, such as the cross.

Active imagination leads to a confrontation with one's sick soul and an acceptance of one's own inner evil tendencies.[17] In *The Varieties of Religious Experience,* William James tells us that Tolstoy, in a morbid psychological state, was drawn to suicide and then an enantiodromia occurred. By confronting death and his pull toward ending his life, Tolstoy let go of the old false self (his then negative persona and dominant ego image), which was in collusion with his shadow. Through a psychology of self-surrender, he contacted a higher power (the Self) and felt the spiritual vitality of being reborn and at one with his true self.

The Hindu god Shiva represents another example of the surrendering of the ego (self) in a dance of destruction and creation. Shiva is commonly depicted as being surrounded by a circle of flames, the circle symbolizing a constant cycle of self-renewal and the flames symbolizing purification. Shiva's dance symbolizes that from destructive energy comes creativity, and from death comes rebirth. In this dance, Shiva steps on a dwarf, which represents the human ego. The implication is that ego death and self-surrender lead to communion with a higher power, the Self.

Certain specific archetypes, or symbolic images, tend to recur repeatedly in depictions of transformations in the human psyche.[18] Outlined below are some of these archetypes of transformation.

Snakes or serpents, particularly poisonous ones, tend to symbolize an individual's fear of death (or insanity, which is a symbolic death of the mind).[19] By facing the serpent and undergoing the dangerous confrontation with death, we are allowing for the enantiodromia of rebirth. In my model of egocide and transformation, the shedding of a snake's skin is connected to Symbolic Death and New Life.

The snake is also an ancient symbol of healing: in ancient Greece, the physician Asklepios carried a staff entwined with a serpent.[20] To this day, the caduceus (two entwined snakes) is associated with the physician and the healing professions in general. Jung clearly acknowledges this interpretation: "The idea of transformation and renewal by means of the serpent is a well-substantiated archetype. It is [a] healing [symbol]." Jung continues: "[The] most significant development of serpent symbolism as regards renewal of personality is to be found in Kundalini yoga."[21]

In addition, the serpent has been identified as a sexual or fertility symbol, both in its masculine aspect, because of its phallic form, and in its feminine aspect, because of its direct contact with water and Mother Earth.[22]

The *cross* signifies an intersection of the vertical (traditionally associated with the celestial, rational, positive, active, and masculine) and the horizontal (traditionally associated with the earthly, irrational, negative, passive, and feminine). Therefore, the whole cross represents a paradoxical union of opposites and an ancient symbol of androgyny. Jung describes it as follows: "In the spontaneous symbolism of the unconscious the cross as quaternity refers to the Self, to [a person's] wholeness. The . . . cross is thus a [symbol] of the healing effect . . . of becoming whole."[23]

Death and rebirth is represented by the serpent in its uroboric form. However, an even more pervasive and influential representation of death and rebirth is a journey to a netherworld and back. One of the earliest myths reflecting this kind of death and rebirth archetype involves the Sumerian goddess Inanna (who later evolved into the Babylonian Ishtar) descending to the Land of No Return, experiencing death, and then achieving a miraculous return to life again. Henderson and Oakes cite an alternative version of this myth that is particularly interesting in relation to my theory of egocide and transformation:[24]

> The chief characteristic of the variant to the descent of Inanna lies in the nature of the mission to the underworld. Here the journey is a kind of mystery in which Inanna accomplishes the quest of herself and emerges as one reborn from a symbolic sacrifice and death.

The *journey of the hero/ine* is best described by Joseph Campbell.[25] In what follows, I am extending Campbell's original thesis to include the heroine, which only makes sense in our post-women's liberation world. The journey of the hero/ine is divided into the following stages:

1. *the departure,* with a call to adventure and the crossing of the first threshold;
2. *the initiation,* with the road of trials: for a man, confronting his shadow, meeting a goddess-like anima figure, and recon-

ciliation with the father; for a woman, confronting her shadow, meeting a god-like animus figure, and reconciliation with the mother;

3. *the return,* which is initially refused, but then effected by a magical flight or rescue that brings about the crossing of a final threshold.

Only when the hero/ine has completed the journey can he or she become whole. As master of the two worlds, the hero/ine has the freedom to create and live fully.

The archetypal journey of the hero/ine is closely associated with the archetype of death and rebirth. As per Campbell, the enemy (the shadow figure) in the hero/ine's journey equals death. Through the confrontation of battle with death, the hero/ine transforms destructive energy into creative energy. By overcoming the fear of death, submitting to the guidance of a divine figure (anima or animus), and contacting the Self, the hero/ine is, in effect, reborn.

Transformative Symbols in Henry Miller's Healing Journey

An example of a creative active imagination process is found in *The Colossus of Maroussi,* a memoir by Henry Miller in which he describes his own egocide and transformation.[26] It took place at Epidaurus in Greece, the ancient healing place of Asklepios himself, just prior to the beginning of World War II. I'll let Miller speak for himself:

At Epidaurus, in the stillness, in the great peace that came over me, I heard the heart beat of the world beat. I know what the cure is: it is to give up, to relinquish, to surrender, so that our little hearts may beat in unison with the great heart of the world. I think that the great hordes who made the long trek to Epidaurus from every corner of the ancient world were already cured before they arrived there. Sitting in the strangely silent amphitheater, I thought of the long and devious route by which I had at last come to this healing center of peace. No man could have chosen a more circumlocutious voyage than mine. Over thirty years I had wandered, as if in a labyrinth. I had tasted every joy, every despair, but I had never known the meaning of peace. En route I had vanquished all my enemies one by one, but the greatest enemy of all I had not even recognized—*myself.* As I entered the still bowl, bathed now in a marble light, I came to that spot in the dead center where the faintest whisper rises like a glad bird and vanishes over the shoulder of the low hill, as the light of a clear day recedes before the velvet black of night. Balboa standing upon the peak of Darien could not have known a greater wonder than I at this moment. There was nothing more to conquer: an ocean of peace lay before me. To be free, as I then knew myself to be, is to realize that all conquest is vain, even the conquest of self, which is the last act of egotism. To be joyous is to carry the ego to its last summit and to deliver it triumphantly. To know peace is total: it is the moment after, when the surrender is complete, when there is no longer even the consciousness of surrender. Peace is at the center and when it is attained the voice issues forth in praise and benediction. Then the voice carries far and wide, to the outermost limits of the universe. Then it heals, because it brings light and the warmth of compassion.

This is also a beautiful description of an archetype of transformation: a place of regeneration activating the healing archetype within. Miller utilizes active imagination as he speaks so eloquently of going to this special amphitheater in the mountains. This healing place of death and rebirth obviously represented a special moment in Miller's private journey of the hero when he realized his own personal myth. He sacrificed his ego and surrendered completely. He then contacted the Self, the center and the totality inside and outside. In other words, he experienced egocide and transformation.

Henry Miller's life following this transformation took on a different character. He continued to write, but it changed as he became more peaceful and reflective. One of his last books, *To Paint Is to Love Again,* was another manifestation of an archetype of transformation, and Miller entered a new active imagination phase, the creative healing expression of the visual arts.[27]

When Miller was in his eighties and married to a young Japanese woman, I read an account of an interview in which he was asked why he was no longer writing or painting, since he was so talented. Henry

Miller paused, reflected and said, "I am involved in the most important art form of all." The perplexed interviewer asked, "And what is that?" Miller responded quietly, "The art of living."

Art Therapy: A Preview

In my analytical practice, I ask patients to create their own spontaneous artistic productions to express their feelings, states of mind, visions, or dreams (daydreams as well as nightdreams). Though it may be hard to believe that archetypal images are *not* willfully produced by the conscious mind, a flexible and meditative ego allows for these symbolic images to emerge from the unconscious wellspring of creativity without reason's direction and control.[28] Patients may choose to draw, paint, dance, make ceramics, sculpt, write, sing, photograph, videotape, or film. Whatever their choice, they don't have to utilize any special artistic skills, but simply creatively respond to their own active imaginations.

The principal value of art therapy is that the archetypal conflict tormenting the patient's soul is made visible in image form, so that the patient can confront it and decide what to do with the part of the psyche to which it refers. Art therapy helps my patients synthesize and transform potentially destructive energy into constructive compositions. When a patient has finished a work of active imagination, I ask him or her to title it. Then I approach it as if it were an actual dream. I ask for his or her personal associations to the work, and I amplify these associations with archetypal references that make sense to the patient.

Let me explain a schema that I sometimes find to be helpful in interpreting drawings and paintings for analytical psychotherapeutic purposes (see Table 5-1). I learned it from Marion Woodman, one of my Jungian training analysts. It's a method of interpretation that attaches particular symbolic importance to different compositional spaces of a drawing or painting. In this schema, the upper left quadrant is associated with the father; the upper right, with the future; the lower left, with the unconscious; and the lower right, with the mother.[29] However, please note that this schema is only one possible way to interpret drawings or paintings, and I do not subscribe to it tenaciously.

Next, I want to emphasize an important point about the artistic

TABLE 5-1
SCHEMA FOR INTERPRETATION OF
ART THERAPY PRODUCTIONS

Father	Future
Unconscious	Mother

productions that are discussed and illustrated in Chapters 6–9: As spontaneous products of active imagination, they come from the patients' unconscious minds and, therefore, contain collective (archetypal) symbols and themes as well as personal symbols and themes. Thus, one challenge in analyzing them is to help patients recognize not only the situation that applies uniquely to them but also the human drama that we all endure and share.

To show how this process unfolds, I am going to shift attention to Sharon, a young, severely depressed and suicidal woman, and two of her many paintings, products of her active imagination. Early in her therapy, Sharon did her first painting (Plate II), which is both diagnostic and prognostic (her case is discussed thoroughly in Chapter 8). Covering the painting is blue rain, which Sharon associated to sadness and depression, but rain also symbolizes life itself. Applying the interpretive template (Table 5-1) to this active imagination product, we see that future therapy will be stormy: the right upper quadrant reveals black clouds. According to Sharon, in the right lower quadrant, there is a green female reproductive organ with yellow, pollen-like seed coming out. It is clear that Sharon will have to deal with the mother, personal and archetypal, in order to become comfortable with being a woman. In the left lower quadrant but near the middle is the origin of a tree (according to Sharon). She identified with this tree which represents masculine and feminine as well as life itself. The tree, which looks more like a sunflower, extends from the left lower quadrant (the unconscious) into the left upper quadrant (representing the father). The patient described it as being ungrounded and top heavy. Nevertheless, it is a promising image that if grounded and balanced could lead to Sharon developing her own inner authority, through resolving her father complex, contacting her animus. Interestingly, Sharon titled this painting "Suspension Between Two States"; one state was called "melancholia" and the other "directed energy." The patient felt empty, which points out the need for Sharon to find her lost soul and feminine identity.

The second of Sharon's pictures that I want to discuss is that of a uroboros (Plate III), which shows how an ancient healing image from the collective unconscious can occur in a creative product of an individual's active imagination. She titled it "Giving Birth to Myself." Sharon's painting offers a numinous depiction of black giving way to light. In the pinkish center, there is an embryo. Thus, we see a representation of transformation—out of Symbolic Death comes New Life.

Overall, this image is what Erich Neumann calls a maternal uroboros, a transitional uroboros which evolves from the basic uroboros and gives rise to the Great Mother archetype.[30] The uroboric circle is a symbol of femininity, the soul, eternity, and the Self; and, as I've repeatedly emphasized, the soul is our salvation in times of dread. It is the *to be* (in Shakespeare's terms) rather than the *not to be*. *To be* is to nurture, to live, to grow, to create, to evolve—which can be considered feminine aspects in a matriarchal sense. On the *not to be* side are the powers of destruction, negativity, devolution, and death—which can be considered masculine aspects in a patriarchal sense. Of course, in the dance of Shiva, it is all one. Out of the disintegration comes reintegration. Viewing the entire, we have a process of re-creation and integrity.[31]

Using active imagination to evoke and render archetypes of transformation is a profoundly effective therapeutic technique. A doctor-patient (therapist-client) relationship of mutual trust assists the development of this process on an internal level, allowing for the healer within the psyche of the depressed or suicidal individual to take charge and continue the process of self-healing.

This internal healing process is the true journey of the hero/ine on the deepest level. Removing the persona (i.e., taking off the mask) and allowing the negative dominant ego-image or false self to be analyzed to death enables the true self to emerge, so that the individual can fully live out his or her own personal myth. The true self, in Jungian terms, is the ego that has been newly reintegrated after the shadow has been confronted (symbolically killed) and the old ego has sacrificed (surrendered) itself. This new ego is secondary to a higher power, the Self, which is now in the center of the psyche and the major archetype of transformation in the individuation process. Subsequently, the individual changes his or her behavior which manifests through new creative actions and relationships featuring service to others as a hallmark of the person's maturation.

PART III

FOUR TRANSFORMING JOURNEYS

CHAPTER 6

Rebecca: Traversing the Dark Night of the Soul

"The feminine in every woman is always waiting."

—IRENE CLAREMONT DE CASTILLEJO

ANALYTICAL therapy proffers a container, or a sacred space, for the patient's healing process to emerge. I attempt to stay neutral and avoid interventions as much as possible. My therapeutic position is to contain and hold the patient's painful chaos, knowing full well that order will, in due course, replace disorder. I view dreams and the creative products of active imagination as manifestations of the psyche's restorative power and see my healing task as offering acceptance, empathy, nurturance, gentle confrontation, and guidance—not as a doctor who promises a cure.

The map of the healing journey as outlined in Chapter 4 (Table 4-2) merely represents a template, to be used as a flexible and abstract guide, not as a concrete, lock-step road map. The egocide and transformation model sounds simple and direct, but it isn't. Like life itself, the process of egocide and transformation resembles a series of advances and retreats. Jung's individuation process consists of "progress and regress, flux and stagnation in alternating sequence."[1]

In this first case study of Rebecca, we will see how depression can be transformed through creative expression. We will learn how the false self (negative persona, ego, and shadow) is pulled into the black hole of severe depression. Then we will also find out how the true self emerges through the repetitious process of egocide and transformation facilitated by dreams, active imagination, and its creative productions.

The unfolding of Rebecca's analytic case is like a detective story, and many clues point to the existence of incest, which happens to be the key to solving and resolving, that is, to transforming her depression. When Rebecca became my patient she was forty-two years old, had three children (a twenty-year-old daughter and two sons, fifteen and ten), and had recently completed a Ph.D. Attractive and coquettish, with a cheerful persona, she told me that she viewed earning her Ph.D. as a major accomplishment after having been at home for twelve years. She had long felt a call to the ministry and had recently applied twice to start seminary training, but both times failed to get in. Deeply troubled by these two rejections, she did not plan to apply a third time, and now wanted to find work that would be meaningful and related to her degree.

Rebecca described her marriage as strained but tolerable. Four years previously, she and her husband had considered divorce, but couples therapy had helped them salvage their marriage. She told me their marital crisis had occurred shortly after her parents' divorce, adding that her parents had been "highly conflicted and emotionally divorced" for twenty years. Now she was parenting them, especially her mother, whom she described as "cold, distant, rejecting, and irrational." She characterized her father as "neglectful, paranoid, and absent." Rebecca stated: "I married my husband to be my father," but then she added, "My husband hooked me into marriage, and he controls me." Her sister, eleven years younger, had just graduated from college, and had always been closer than Rebecca to their father.

The initial dream in any in-depth psychotherapeutic experience is important.[2] It reflects the patient's overall attitude toward analytical psychotherapy, gives the therapist key information about the patient's problems, and about possible outcomes of those problems. It also enables the therapist to assess the patient's ego strengths, which need to be enlisted to effect positive treatment.

Rebecca's first dream was particularly revealing.

> DREAM: *She is a student teacher around the age of twenty, and her assignment is to write the story of the three bears as a teaching device. Her husband helps her rewrite the story. On her way to school she sees a red car and thinks that her mother and her mother's best friend are in it. After she arrives at the school and parks her car, she looks for a man who is to be her partner in student teaching. Going into a large auditorium, hot from the drive to school, she takes off her sweater and only has on her bra. She walks against a crowd of students, as if school were over. Once she finds her classroom, she*

*sits down. Her teacher, an older woman, and the male student for
whom she had been looking are in the middle of a discussion. After
a brief time, the teacher tells Rebecca that her three bears story is
trite and suggests that she use kangaroos coming out of a cave
instead. Rebecca thinks her male partner has a better idea, which is
not disclosed. She feels uncomfortable wearing just her bra, so she
puts on her sweater as she leaves. At the end of the dream, on her
way out of the building, she notices three women performing on stage.*

Rebecca felt that student teaching represented her frustration
with being a student for so long and her need to leave that role (or,
by extension, to avoid dependence on authority figures). She associated the three bears with the story *Goldilocks and the Three Bears*
as well as with the Christian Trinity. However, it is noteworthy that
in the dream Goldilocks is absent, and this may be related to something amiss in Rebecca's childhood. Then she talked about being at
a shamanic drumming led by Dr. X, her former therapist, and taking
a journey into the underworld, where she discovered the bear as her
power animal.

When Rebecca discussed rewriting the three bears story, she
stated, "I can't do anything on my own. I am dependent on my
husband, but I dislike it." Given her linkage of husband and father,
this statement reveals a core conflict with father or a negative father
complex. Likewise, her possible sighting of her mother in a red car
suggests a problem with mother enveloped in red or angry emotions.
Associating with the teacher's recommendation to write about kangaroos coming out of a cave, Rebecca described kangaroos as "primitive, funny, and odd creatures" and the cave as an "unknown
crevice in Mother Earth." I could see that she was making some
connection with archetypes from the collective unconscious—the
kangaroo as a primeval animal from the ancient down under, the
cave as a Mother Earth womb image, and the teacher as a wise old
woman. These particular images seemed to suggest that Rebecca
ought to work toward accepting herself by contacting her own animal, rather than the bear she was led to by Dr. X, an outside
authority.

Rebecca described the male student teacher as a potential partner
and guide (an animus figure), since he seemed to have a better but
undisclosed plan. The fact that the Rebecca figure near the end of the
dream felt uncomfortable and put her sweater back on suggested

positive ego strength: She realized that she was exposing herself and assumed a more respectable persona. The three performing women at the end of the dream, Rebecca said, represented the extraverted (shadow) side of herself—a feminine trinity as opposed to the male Christian trinity that had dominated her childhood.

After this first meeting, I could tell that Rebecca was bright, with sufficient ego strengths, but she seemed to be arrested emotionally at a younger age (around twenty years old, as indicated in the dream). Her current situation with her husband mirrored a dependent, but ambivalent, father-daughter relationship. However, the fact that her dream referred to a better but undisclosed plan, associated with a positive animus figure, appeared to indicate her willingness to be involved in in-depth therapy with me. I liked her, but I had the sense that she was hypersensitive, vulnerable, quite depressed, and perhaps more disturbed underneath her pleasant facade. Her subtle seductiveness suggested that her feelings toward me might take an erotic turn in the future.

Rape and Wounded Instincts: Connecting Past and Future

At our second session Rebecca said that she was anxious and feared that I would not want to work with her. I explained that she was evaluating me as much as I was her. Her focus on a fear of rejection pointed to mistrust, a typical Stage I symptom which was also indicated by a new dream she reported.

DREAM: *She is at the rape crisis center on phone duty (a volunteer job she actually held at the time). A woman calls and asks what is going to happen to a male rapist who is on trial. Rebecca explains that the center is for rape victims, but that she can get someone else to talk with her. Then the scene shifts. Rebecca is in a large, open place with an orchestra on a lower level. The woman caller is talking with a man at the rape crisis center (apparently she is being interviewed). Rebecca feels that she has been receiving hotline calls at home and tries to cancel the call forward function that is making this happen. Then she realizes that she has to go to the basement and deal with unfamiliar electrical equipment. She goes ahead, because she thinks it is right.*

Rebecca identified the woman caller as a shadow figure and linked the rapist to Dr. X, whom she said she hadn't really trusted. She added that the dream suggested a fear that she had done something wrong, or was actually insane, and that she would be found out. I began to suspect that she may have suffered some kind of sexual transgression in the past, possibly by Dr. X.[3]

Rebecca associated the shift in the dream to the open place with her feeling useless at home, and wanting to take a new job and restructure her life. To Rebecca the orchestra represented "beautiful harmony based on some special order"; the male interviewer suggested me as possibly a helping animus figure. She perceived the basement as a "place below, dark, and unknown"; a classic representation of the personal unconscious. When she talked about having to deal with the electrical equipment she looked sad, even though it was a source of energy, because she feared electrocution. She interpreted her ultimate willingness to descend and deal with the scary equipment as a metaphor for exploring the unconscious and the analytical process.

Rebecca's real-life rejection by her mother and father began at the age of eight months, when Rebecca was given to her maternal grandmother to raise. Her parents were working and going to college. Because her parents were physically far away, frequent visits were out of the question. For a child of this age, separation anxiety is at its peak. Rebecca was deprived of her mother and father for the next three years—a crucial developmental period, when Rebecca was becoming her own unique self. The fact that she had accomplished so much in her life and had sought in-depth therapy was a testament to her positive ego strength despite such severe emotional wounds.

Rebecca's first two dreams and her personal history convinced me that she had been hurt, neglected, and abandoned as a child, and that her being rejected for ministerial training, as well as her fear that I'd reject her, was a displacement and condensation of all the losses she had endured over the years. She seemed to be suffering from dysthymia, a depressive neurosis, related to her early losses.

We resumed analytical therapy after the summer break. She said that over the summer she had read books about feminism and had become angry at men, especially her husband and Dr. X. I explored the possibility of her being angry with me, but she denied this. She had dreamed many times of wild little boys and shadowy men, which she felt indicated a problematic masculine side of herself and difficulty in relating to men. She was angry at letting others, males in particular, control her. She was also angry at God because he didn't respond to her call to be a minister. I suggested that her call to be a minister could also be an impetus to become conscious of her own animus, that is, her own female authority.[4]

After nearly two months of therapy, Rebecca shared an important three-part dream.

> DREAM: *First, Rebecca and her husband are baking cookies that burn, and then she goes with her husband to an open, sandy place, where they lie down and she strokes his penis. She notices a black-haired woman watching and becomes embarrassed. Second, a black woman physician (a former employer in her day-to-day life) climbs on top of Rebecca, but Rebecca whispers "not now" because her daughter is beside her. Dr. X, who is also there, kisses her. Third, Rebecca is at a beach house with many family members and Dr. X. She wants to be with Dr. X. He parts her lips with his finger and enters her mouth with his tongue, which sexually arouses her. At that point, a black-haired man walks by and looks at them.*

Rebecca associated making cookies in the first part of her dream with her maternal grandmother, which was one of the few essentially positive memories from her early years. Referring to her husband in the dream, she said that he could be supportive and that she felt good about stroking his penis, as if she were contacting positive male energy within herself, in part through her relationship with her husband. She associated the black-haired woman with her mother, since the woman, in her late twenties, was the same age Rebecca's mother had been when her parents came to take her back from her grandmother: another separation-and-loss experience.

Rebecca said that her relationship with the black woman physician had actually been very confusing. Although she did get some affirmation of her managerial skills from this doctor, she was distressed because this woman, like her mother, intruded into her personal life; at one point, she dragged Rebecca to an EST meeting. In the dream, Rebecca was afraid of being raped by her, which was linked to similar worries about Dr. X.

In the third part of Rebecca's dream, the fact that Dr. X aroused her sexually suggested a past eroticized transference and possible unethical sexual conduct. Even though she talked about Dr. X as nothing more than a former therapist and friend, her dream seemed to indicate that something sexual had occurred with him. If nothing sexual had occurred with him, then perhaps it occurred with another man in a similarly powerful role, such as her father (suggested by the black-haired man who walked by, who resembled her father).

Five months into her therapy, Rebecca talked about a letter she had just received from the bishop reiterating that she was not to be considered for the ministry. She felt rejected, but she also felt a sense of resolve. The next day, she resigned from her job as assistant to the pastor at the student religious center of her denomination. Then she went on a four-day spiritual retreat. Rebecca's husband supported her healing sojourn, which meant a lot to her. The night she arrived at the retreat house, she had a pivotal dream.

> DREAM: *She journeys to a religious place. After going to bed, she notices a man at the right side of her bed facing her at a right angle. She is afraid and flings off the covers and runs out of the building. Looking back, she sees the man in her room, watching her. Then one of the religious sisters, an old, large, buxom woman, rushes out to help her, and Rebecca throws herself into the woman's arms and is comforted.*

Although the dream frightened Rebecca, she thought it represented a turning point. She sensed that it was about getting away from a negative father figure: a symbolic reaction to her leaving her job and abandoning her desire to be a minister. The image of a wise old woman embracing her, and of Rebecca allowing herself to be embraced, represented a meaningful metaphor of self-acceptance.

The Divine Child, On the Edge, and the Chalice

Next, Rebecca shared an important dream fragment containing a divine child image, a symbol of both rebirth and the Self. In the dream, she is holding a baby girl and being helped by her pastor. Most likely the pastor in this dream represented inner contact with her own affirming animus and indicated a positive transference and growing therapeutic alliance.

At a subsequent session, Rebecca announced that she had resigned from the rape crisis center, the Parents Anonymous group, and a church committee. She said, "I want to stop helping others and help myself." I supported her decision. I reminded her that her resignations represented losses of parts of herself, and that it was understandable that she felt sad.

She then described herself as a four-part being, fragmented, yet struggling to be whole. One part was, figuratively speaking, behind a chair; another, an angry part, was running around screaming; a third was participating in the therapy session; while a fourth was hiding altogether. She said the fourth part was like a mold of her, which sounded like a possible future persona or ego-image more true to herself.

In an effort to help unify her fragmenting psyche, I suggested that Rebecca create something, perhaps draw or paint images of her feelings and dreams. She responded that it would be difficult. Then her angry part, which she said was like a three-year-old child, took over, and she blurted out that she wanted to kick me in the shins. She reported that she used to be all feeling, like a three-year-old, angry all the time and wanting to kick and bite. I replied that she had reason to be angry, because at the age of three she had to deal with being abandoned by her parents and being replaced by her unwed aunt's new baby.

Five weeks later, Rebecca said she felt as if she were "on hold, waiting for some catalyst to come along and change something." Then she started crying and said that she had an image of herself standing on the edge of a void, afraid of falling into it. I asked her to immediately draw the image (see Figure 6-1). At the top, to indicate where she was a year ago, she drew herself as a circle on the periphery of a giant spinning disk. To represent herself at the moment, she drew another circle much closer to what she called the abyss at the center of the disk. Lines to the left of the disk represented the void underneath.

I felt that Rebecca had come near to the end of Stage I and was on the verge of egocide and surrendering to the unconscious void. She trusted me and her therapy enough to talk openly about her fear of falling into a bottomless pit where she would drown, suffocate, be eaten alive, or float forever. We both realized that her former ego-identity was breaking apart so that she could contact the Self, undergo a transformation process or death-rebirth experience, and continue on her path of individuation. Nevertheless, at the end of the session she could not make a commitment to resume analytical treat-

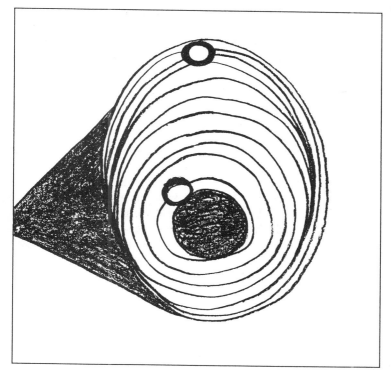

FIGURE 6-1
On the Edge of a Void

ment. A decision to commit egocide—like suicide—is an ambivalent
one because death is involved, although it's symbolic.

Rebecca called five days later and asked for an appointment.
When she came in, she brought with her a series of drawings. Figure
6-2 has seven spirals, which symbolize the individuation process;
the number seven is the number of transition, creation, illumination, and completion. She identified the three top-row spirals as
clockwise, symbolizing evolution, progression, integration, and constructive change. The four bottom-row spirals were seen as counterclockwise, symbolizing devolution, regression, disintegration, and
destruction.[5] The outside of the composition is dark and the inside
is light, suggesting the inner light of her psyche. However, in five of

the spirals, the centers are dark, which seems to suggest an overall yin/yang union of opposites. Rebecca thought that the lighter central composition looked like intestines and commented, "It takes a lot of guts to do this kind of work, to be on this inner journey." She had drawn more counterclockwise spirals than clockwise spirals and she identified more strongly with the former, particularly the one near the exit point. It seemed that was why she came back to therapy: She was more interested in egocide (Symbolic Death) than in self-destruction.

Figure 6-3, entitled "What Is This Sinking Feeling?," referred to a question that Rebecca had once asked Dr. X. He hadn't had an answer. Now, as then, she felt she was on the edge, naked, and, in her words, "being pulled head first down into the depths." She further explained that she had an inner drive to go deeper, that is, to continue therapy, despite her fear. She associated the shape of the container in the drawing with the womb and the birth canal. While

FIGURE 6-2
Spirals of Existence

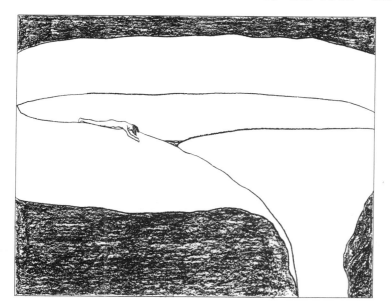

FIGURE 6-3
"What Is This Sinking Feeling?"

talking about this, she felt nauseated with an urge to vomit and stated, "I can't bear the pain anymore." To me, this constellation of nausea, pain, and female private parts seemed, once again, to point to possible sexual abuse in Rebecca's past.

Eight months into treatment, Rebecca got a job (related to her Ph.D. degree) mainstreaming the mentally retarded into the work force. This involved training, support, and much patience. She commented that it was like training her own emotionally retarded inner child. She had recently gone back to Arkansas, where she had spent most of her childhood, to attend her uncle's funeral. (Her mother refused to go, even though it was her brother who had died.) During the trip, Rebecca had felt as though a part of her was dying and now she felt more separated from her mother, her past, and her roots. After returning, she made two drawings.

Rebecca associated Figure 6-4, "Worms in a Jar Lid," with a childhood rhyme, "The worms crawl in, the worms crawl out, the

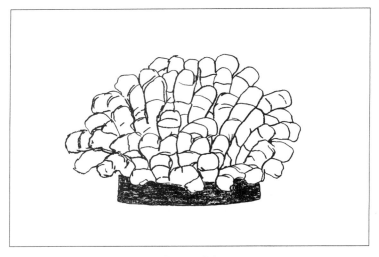

FIGURE 6-4
Worms in a Jar Lid

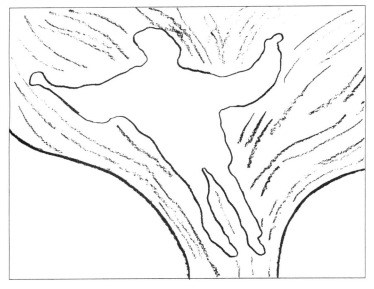

FIGURE 6-5
"The Chalice of Birth [and Rebirth]"

worms play pinochle on your snout," a playful image but an image of death, since worms help to decompose corpses. Rebecca also associated worms to penises. The fact that she didn't like worms or penises meant that she was confronting something in herself that she didn't like. Again, I thought of the possibility of childhood sexual abuse. In the drawing, the lid is off the jar, so we see a symbolic release of pent-up emotions.

Rebecca called the other drawing "The Chalice of Birth" (Figure 6-5), which she described as a male figure falling, yet being born in the womb. It represents a mixture of opposites: the masculine and the feminine elements. The man with his arms up and open (symbolizing Rebecca's new animus or inner masculine spirit) is totally accepting of the birth process (symbolizing Rebecca's rebirth). To Rebecca, the drawing felt integrative, because the falling male figure is being held and was experienced as uplifting. She also pointed out that the composition as a whole had a stable bottom line and was shaped like a tree, rooted and grounded: a symbol of reaching to the sky (father) but having roots in the earth (mother). In addition, she could look at the falling masculine image as her own falling patriarchal identity. She was letting go of it, and it was being contained by the feminine chalice. She further associated the chalice with the communion cup, containing the blood of Christ, thus suggesting a unity with life by taking in a new animus (spirit). I considered this drawing to serve a very important transcendent function for Rebecca, helping her to rise above her negative father and mother complexes.

Before the next session, Rebecca had an experience that deeply affected her. She had looked in a mirror and said to herself that she was not a scientist, but an artist. Rebecca's egocide had taken place. She saw herself as she truly was in the moment. Rebecca felt independent (her parents' hold on her was no more). Most significantly, she said that she wanted to work with clay and, thus, redirect her anger, sadness, and a sense of disorganization into something creative and reflective of her soul.

To the following session Rebecca brought a chalice made of wet clay, which, like many of the images in her drawings, was womb-shaped. She said that it was crude, ugly, and misshapen, but it had potential and represented a transitional period (Stage II) in her movement toward wholeness. The chalice, she said, reminded her of communion, so it suggested healing. She further associated the chalice with the perpetual quest for the Holy Grail. Her chalice stem was open, unlike the stem of the chalice used in the patriarchal church, which is closed.

Confirming the maxim that outer behavior parallels inner life, on Sunday Rebecca had gone to church and served the chalice during communion. However, she became very angry about some of the minister's sexist comments, so she gave the chalice to someone else and left the church for good.

Sacrifice: Goodbye Dr. X, Hello Inner Healer

Eleven months into therapy, Rebecca was going on an extended trip with her husband and daughter, so we had our last session for a while. She was angry and hurt at the time because she had not been invited to her mother's second wedding. However, to her credit, she was determined not to play her mother's petty games and worry about it, which was a good sign that she was on her way to finding her own true identity.

During this trip, Rebecca's daughter was critically injured in a car accident and lay in a coma. From a distant hospital, Rebecca wrote a long letter to me about how alone and desperate she felt. She stated, "I am going to stop controlling the world, and I am going to live now. Not do, but be. I am back to my belief that I am a priest inside." From my point of view, Rebecca was drinking from her chalice.

Upon her return, Rebecca did not see me for three months because her daughter, in a hospital closer to home, needed so much care. When she did resume therapy, she said that she was "coming unglued," having lost sight of herself while tending her daughter. She was lonely, having cut herself off from the church and her associated friends. As it turned out, her daughter amazingly regained consciousness and subsequently returned home.

At an ensuing session, Rebecca talked about feeling increasingly depressed, despondent, and angry at her husband. She said some irrational fears going back a dozen years had resurfaced; among them were a fear of being home alone after her kids had gone to school and a fear of being attacked while taking a shower.

In the next session, Rebecca complained that her mother, whose second marriage had failed, was going to move closer to her. Rebecca was very concerned that she would be "sucked up" or "devoured" by her mother. She was passive, whiny, and talked in a childish, and at times confused, manner about her fear of being trapped. Having her daughter at home was not as bad as Rebecca had feared it might be. However, Rebecca awakened the night before our session feeling panicky and experiencing unrecalled nightmares. Her husband was out of town, and she was upset because he was not there. She was afraid that she might be abducted in order to be sexually assaulted and possibly killed.

Rebecca came to the subsequent session very depressed, with what she described as an "I am stuck" feeling. She said, "I feel like a worm in a cocoon," and she associated the cocoon with the years she spent getting her Ph.D., pursuing the ministry, and undertaking therapy. In contrast to the worm as penis and death (Figure 6-4), here the worm is transforming Rebecca's depression. She added that she was sick of being in the cocoon and prayed for help in getting out. From my perspective, the cocoon feeling indicated that she was in another incubation phase. Feeling forced to wait conformed to a classic Stage II pattern (the Death-Rebirth struggle). Eventually, the butterfly would evolve and her true self would emerge.

Rebecca also said she was not finished with her therapist, Dr. X. Because of overwhelming anxiety about a recent long dream and her desire to tell the truth regarding Dr. X, Rebecca scheduled an additional session.

> DREAM: *First, she is in bed with me, and we are married or conjoined. She wonders what I will do and if she can ever have sex with me. Second, she is looking through a Jungian booklet or folder. Between us is an eight-year-old girl with long golden hair who she assumes is one of my daughters. I take the girl out of the bed to her own room and tell her that she does not belong in our bed. Third, while I am gone, Rebecca notices a lumpy female sleeping across the room. She wonders if she can have sex with me with this woman present. Fourth, I am punching data into a computer, trying to get a program to run. She looks at what I'm doing and realizes that the program is going to work. Fifth, I am reaching over to her (she is on my left), and she buries her head in my chest and decides that she can have sex with me.*

Rebecca maintained that this dream did not reflect an erotic transference. Rather, it suggested that she would unite with the part of her (inner doctor/healer) that I represented. Looking through the booklet reflected her interest in Jungian psychology. The young girl with golden hair belonging to me represented, according to Rebecca, the positive fathering experience I was providing her. The girl also could be the missing Goldilocks, suggesting that some of the sexual abuse may have occurred when she was around eight. The lumpy female was an obscure mother figure; and the computer scene indicated optimism that the therapy program would work. Rebecca's contact with my left side could be interpreted as her establishing a heart link with me and my anima. She felt that she could successfully complete her analytical work because her union with me represented an *inner marriage* with her inner doctor/healer or positive animus, which agrees with Jungian theory.

Given the encouragement of this dream, Rebecca said that she wanted me to know the full story about Dr. X. She had fallen madly in love with him (an erotic transference). They had broken off the therapy but had remained involved (indicating an obvious sexualized countertransference problem on Dr. X's part). She said they met once at his home when he was separated from his wife. After moving to her current home, before she ever saw me, she wrote him a letter saying that he had "mind-fucked" her. (He could have actually had intercourse with her, that is raped her, while she was under hypnosis.) She had gotten no response to her letter.

Later that same year Rebecca's daughter had tried to commit suicide, and Rebecca took her to Dr. X (perhaps unconsciously recapitulating a form of parental abuse: the mother handing over her daughter to the abusive father). The renewed contact between Rebecca and Dr. X rekindled their relationship. Following a sexual advance from Dr. X, Rebecca decided that Dr. X was disturbed and that she should protect him. I wondered whether this pattern of feeling abused and then being protective of the abuser was repeating a much more serious pattern from her childhood.

In the next session, Rebecca admitted that she feared I would not want to see her anymore, that I would think she might be trying to do with me what she had done with Dr. X. I reassured her that by being aware of all the issues and still disclosing her thoughts and feelings, she had made a choice to trust: in herself, in me, and in the healing therapeutic relationship. Then, going on to talk about Dr. X, she made this perceptive comment: "If I had had sex with him, I would have devoured him and hurt him badly. I would have attacked him like a lion and pulled him apart." She said that she had an immense rage toward Dr. X because she had trusted him and he had failed her. I underscored this as a major insight, pointing out that she had not failed, but Dr. X had failed her.

Several weeks later, Rebecca told me that she had celebrated communion with a female friend at the same religious retreat center. While there, she had also used active imagination to work through some difficult personal issues. Her initial mental image was of going through a tunnel and opening three doors but being stopped by fear in front of a fourth door. When she finally opened this door, she saw a reflection of herself as a rosebud (symbol of the Great Mother). The rosebud blossomed into a multicolored rose window with a cross in the center (mandala, sacred circle, and symbol of the Self), which made her feel hopeful.

In a session shortly afterward, she reported a brief but very important two-part dream. In the first part, with a four-day holiday coming, Rebecca bakes cakes for each day. She drew the image for me: one large square pan in which four cakes bake simultaneously. Recalling the description of herself as a four-part being, I interpreted this image as an indication that her fragmented psyche was coming together—a real cause for celebration. In the second part, Rebecca is pregnant, suggesting that she was being procreative with herself in both her inner and outer worlds. In fact, she felt integrated enough to talk constructively with me about abandoning for good her on-again, off-again idea of becoming a counselor.

All the evidence told me that Rebecca was now in the latter part of Stage II of her illness and therapy, after 55 sessions with me covering a year and a half. Her dreams and disclosures about herself revealed the faith that she now had in herself and in the therapeutic process. She displayed an increasing ability to rework traumas of the past with conscious awareness. Rebecca's outer life manifested better relationships with her immediate family, due to her letting go of an unrealistic and grandiose conception that she should be an ideal person. On reflection, I considered her to be well along the path of individuation, and clearly there was light at the end of the dark tunnel.

Letting Go and the Sacred Kangaroo

Two months later, Rebecca abruptly announced that she had dropped the educational program that would have enabled her to become a counselor. She gave two reasons: (1) She wanted to stop pursuing external validations of herself, and (2) she wanted to stop postponing her life. She also was "divorcing" her mother. Her mother had been living with her temporarily after divorcing her second husband. Rebecca's mother had abandoned her, and now Rebecca was turning the tables and shutting her mother out of her life. She stated, "I won't rescue her anymore. I am tired of mothering my mother." Following these events—quitting school and divorcing her mother—she was able to interact much more positively with her husband. She also commented that there was more family cooperation, fun, and happiness.

In the context of a new sacred space inside (her revitalized psyche) and a new sacred space outside (a studio for doing ceramic work), Rebecca began a program of active imagination utilizing clay. Her first products were five little boxes featuring broken pieces of jewelry, mementos that she had saved. She called them "spirit boxes," and said, "I have a desire to resurrect the parts of me that have been hurt and rejected, and I am doing just that." Her term "resurrect" was especially appropriate in regard to the process of egocide and transformation she was undergoing.

At one year and ten months into therapy, Rebecca felt confident enough to talk about how difficult it always had been for her to experience pleasurable sex with her husband or to discuss sexual matters with him. She said that communication between her and her husband had improved somewhat, and, as a result, their sex life had gotten a little better.

In a subsequent session, Rebecca reported an intense dream.

DREAM: *First, she is walking down a street with a baby, and there are two animals in the street that are entangled with each other: a bear and a kangaroo. Lots of people are around. She and the baby get into a safe place, but she is afraid of all the people. Second, she sees a man talking to a little girl who does not respond verbally. The girl is sucking an extra-long pacifier that is somehow connected to drugs. The man takes the pacifier out and knows that it is bad. The*

girl has a numb white tongue that is abnormally smooth because of
damage from the pacifier. Third, Rebecca goes to a health food store.
She leaves her valuables in the car and discovers upon entering the
store that it has been changed into a fast food place, with health food
in the back. She looks for sponges, but they have none. She goes out
and discovers that her valuables have been stolen. She hurriedly
copies the license plate numbers from several nearby cars because she
feels that the culprit, a male driver, can be caught with one of these
numbers.

Discussing the dream, Rebecca felt that the baby was less than a
year old and represented herself as an infant when she was abandoned. The fact that she was going somewhere with this baby signi-
fied that her new ego was integrated (the baby serving as a divine
child archetype of transformation). She associated the bear with the
three bears and the masculine trinity in her initial dream and with
the power animal she had been led to adopt by Dr. X. However, the
bear also represents mother and Self symbols as well as a healing
force.[6] As for the kangaroo, she remembered that a kangaroo had
appeared in the first dream that she brought to me. The kangaroo,
like the bear, is a healing mother symbol: The female kangaroo is
well known for nurturing her young in a pouch and carrying them
with her everywhere she goes. Rebecca acknowledged that the conflict between the bear and the kangaroo suggested her own internal
conflict regarding her mother and her motherhood.

After seeing these animals in her dream, Rebecca goes into a safe
place but is afraid of being hurt. In the second part of the dream, the
fact that badness (drugs) and abnormality are linked with the extra-
long pacifier intimates the possibility of oral-genital sexual abuse
between a male and Rebecca as a little girl, who is unable to say
anything about it. The man in the dream could be me, the doctor
who facilitates the removal of the pacifier (the defense of repression),
examines the patient, and notes that damage has been done; of
course, the man is also Rebecca's own animus/healer. The third
sequence of the dream, when she goes to the health food shop, could
represent her attempt to renew her own body with a sponge, which
she associated with cleansing and/or birth control. But when she goes
in to buy this sponge,[7] a male culprit steals her valuables, which
again indicated to me that she might have been molested as a young
child.

It is noteworthy that in the above session, for the first time, she consciously raised the possibility that some sexual abuse—even incest—might have occurred when she was a child and been forgotten. Soon after this breakthrough speculation, Rebecca brought in two ceramic pieces to show me. They were like paintings but drawn on panels of clay and then built out and etched in, creating a bas-relief. The first "Sacred Kangaroo," was a kangaroo mother with a baby in its pouch. I thought that it reflected her own sense of accepting herself, her own buried child that had been abandoned, neglected, and damaged. This mother/child archetype (like the chalice before) served a transcendent function, allowing her to nurture herself.

The second bas-relief was called "Peace." A moon is in the sky and there is a tree behind which a kangaroo advances. A figure representing Rebecca stands with her back to the viewer, facing the kangaroo, the moon, and the tree. There is also a second tree further in the background and a bear who is receding.

In showing me these ceramic productions, Rebecca stated, "I feel anxious about something I am going to tell you." She said that it related to her last reported dream of the little girl having something removed from her mouth; she felt as if she may have gone through periods in her past of forced oral sex, with no sensation or ability to speak. She noted that it was this type of sexual activity with her husband that nauseated her. She then related a curious incident that took place the previous weekend—a recurrence of an old problem. Before she was fully awake in the morning, she had the feeling that there was pressure from a hand on her crotch. Then it disappeared, and she heard her name spoken by a woman.

Rebecca told me again that she sometimes didn't have any sensation in her genital area. That weekend morning when she felt the pressure, she thought, "I *have* been sexually abused. Why else would I have no response to sexual stimuli, either by myself or with my husband?" Rebecca then disclosed something that disturbed me very much. She said that Dr. X had "probed the sexual area" several times while she was under hypnosis. However, she couldn't consciously link this probing to the hand pressure she had felt that weekend morning. Instead, she associated it with her father or grandfather. She thought the voice she had heard belonged to her mother or maternal grandmother. She also said that she went into hypnosis easily because she used to put herself into a trance. Trance-induction is a common, defensive dissociation employed by children who are abused and by women who were abused as children. Rebecca was scared to talk about this topic, admitting that she was afraid I would tell her that she was bad or making it up. I reassured her that I would not tell her either thing.

After a two-month break, Rebecca began a new year of in-depth analytical work. She reported an affirming visit with a local professional potter who was excited about her ceramics. She also confided that she had originally wanted to major in art, but that she had not had the freedom or courage to do that, so—like her parents—she majored in education. Later, she had thought of entering a healing profession like the ministry or counseling, but now she realized that her only motivation was a desire to help herself. By contrast, the clay work was fun, spontaneous, and creative. She added, "I'm not really well suited to be a counselor or therapist. I've got too much of my own pain, both historical and current." I supported her insightful viewpoint on this matter. She went on to say that her husband had been quite encouraging in helping her set up her studio at home. At the end of the session, she reaffirmed that she was going to mother herself.

Egocide and Transformation:
Death of Incest Through Dreams

A little over two years and two months into therapy, Rebecca shared a dream in which a woman driving a car, with a three- to four-year-old girl, deliberately kills herself. Miraculously the girl survives. Rebecca saw the woman as a self-destructive part of herself, related to her mother. She commits suicide, but the little girl—her reborn self—is actually saved. Rebecca then talked at length about how she was saving herself while killing her negative mother complex; thus, I interpreted this dream suicide as the equivalent of egocide, because it was a symbolic suicide. This aspect of Rebecca's case illustrates clearly that patients usually have to experience egocide and transformation more than once and often several times.

Two weeks later, Rebecca reported a short dream about a wedding (always a significant image), after which she was being congratulated by me. She associated the wedding with an inner marriage and a new beginning. The people she saw getting married were her friends. The woman was a confidante and a positive, intelligent, and affirming person; and her husband-to-be was described by Rebecca as "an unfinished person"—someone who felt like a failure but actually had achieved a lot. She saw him as her negative, wounded animus that needed a great deal of nurturing. She interpreted my congratulations as supporting her inner union with her self-doubting masculine part. Another association to the dream was that the day before she and her husband had happily celebrated their own twenty-fourth wedding anniversary.

At two years and six months a critical period occurred in Rebecca's therapy, equivalent to the onset of post-egocide metamorphosis. The source of the decisive period was a dream of union with a positive shadow figure, represented by the professional ceramicist who was her mentor. In the dream, she is intimate with this woman. They embrace, and Rebecca strokes the ceramicist's hair. Then the ceramicist has to leave temporarily. Rebecca marvels that the ceramicist stores her silver in her freezer to avoid getting fingerprints on it, and she thinks about moving all of her own silver into her freezer. Then the scene shifts to her mentor's garden. She strokes one of her ceramic animals, a wolf: a very territorial, nurturing, and elegant animal.

The hug with the professional ceramicist in Rebecca's dream was symbolic of Rebecca's acceptance of her new feminine ego identity and herself as a creative person. The silver in the freezer related to her past freezing of her core femininity. The notion of not wanting any fingerprints on her silver could be linked to her not liking the strange pressure she occasionally felt on her genital area. This dream set the stage for what Rebecca's next reported dream revealed: She had been sexually abused by her father.

> DREAM: *Rebecca is her current age. Her father comes to her when her mother is gone, and one of them notices that a living room window is open. She goes to close it and discovers that there are two windows, like a storm window with a stained glass window on the inner side. Her father comes to her again, bulgy and strangely shaped. He approaches her with a hug and says he needs a plug. Then she is holding an armful of wet clothes. She hangs them out in the bathroom and tells her father that she doesn't think they should have sexual relations anymore. Next to the bathroom is a room full of clutter. There is a bed at one end of the room, and a woman speaks*

from the bed. She wonders if the woman is her mother. She apolo-
gizes for being in the bathroom, and she hangs up a green bathing
suit.

Discussing this dream, Rebecca confessed that she had difficulty
accepting that she and her father had had sexual relations, but she
was certain that it was true. She did not think that Dr. X had actually
had sexual intercourse with her, although she had no way of knowing
for certain, because she had been often under hypnosis. She then
started crying and saying that she felt very sorry for her father, that
he was a pitiful, disturbed man. She told me she had shared this
dream with her husband, and he had responded, "Yes, your father
could have done that." Then she expressed rage toward her mother
for not intervening to stop the abuse.

Next, Rebecca told me an associated memory that she had not
recalled before. When her sister was almost five years old she became
allergic to dust, and her doctor said that she had to sleep in an
allergy-free room. Accordingly, her mother cleaned out Rebecca's
room and slept with her sister there, while Rebecca, then fifteen-
and-a-half years old, moved into her parents' bedroom and slept in
the same bed with her father. This arrangement lasted for a year and
a half. Apparently, she had had no fully conscious memories of the
arrangement until this moment in her therapy. Now that she knew
she had been sexually abused, she realized that the guilt she had been
harboring for so many years was properly related to her father's
problem, not hers. She also wondered if her father had sexually
abused her sister, who had been sexually active at fourteen and had
become pregnant the summer after graduating from high school.

We spent an additional session reanalyzing the critical dream. She
realized that earlier when her mother was not present, her father had
had sex with her. Now, following her divorce of her mother and the
death of her negative mother complex, her father had come to her
in a dream wanting sex again. Repulsed at what she was coming to
understand, she started crying; but I reminded her that in the dream
she had said that the sex had to stop. She said she had the feeling that
if she accused her father "it would hurt him so badly that he would
die; the rage would just kill him." Of course, what needed to happen
was a Symbolic Death of Rebecca's negative father complex, which
could only happen by bringing her rage and anger against her father
into her conscious life. Exploring what kinds of sex she had had with

her father, Rebecca reflected on her symptoms—irrational fears, aversions to fellatio, frigidity, pain during intercourse, and nightmares involving sex—and determined that they had engaged in oral-genital sex and intercourse. She reported that throughout childhood she couldn't stand creamy things in her mouth, such as tapioca and meringue. During this session she repeatedly exclaimed, "It is just so hard to believe. I feel so angry that these memories are coming to me now."

In a third session, Rebecca kept reworking the dream. She associated the worry about the open window with her stormy feelings about what the dream was revealing. She associated the inner window with insight. The stained glass represented fragile pieces of her broken self put together in an integrated and beautiful pattern: her creatively rebuilt true self. Her father being bulgy suggested that he had an erection, and his needing a plug suggested oral sex (like the extra-long pacifier in her earlier dream). She thought that her washing clothes symbolized her effort to cleanse herself, that is, rid herself of the problem. She connected the room next to the bathroom with her own inner room, which she thought of as cluttered, and the green bathing suit with growth and healing (in actuality, she currently wore this suit to her water aerobics classes).

At this point in Rebecca's individuation process, she was facing a dilemma regarding what to do with her discoveries about her incestuous past. She joined a group for victims of sexual molestation. The group process included writing letters to her parents (without necessarily mailing them), which she found to be very therapeutic. Her predicament was also played out in a transference relationship. She pleaded with me, "I want you to stay with me until I'm through this. I don't want you to leave me." She was crying, knowing that this request was neurotic and irrational, but she felt that she needed to make it. To me, her behavior and feelings were clearly illustrative of Stage II in the egocide and transformation process, when the therapeutic alliance is so intensely symbiotic and potentially so positive.

Two years and seven months into her therapy, Rebecca, describing her feelings metaphorically, stated, "I'm sitting in a puddle of rain. The major storm has gone. I have scraped away many layers of pain and confusion in my life, but what to do now?"

As she had many times before, Rebecca then switched from the rage she felt toward her father to the rage she felt toward her mother. She was infuriated with her mother for letting her sleep with her father during her vulnerable teenage years. The only saving grace in those years was that when Rebecca was a senior they moved to a new town and Rebecca got her own bedroom. She felt that her mother allowed her to choose the biggest room (actually, the master bedroom with its own private bath) out of guilt and to keep her at home. When Rebecca talked to her mother about wanting to go away to college, her mother would say no and that Rebecca was killing her. After she graduated from high school, Rebecca ran away to live with her cousin. She described her mother as a witch who just lived in the dark, hiding behind blinds, and as someone who almost killed her as a little girl. When Rebecca used to speak to her mother about her father's profound loneliness, her mother would say that he was paranoid and abusive. Now Rebecca was enraged at her mother, because she had known this and yet had stayed with him for thirty-six years, allowing him to vent his paranoid and abusive nature on Rebecca. Rebecca recalled that she had married her husband to escape her home and to help her establish boundaries for herself—an objective that she now related to having permitted her father to do anything with her. At the end of this session, she talked about not having had any fever blisters on her mouth for many years until she had the dream about her father, after which she came down with massive fever blisters on her mouth. She considered these fever blisters to be graphic, psychosomatic confirmation of past oral-genital sexual abuse.

"The Letter Killeth, But the Spirit Giveth Life"

Rebecca finally decided to tell her sister about her incestuous relationship with her father. She wrote her a letter explaining her revelation and asked her not to mention it to her mother or father. When she mailed the letter, she felt as if she were violating a secret. It made her recall that her father always told secrets to her and to her sister; and then, again, she realized that it was her father, not she, who was the real violator. She remembered how he was always ashamed, guilt-ridden, and embarrassed about things. As for herself, she thought that her father had "murdered her soul"[8] but that "something inside survived."[9] Years later, when she acted out her incestuous complex with Dr. X, he convinced her that she could trust him; but then she felt betrayed by him when he abandoned her.

Until very recently she had been bound up with protecting Dr. X, and now she no longer wanted to do that. She felt the same way about her father after mailing her letter.

It wasn't long until Rebecca's sister called her and conveyed that she was sorry that Rebecca had been in such pain. Her sister admitted that the letter made her feel as if someone had kicked her in the stomach; she didn't know if she herself had been abused or not, but now she was forced to wonder. After Rebecca told me about this, she brought out all the letters that she had written to Dr. X but had not mailed, and all the letters he had written to her. Then she tore them all up. She screamed, cried, complained, and said that she felt as if she were going to vomit. She also complained of aching sensations in her pelvis and anxiety throughout her body. When she calmed down, she shared something very private and difficult for her to express: She had always cried after having sex with her husband, feeling a sense of fragmentation and emptiness, as if she had done something wrong. I indicated to her that this pattern of behavior only underscored how deep and long-lasting the damage suffered in childhood can be. We talked about how she now had a new identity as a woman; and although it was difficult for her to talk about sex, she was, indeed, doing it, which she hadn't been able to do before.

At two years and eight months into therapy, and characteristic of Stage III, with its creative new actions based on the true self, Rebecca at last mailed a letter to Dr. X, confronting him with everything that he had done to her and letting him know that what had happened with him was related to her incest with her father. As anticipated, she never heard from him. Subsequently, she filed a formal complaint with the appropriate state licensing board.

She also sent letters to her mother and father in conjunction with attending the group for survivors of sexual molestation. She outlined the incestuous relationship, how she felt about it, and that they had to accept responsibility for this tragedy and get therapeutic help for themselves. Both of her parents wrote back but addressed none of the issues outlined in Rebecca's letters. It was blatant dissociation and denial now on their part.

Nevertheless, Rebecca felt she could resolve her problem with her mother and forgive and accept her, but she refused ever again to take care of her. She felt hopeless about resolving her problem with her father, but she wasn't going to let that get her down. She felt good about her own reintegration and renewal as a woman (self-Self axis, which is central to Stage III) and her continued creative active imagination work in ceramics.

At our next session, Rebecca brought in two very meaningful ceramic pieces. One was a woman with a green ball in her navel. Rebecca associated this orb with the life force and the navel with the ground of her being. Thus, the sphere was a symbol of the Self and healing.

The second ceramic piece consisted of many parts, which she assembled on the floor of my office. The main part consisted of a female figure which represented herself. Flayed open, with a hole through the top of her head, a worm was going into the hole all the way down into her stomach. Her arms were up, her legs were spread apart, and there was a small sphere in her navel. Four worms were entering her left side and three worms were entering her right side. Two serpents, a male and a female, were devouring her genital area. Next to the figure, on her left side, was a vessel that was empty and ready for receiving the spirit (a classic Taoist image).

This second, multi-faceted ceramic creation was very significant with regard to Rebecca's egocide and transformation. Treating it like a dream, she associated the worm entering her head and going down into her stomach as symbolic of being violated by her father's penis. The four worms entering her left or feminine side (her murdered soul) and the male serpent represent further incestual abuse. Her mother's collusion is indicated by the three worms entering her right or masculine side (her crushed spirit) and by the female serpent devouring her genital area. In a healing vein, worms eat decaying matter, break it up, aerate it, and, thereby, help regenerate it. The serpents are also symbols of healing and transformation. Now the worms and snakes which represent phallus have transfigured into *phallos,* a sacred principle of generativity.[10] Rebecca interpreted the whole active imagination product as her fragmented self lying down dead, which fits with a post-egocide creative synthesis leading to rebirth. She also saw it as her being in a cave. A cave is like a womb of Mother Earth (recall her initial dream with the kangaroos coming out of a cave); so perhaps the cave she imagined was the symbolic place in which she was giving birth to her own individuality.

Several weeks later, Rebecca came to a session very excited, saying that she had been making hair ornaments, necklaces, and earrings out of ceramics. She felt this activity was truly an immersion into the feminine side of herself. She called the necklaces "primitive death-rebirth pieces" and pointed out that the neck is a critical body part, since it contains the spine, esophagus, trachea, and major blood vessels, holds the head up so that it can rotate, and connects the head and the body. It is meaningful that she now reported mutually satisfactory sexual relations with her husband and she added that she actually enjoyed their physical intimacy.

Immediately following this period of intensive ceramic work, she had a beautiful dream.

> DREAM: *A woman is having a baby underwater. Her male partner is there with her. Rebecca knows that an underwater birth is good for the baby, but she wonders how the two parents are breathing. She sees a doctor beside them, and then she watches the couple surface, take a breath, and go back underwater, like dolphins.*

Associating with the images in this dream, Rebecca thought that the couple represented her inner marriage of the masculine and feminine, and that the birth reflected that she was now involved in a rebirthing process as well as being involved in giving birth to ceramic creations.

For all her progress, Rebecca admitted that she still had rough days. However, she made it a point to keep on working and creating. She was determined never to stop pursuing the truth, and to remain ever in contact with her true self.

Near the end of Stage III, and after almost three years of therapy, Rebecca wrote me a letter that contained the phrase: "with gratitude for your acceptance." Revealing that these words were an outer expression of an inner process, she also wrote, "I am my mother, self-birthing being, transforming life into living. Embracing father [her own inner archetypal father]. Welcoming fecundity. Peace."

Peace with oneself is a first step to making peace with others. The word for peace in Hebrew, *shalom,* does not mean the absence of war but rather well-being or peace unto you. Shalom is a sacred circle— the symbol of the Self.

After her analytic treatment with me, Rebecca moved with her family to a different state. She is now seeing a woman analyst. It is common Jungian practice to see analysts of both genders. Rebecca's ceramic work continues to be important to her, but more as an avocation. Currently, she is working in an area related to her Ph.D. degree and teaching a course at a women's college.

CHAPTER 7

Gary: The Dance
of the Dragon

"The chief benefit of dancing is to learn how
to sit still."

—SAMUEL JOHNSON

IN our rapid paced way of life, rootlessness is commonplace. In order to find ourselves, we must stay in one place and be silent. Once the seed is planted it needs to germinate, to be held and nurtured by the dark earth. Creative change is slow and takes quiet time for the eventual growth and development to occur.

Gary's story illustrates how important it is to be grounded and at peace. No easy feat for Gary, who is a dancer and racer. Gary had been adopted and once he decided to find out who he really was, he labored hard to trace his roots of origin. This was a transcendent and healing process for him, basic to his egocide and transformation and the unfolding of his personal myth.

When I first met Gary, he appeared younger than his thirty-five years. A married professional dancer and college instructor, Gary dressed more like a student, in colorful T-shirts and jeans. Underneath this casual, upbeat surface, however, he was depressed and stuck. He complained of a loss of soul, which he attributed to a lack of creativity and meaning in his life. Gary said he wanted to get back on track and be more like he was in college when he was a free spirit and a poet. He boasted about his attraction to danger. He had previously raced motorcycles and now raced cars and had had numerous accidents. Like a typical *puer aeternus* (eternal boy),[1] he proudly declared, "I love speed and power." He was not sure why he continued his dancing career instead of devoting his time to racing, which he really loved to do.

Gary believed that he was developing into a good choreographer, but felt troubled because he had built so many grids around himself and had no time for imagination. Nevertheless, he thought of dance as a valuable aspect of his life because it offered him a means of blending imagination, movement, and power in order to feel whole. Dance was difficult for him, however. He started dancing relatively late, when he was twenty-five. It did not come naturally to him and he had to work very hard at it.

Gary's uncertainties about his future mirrored uncertainties about his past. Like many adoptees, he was ambivalent about tracking down his biological parents. Gary believed that he had been given away for adoption at the age of eight weeks after his biological mother, a poor woman with too many other children, was abandoned by his biological father, a soldier. Later, he talked with his adoptive mother, who told him that he had been adopted at the age of three days, not eight weeks. She discounted the notion that his biological mother was poor and overburdened with other children and claimed she knew little about his biological father. Gary was frustrated by his adoptive mother's response; but with my support, he began searching for his biological parents. He was encouraged in this process by several illuminating dreams.

Gary described his adoptive mother as stable and devoted to him and home life. He felt that she had met all of his basic needs for nurturance, but that she had little understanding of his educational or professional development, perhaps because she had not gone to college. His adoptive father, a cobbler who died thirteen years previously, had been kind but distant. He and his adoptive father had gone go-cart racing together until Gary was eighteen. When Gary went away to college, however, their relationship grew strained because Gary became hippie-like. It was only after his father's death that Gary decided to pursue dance.

Gary was married to a dancer whom he met in college, when both of them made extra money dancing in go-go bars. She also taught in the same performing arts department where he worked. They were both very committed to dance and did not want to have children, so Gary had had a vasectomy. Early in their marriage, his wife had an affair, and his sense of rejection and abandonment probably opened up old wounds about being abandoned by his biological mother. He and his wife dealt with this difficult situation by mutually agreeing to have an open marriage, which put an even greater strain on their relationship.

Despite their intellectual kinship, Gary and his wife had little emotional intimacy. His wife coped by drinking. She had a significant alcohol problem, often embarrassing him in public. He coped by working excessively. His wife complained that he abused her through his self-imposed workload, because it took him away from her and made him more aloof and detached. Also, she claimed, it took him away from his playful and creative soul.

Confronting Shadow and Befriending Anima

Gary had a powerful dream the night before his first therapy session.

> DREAM: *He has an angry exchange in his house with a colleague (in real life, a technician in his dance company). This man wrestles with Gary, but Gary gets him out of his house. Then the scene shifts, and Gary is confronted by another man, a black colleague.*

To me, the dream clearly symbolized that Gary was undergoing confrontations with shadow figures; he was fighting with the technical, competitive, dark sides of himself. It also indicated some issues that would come up in his relationship with me.

During our initial session, Gary expressed concern that his relationship with his wife was too symbiotic and that he abused her (the same term she had used). He talked about how self-deprecating he was and about the many motorcycle accidents he had had, which I translated to mean that he was feeling guilty about what he was doing to his wife. It seemed that he was stuck in his own development and that he and his wife were stuck in an interrelated mutual abuse.

In subsequent sessions, Gary spoke about having "fallen from the path of my heart," but also of having a sense that an angel was watching over him. He complained about being irritable, frustrated, and too engaged in the outer world, whereas he used to write poetry, draw, and paint. At this point I prescribed—literally wrote out on a prescription pad—that he paint his dreams and visions at least once every two weeks, thus confronting him just as the two men in his first dream had. Of course, he was actually confronting himself by starting in-depth therapy.

Later, when speaking of his vasectomy (which was performed

when he was twenty-eight years old), Gary said, "I killed the child within." I asked if that feeling was related to his feeling of falling from the path of the heart. He responded that both feelings were associated with his adoptive father's death thirteen years ago. It was as if he were identifying with his lost fathers: his adoptive father and his biological father. Gary himself would never be a father and if he did not resolve his father issues, he would remain a *puer aeternus*.

During this period, Gary's wife was having one of their agreed-upon extramarital affairs, and Gary had a related dream of an anima figure. In real life, this figure was a fifteen-year-old dancer with whom he had worked and to whom he was sexually attracted. Gary had actually given her an anonymous gift of dance lessons with a famous dancer, which had cost him a good deal of money. In the dream, he was trying to make contact with this anima figure in a non-sexual way; he was befriending his feminine side.

Later, Gary reported a dream about himself and his wife.

> DREAM: *They are at their home in the country. Some renters have been there and have not taken proper care of the house. Both he and his wife are about to take a test in a chemistry class. The test is on improbability equations having to do with Heisenberg's principle of uncertainty.*[2] *They are not prepared for the test but are relying on their innate abilities. Then the scene shifts, and Gary is driving fast the wrong way on a one-way street. Following this, he and his wife are visiting his wife's parents, and they end up very angry because they have missed the chemistry test.*

Gary felt that something was not right with the feminine side of his own emotional house, as represented in the dream by his real-life relationship with his wife. Regarding the test, he stated, "I can't know what is going to happen; I must accept the uncertainty principle." Regarding the fact that he was speeding the wrong way down a one-way street, he said, "I have been generating my own turmoil and anger and I need to confront that." I thought his associations and interpretations were very insightful.

Ten weeks into the therapy, Gary confronted his wife about her drinking, and she decreased her alcohol consumption. They were now communicating more. His wife told him that she loved him but that he seemed like a stranger to her. In this context, he asked himself, "Who does my wife love? Me? Who am I?" I thought that his wife had been quite perceptive in identifying a central issue, i.e., Gary's identity, that was troubling him.

Gary then reported two meaningful dreams.

> DREAM I: *He is upstairs in an attic loft in the town where he went to college. An occult group meeting is in progress. He believes that his wife is there and tries to find her. He decides to explore and challenge the group. The walls of the room consist of illusionary or trap doors of rough-cut wood. He senses danger. He can't find the source of it, but he knows it is masculine in nature. He feels that he is different from the group, and the group also feels this. Then there is music, and people dance. The room clears, and there are fewer walls. He cuddles Bamfa, his dog in real life. Finally, Gary turns into a female child, five to seven years of age, who is hugging the dog. The dog disappears, and the girl is embracing herself.*

Associating with the images in this dream, Gary said that he was interested in the occult and that he dated a woman in college who claimed to be a witch. At that time, he also took hallucinogenic drugs, which he associated with the disappearing wall images in the dream. To me, these wall images seemed to indicate a lowering or removing of inner defenses. He thought his efforts to find his wife represented his attempts to find the feminine part of himself, i.e., his anima, which he also related to his search for his biological mother. He thought the danger he felt in the dream was like the challenge that he faced in real life whenever he was the racer or the rebel poet-dancer. Gary said that Bamfa, his twelve-year-old female dog, provided him with unconditional love. I saw Bamfa as representing the instinctual and sustaining maternal feminine. The dog is also a symbol of healing.[3] His changing into a girl meant to him that he was identifying through and through with his own anima or soul. Then the dream ended with an image of him accepting, embracing, and loving that feminine part of himself.[4]

> DREAM II: *He is living with his wife in the state where he went to graduate school. His wife is kidnapped, and he wonders who did it. He goes to the police to try to find her, but they are not much help. His wife then approaches him on the street and tells him she was kidnapped by a young man in a tan van. She says that this man turned up his stereo loud and said he wanted to have sex with her.*

He then took out his penis, which had a French tickler on it, and raped her. His wife also reports that another man with the last name "Uill" hexed her and that she is under his spell. She then leaves to return to the Uill man. Gary returns to the police, but again they are not very helpful. Then he calls his wife's parents, and they hire a private detective.

Gary associated the Uill man with you-ill, referring to a part of him that was sick and upsetting to himself and his wife. This evil shadow part, he thought, had also captured and raped his anima. Gary then wondered out loud if maybe there were some truth to his wife's statement that he abused her through his excessive work. In addition, he considered the possibility that he was hurting himself this way. He associated the private detective in the dream with the analytical therapy process and his efforts to heal himself. Reflecting further on the therapeutic process, he said, "Sometimes you need to get sick in order to get better."

The Flying Dragon Learns to Dance

Almost three months into the therapy, Gary brought in his first active imagination painting, a watercolor of a flying dragon (Plate IV). He associated it with a poem entitled "Young Dragon" that he wrote after his adoptive father died. Gary also mentioned that there was a young dragon tree (he so named it because it had a dragon shape) near the farmland that he bought with money inherited from his adoptive father. In his poem, the dragon is crippled, but it learns to fly; the dragon joins a circus and does a trapeze act without a net. Gary associated the dragon he painted with his father's death and with his own rebirth at the time.

Gary also told me that he was performing in a dragon dance choreographed by a woman dancer at a nearby university. The dragon, blind, dances with three women. The first woman is nurturing; the second woman (danced by Gary's wife) is spiritual and the "coolest" one; and the third woman is sensual. The dragon (danced by Gary) starts out as an earth creature and then learns to fly to heaven.

At a little over four months into therapy, Gary thought about stopping treatment, because he felt much better. I said that I felt his problems were still not resolved. He agreed to continue after some discussion of the advantages and disadvantages. Near the close of the session, he reported a funny dream from the night before that seemed to contradict his inclination to leave therapy. Gary interpreted the dream to mean that he should continue analytical treatment and that his feminine, feeling side was attempting to connect with his intellectual side.

In the next session, however, Gary again reported that he was feeling better and wanted to stop therapy. As before, I interpreted this request as resistance. He was, in effect, like the flying dragon who really needed to be grounded in the dance of life. He kept talking enthusiastically about his new sports car, another indication that he wanted to race away from his problems. Once again, after discussing the issues at hand, he decided to remain in analytical therapy.

At five months into the analytical process, Gary said that he was having difficulty remembering his dreams; this seemed to represent a new and subtler form of resistance to therapy. He talked a lot about his work situation, where he was being groomed as interim chairperson for his department. He had received a vote of confidence from the faculty, so his ego was somewhat inflated. He wanted to try out this vocational path to see if he liked it. Then he talked about a new dance he was planning that would be performed the following spring. It was a solo concerning a spiritual struggle.

A month later, Gary reported a dream in which he was a prisoner of war. The guards were trying to kill him, but he was invincible. He decided that he must find a way out of this prison. In discussing the dream, he said that he felt that he was a prisoner both inside and outside. He vowed to overcome his sadistic, guard-like shadow and patriarchal side. Gary wanted to break out of the negative-ego power complex; in other words, he wanted to commit egocide and shadowcide.

At seven months into therapy, Gary said that he felt better and was coping and dancing better. However, he described his work situation as strained. He also talked about increased tension in his marriage and decreased intimacy with his wife. He said that he had always felt that he couldn't do anything right. He complained, "From the sixth grade on, I have felt as if I were punishing myself and that I was different in a negative way."

Then Gary showed me three watercolors he had completed the

day before. The first (Plate V) depicts a lost young girl suspended in a vortex, a black hole. She has blonde hair and a red vulva. The second picture (Plate VI) shows the rape of Persephone (only her giant pubic area and vagina are visible). Gary called it "a cosmic rape by a blue sword or phallus." He pointed out a "skyhook" in the upper left corner of the drawing that holds things together but, like the patient, it isn't connected to anything. These two active imagination pieces point out a major and painful problem with Gary's anima (soul): it is lost and raped.

The third image (Plate VII) is very significant and confirms the innate healing force of the psyche. This work of active imagination is an attempt at androgynous integration, i.e., a union of opposites. The red phallus shape (masculine) penetrates and is between the blue concave shapes (feminine). The painting is nearly balanced with green (growth) in every corner except the left upper quadrant, which represents the father space that Gary was working on. This picture symbolizes the psyche centering and healing; it's a lovely image of what's to come.

Egocide and Transformation into the Consciousness of the Wounded Healer

Over the next several months, Gary gradually experienced less discord in his work and in his marriage. He told me about a holiday, from both work and therapy, at his adoptive mother's house. While there, he realized for the first time that it was not his home; he then sold the land he had inherited from his adoptive father. Gary was severing connections to this part of his past and letting go of his adoptive parents. He also visited an old mentor in the town where he went to college. The mentor was a mystic, and he had supervised Gary on a book of poems and drawings that Gary had printed and bound. Titled *Manfred*, it is about a boy who becomes the sun. Gary said it is all about light, optimism, and cosmic wonder. I was struck by the fact that his scenario omitted groundedness, darkness, and reality. This is typical of men who are stuck in a *puer aeternus* complex.

Toward the end of his first year of therapy, Gary came in feeling frustrated, bored, and empty. He again had thoughts of becoming a race car driver. Gary then reported a dream from the night before.

DREAM: *He is observing himself with a young boy, a Korean refu-
gee. The boy has an unusual, one- to four-inch-thick creature like
a sea serpent in a large container of sea water. The boy is accompanied by a large male bodyguard, because an assassin is after him (as
he is one of the last of his kind). The assassin appears and wields his
sword. Then the boy hurls the serpent against the wall and it
shatters, at which point he assumes his full power. The bodyguard
takes on the assassin, wounding him with multiple cuts but not killing
him. The now powerful boy then battles the assassin, but he gets
stabbed with a single sword thrust through the head and arm. The
boy removes the sword from himself and miraculously is not only
alive but unharmed.*

The dream portrayed a moment of egocide and transformation
into the consciousness of the wounded healer. I considered this
dream to be significant and healing because of the presence and role
of the serpent. Gary associated the boy with a part of himself that
was growing and grappling with a negative shadow, then being
wounded by the shadow and surviving because of an inner strength.
The divine child archetype within himself was still somewhat for-
eign, as indicated by the boy's identity.

At the next session, Gary told me that he was working on a new
creative dance production that he had choreographed for students,
symbolically entitled "The Perfectly Dead." It concerns a helper of
Charon, the man in Greek mythology who transports the newly dead
across the River Styx to Hades. Gary also talked about how busy he
was as interim chairperson and about his need for contemplative
time. Paradoxically, he had just purchased a new Porsche special
edition with money left to him by his paternal grandfather. He loved
it; the new car was quick, elegant, and balanced like a dancer. With
his history of accidents, Gary seemed in danger of acting out his
desire to visit the underworld. As if to reassure himself, he stated, "I
never have gotten hurt racing cars, but I am not saying I am invul-
nerable." Gary was being pulled in two opposing directions: his
dance and academic career vs. his interest in professional racing.
Reflecting on his therapy, he said, "I am here to learn, to cast a
shadow, to know my dark side. I need to get in touch with myself
and my feelings."

After making this insightful comment, Gary recounted a dream
that indicated, to both of us, his psyche's wish for introversion in

order to facilitate a healing inner journey. The dream also revealed his feelings about his self-torturing anima and negative mother complex that were being expressed outwardly as depression.

Confronting the Witch Within

In the next session, Gary's depression spilled over into rage over his wife's extramarital affairs. He was still furious about the initial affair because he had trusted his wife and then she had betrayed him. Gary confided that when he first learned of this affair, it was doubly upsetting to him because it was with a friend. She wanted to move in with this man, who, ironically, was a mental health worker. Gary felt that he was advocating their mutual abuse by supporting the continuance of their open marriage policy. He also revealed that his wife had a fear of death and severe conflicts with her parents, particularly her mother, and these problems contributed to her reasons for drinking so heavily. We discussed the possibility of his wife seeking therapy. However, she consistently refused therapy, claiming that she was happy with her current state of mind and situation, despite her trouble sleeping and her problem with alcohol.

Gary then recounted a dream that spoke about his own negative mother complex.

> DREAM: *It takes place in a country house in a small farming community near the university he attended in real life. A young woman who is a stranger in the community is hit by a car. She is lying in a grave with a glass cover. The glass shatters and, surprisingly, the woman is not dead. She then rises up and walks away. Gary, his wife, and other people follow the woman and her male companion into the country house through a narrow passageway. Inside they encounter a witch. Gary and his wife are carrying a black scarf that they found in the supposedly dead woman's coffin. The black scarf protects them. They then come to a burial vault at the end of the passageway. The dead-reborn woman and her male companion are there. Gary's wife wants to go into this chamber, but Gary doesn't because he's afraid. He suspects that this is part of a sinister plot that the witch has devised to steal his soul. To his*

amazement, after he gives her the black scarf so that she will be protected, his wife goes into the vault without him.

Gary felt that his own image of the feminine (his soul) was dead. The problem had to do with a witch who was somehow connected to his wife and mother. He thought that he was projecting his anima onto his wife and that it was his anima that was going into the vault to confront his negative mother (the witch), with a black scarf (Symbolic Death) to protect her. Confirming this overall interpretation linking wife, mother, anima, and witch, he dreamed before the next session about his wife as a witch. He also slipped and called his wife "mother" at their dance studio! Furthermore, he reported that he was currently distant from his wife, felt a lot of emptiness and rage, and was disturbed because she was again drinking excessively.

A year and a half into his therapy, Gary had a dream that he thought symbolized his problem with control and his working through his resistance to the analytical process. Referring to the resistance, he stated, "I have let myself go," which indicated a growth in trust on his part. Gary said that he had "submitted to an inner healer or authority, the father within." He described it as a feeling similar to one he experienced when he was racing cars: In racing, he explained, one must surrender to the right speed in order to get around corners effectively and avoid crashing.

Rebirth of the Soul Through a Transcendent Symbol

At twenty months into the therapy, Gary reported that he had dreamed of making love with his adoptive mother. After intercourse, she nurses him, first as if he were an infant (by breast-feeding) and then as if he were sick. Recounting this dream, Gary was visibly touched and tearful. He wondered out loud whether his relationship with his adoptive mother was like an alchemical vessel leading to something else. He then had a crucial insight—a feeling that this dream was connected with his desire to have union with his biological mother or, as he put it, with his "earth mother." It seemed that Gary was clearly in Stage II, the middle or transitional phase, of analytical therapy.

Gary came in nearly two months later with a lot of stress showing in his face. He complained about ongoing problems in his work and marriage. He related a dream involving an earthquake and an ancient reptilian creature that goes after his wife.

Gary said he was no longer merely observing what was happening to him but was now involved in the process. The earthquake was like Mother Earth opening up. He was shaken emotionally, and connected the opening up to wanting to contact his biological mother (which he had not wanted to do when he started therapy). He associated the reptile with being cold-blooded and not nurturing; Gary saw the creature's going after his wife as revealing that she was cold like the reptile, having had the initial extramarital affair. At that time, Gary confessed, he had condoned her behavior (as well as the behavior of the friend, rationalizing that his wife was irresistibly attractive). However, he had been secretly outraged and despondent. When he talked with his wife later about these feelings, she said that at the time she had felt guilty and had wondered if he would leave her. Gary was close to seeing that he projected his own, cold-blooded anima onto his wife and possibly contributed to her initial and subsequent affairs.

Following this dream, Gary made a firm decision to seek information about his biological mother. It was as if he wanted to contact the warm-blooded, maternal source of himself. He then had a pivotal dream: one that was very humbling. It takes place in a research teaching hospital.

> DREAM: *Gary is involved in research projects having to do with test-tube babies. He is a student there, but doesn't know why. He walks down a hall, opens up a utility service door, and sees two dark-gray pipes that turn into two dark-haired women. A vertical tower rises up between them and turns into a huge maternal figure. The three figures form a feminine trinity. Feeling frightened, he shuts the door and walks to the lab. There are babies on the shelves in plastic incubators. Then, one of the babies gets out of its incubator, steps off the shelf, and grows into a four-year-old child. This child says: "I am your dream world, I am your dream life." The child ages quickly, becoming first an adult, and then very elderly, near death.*

In discussing this dream, Gary said that the first part of it had to do with the medical center where he came to see me, his meetings with me, and our analytical work. In his own way, he was coming to terms with his adoptive mother as well as his biological mother. He had long had a fantasy image of his biological mother as ideal, but now he was tempering it by an image at the other extreme: "Because I was born out of wedlock," he said, "my mother was like a whore." Since these two possible aspects of his biological mother were in the dark, he opens a utility door in his dream and sees two dark-haired women, whom he associated with the Virgin Mary and Mary Magdalene (the classic Madonna/whore archetype).[5] He also thought the two women could be his adoptive mother and his biological mother, who then came together as one looming Great Mother edifice. He went back to the out-of-wedlock theme and said that he felt illegitimate as a child, like a bastard. When he was young, he had asked his adoptive mother if a woman could have a baby when she wasn't married. His adoptive mother replied that a woman could, but it wasn't legal, so he then assumed that it was a crime.

To Gary, the second part of the dream, where he went into the lab and saw babies on the shelves, symbolized the place where his adoption experiment began—a nursery that was also a laboratory. He thought that the experiment was not right and that this feeling might relate to a trace memory he had of being in a nursery after he was born. Then he discussed the baby-turned-child who stepped off the shelf. He described the child as a hermaphrodite, a symbol that signals psychic transformation.[6] He thought that the child must have grown into an adult too rapidly and had to die in order to be reborn. This seemed related to the analytical process and to the death-rebirth experience involved in egocide and transformation. He then recalled his fear that his vasectomy had "killed the child within." However, now through his submission to his own inner father, the child was reborn.

Gary deduced from this important dream that separation from his adoptive family was possible, and he was right to search actively for his biological mother. His coming to these conclusions represented a critical point in his analytical therapy. It had now been nearly two years since his therapy had begun. For the moment, his work situation was stable. Interestingly, he also had an affair at this time with a woman who had formerly been in his dance company, and who had once been arrested for prostitution (noteworthy because of Gary's recent image of his mother as a whore). Gary's wife had a simultaneous affair with this woman's husband.

Reunion with the Source:
Another Experience of Symbolic Death and New Life

The next time I saw Gary, he had visited with his adoptive mother and had asked her many questions about his adoption. To his amazement, he learned that his biological mother lived in the same town where he grew up and where his adoptive mother still lived. His biological mother's name was Mary, and she was still unmarried—a clear example of synchronicity, given Gary's dream of the Virgin Mary and Mary Magdalene. He also learned the name of his biological father, who lived only fifteen miles away from his hometown. His adoptive mother felt it would be okay for him to visit his biological parents, although she was equivocal.

Gary decided to write his biological mother to explore the possibility of seeing her, because he was afraid that she might reject him. Before leaving his old hometown, he drove by her house. To his surprise, she lived in a middle-class instead of a lower-class neighborhood, which he had once imagined as more appropriate for a whore. On his way home, he developed yet another fantasy about her: She would have a warm and friendly face, blonde hair, and be about five feet four inches tall. In contemplating a visit with his biological mother and father, he said that he felt good about himself and about life in general. As he put it, "I felt a connection was now possible with the human family." Here was a glimmer of future movement into Stage III (see Table 4-2). In addition, there seemed to be a positive turn in our relationship, in part because his wife told him that she was jealous of his relationship with me. The fact that he was on the brink of establishing a new relationship with his biological mother also might have been threatening to his wife.

Gary received a letter back from his biological mother saying that she was extremely pleased to hear from him. She was a very religious person and had prayed for many years that her only child would find her and return. She closed the letter by inviting him to visit her, which he did. When he first met her, he felt an instant connection with her, as if he had known her all his life. As he had imagined, she had an amicable and glowing face, blonde hair, and was around five feet four inches tall. She asked Gary to call her by her familiar name, Marm, which, to me, sounded like a combination of Ma, warm, Mary, and Mom.

Marm, like his adoptive mother, was somewhat resistant to the idea of his seeking out his biological father. She veiled this initially by saying: "It would upset and distress him," as he had recently been in the hospital recovering from a stroke. Gary did eventually meet him and it was a very moving event. His father responded incredibly well, and Gary visited him frequently thereafter. According to Gary's previously unknown half-sister, these visits actually helped his father's healing process—just as they did Gary's.

During the last year that I saw Gary in analytical treatment, his relationship with his wife became strained to the limit. Her alcohol problem became severe, and Gary threatened separation and divorce unless she got help, which she subsequently did. During this difficult time it was my sense that there was a deep love that held Gary and his wife together. After his wife got help, they both seemed to be working hard on their problems and themselves; their marriage was solidifying as a result. Gary also became more creative in his dance work and more comfortable with being an authority from an academic perspective as opposed to a performer's perspective.

When I told Gary that I would be moving to Texas, he seemed sad. Then he talked a lot about becoming a choreographer/teacher rather than a performer. Just prior to ending our therapy, he injured himself, necessitating just such a change in his career direction. Specifically, in a freak accident at work, he cut his left Achilles tendon (the feminine side) nearly all the way through. It was interesting to me that in Greek legend Achilles' heel is the only part of him that is mortal and vulnerable, his mother having held him by the heel while dipping him into the River Styx (the river of death) to make his body invincible. Gary had proven himself mortal; he had died in a symbolic sense and was afterward reborn—again, another example of egocide and transformation.

Gary denied feeling angry or abandoned by my leaving. However, he stated, "No one has ever been there for me." He *was* upset with me for leaving, and I felt bad about doing so, knowing his vulnerability. I shared that I was fond of him and that I would miss working with him. In that context, I referred him to another Jungian-oriented therapist.

At our final meeting, after he had seen the other therapist, whom he liked, Gary told me a prodigious dream.

DREAM: *He is in an intensely troubling and dangerous situation, walking through a room of sleeping snakes in which there is an unusual, primitive ape. Gary is trying to leave, but he can't get out of the center of the room. He becomes quite scared. Then a tall, black woman in her early forties leaps into the center of the room and comforts him. She smiles and leads him through the snakes, past the ape, and out of the room. He then feels safe.*

According to Jung, "the serpent is a well-substantiated archetype" of transformation and renewal, a healing symbol.[7] Gary's last dream seemed to foretell a good outcome for Gary's continued therapy. He was able to call on a strong, healing anima figure to guide him through the dangers of the healing serpents and past the wise ape,[8] so that he could continue his process of individuation, his journey toward wholeness.

Let me share a five-year follow-up: Gary is doing well. He saw the other therapist for two years, and has permanently separated from his wife. Gary continues his academic work as an educator and choreographer but is no longer involved with performing or administration. Interestingly, his role as mentor has expanded to include being a professional racing instructor during the summers. Gary has transformed his depression, held onto his soul, and become a doctor to himself and others, in the true etymological sense of the word—which means teacher in Greek. He also has continued on his journey of individuation, which was grounded in discovering his roots and propelled forward by the healing power of the psyche.

CHAPTER 8

Sharon: Death of the Inner Witch and Birth of the Creative Self

"Long have I resisted,
Finally I yielded:
When the old ego disintegrates
The new ego awakens."

—GOETHE

SHARON suffers from a self-destructive depression and border-line condition, along with related ego deficits.[1] She rapidly swings, often in a whip-sawing manner, between conflicting feelings. The following contrasting images and themes will be discussed: life/death, female/male, independent/dependent, mother/father, fire/water, hopeful/hopelessness, creative/destructive, love/hate, light/darkness, good/evil, and solar/lunar.

Sharon's case reveals how egocide and transformation facilitate the individuation process and promote healing in a seriously disturbed person. The crossing is rough, even turbulent at times, but hope and wholeness are the rewards of Sharon's arduous journey.

Sharon, twenty-six years old and a new graduate student, was referred to me by a therapist in a distant state, whom she and her husband had seen irregularly during the previous year. With their former therapist, they had talked about their own individual depressive states and problems in their marriage.

Although Sharon was very depressed and suffered from anorexia and a distorted body image, she reported no insomnia or thoughts of suicide. During the first year of her therapy with me, she was physically separated from her fatherlike husband, a college professor, having moved away from him to enroll in a Ph.D. program at a top-ranked school. This move represented a painful beginning for her independent healing journey. At the time our sessions began, she was planning to follow a family script and study in a business-related field. Her realization that she didn't want to do this was the impetus for her egocide and transformation.

The Initial Dream: Addiction to Perfection

Sharon brought a two-part dream to the first session that revealed one of her most serious problems, an addiction to perfection.[2] In effect, this addiction was a product of her general sense of feeling worthless—a major symptom of Stage I of the map of the healing journey (see Table 4-2).

> DREAM I: *Sharon moves to a new apartment that her former therapist owns. She leaves her old apartment, also owned by her therapist, spotlessly clean with the floor shining and the refrigerator door ajar. Later, when she runs into her former therapist, he tells her that she has to clean the old apartment. This makes her feel guilty. Her new apartment is full of books, especially paperback novels. A young boy who lives down the hall is visiting; and when he has to go home, he leaves the book he was reading. He returns upset and wants his book, but she won't let him have it and blocks the door. The boy's mother then comes and gets the book, a war novel, and she notes that the mother looks sad.*

> DREAM II: *Sharon is driving downtown to a travel agency located above an ice cream parlor. She is helping with a fund-raising effort. The scene shifts to the sound of a radio ad for a child-care center. "Drop off your kid at Rocky Mountain Chocolate Factory," the radio announcer says, and he adds that a child can get balloons and ice cream and go to the movies, and that, for a special fee of $50, a child can get a chauffeur and a companion: either a nurse or a college professor.*

In discussing the dream, Sharon focused first on the image of her moving from one apartment to another. She thought it meant that even though moving to a new apartment seemed to represent a change in her life, the fact that her therapist owned both apartments revealed she still had to deal with the same psychological issues that had bothered her in the past. However, she told me that she was

DEATH OF THE INNER WITCH

motivated to get to the bottom of her problems and that she wanted, and needed, in-depth analytical therapy.

Addressing the next dream image of paperback novels, Sharon said that she had a natural alliance with her father because they both loved paperback novels. In real life, Sharon's appearance was decidedly boylike, and she seemed to identify strongly with her father— perhaps reflecting her father's wish for a boy. I interpreted the young boy in the dream to be an animus figure attempting to gain distance from the sad mother; the fact that the novel he wanted was a war novel possibly indicated a future battle with mother.

Sharon thought that the positive nature of the downtown locale and the fund-raising in her dream could be tied to her positive feelings about living in the inner city and to her interest in power and money. Overall, however, she felt that she was very vulnerable and about to fall apart under the stress of starting graduate school. She related the child care, balloons, ice cream, and movies in her dream directly to her childhood, in which she was given a lot of things; but they were without lasting substance, and were given coldly (as symbolized by the sealed-up air of the balloons and frigid nature of the ice cream); and she was basically aloof, often watching others as if seeing them on a movie screen. Sharon said that she did actually feel the need for a companion—her husband or, perhaps, a nurselike person—to comfort her, since she felt all alone and abandoned (key Stage I feelings). Her husband, she admitted, used to mother her as well as father her. He would get her up in the morning, pick out her clothes, help dress her, feed her, and pack her lunch.

When Sharon was eight years old, her parents left her behind when they went to Europe; consequently, she attempted suicide by overdosing on aspirin. Symptomatic of how alienated she felt then, she told no one about the attempt, not even her baby-sitter. Instead, she explained her vomiting and lethargy as a mild case of the flu.

My impression of Sharon after the first session was that she was unstable and aware of it. She was quite anxious and very depressed— suffering from decreased concentration, alienation, guilt, poor self-image, and despondency. My working diagnoses were: major depressive episode (acute), dysthymia (depressive neurosis, chronic), eating disorder (anorexia nervosa), and a possible borderline personality disorder (later confirmed by psychological testing).

Preoccupation with Failure and Suicidal States

During Sharon's second visit, she expressed a nagging fear that she would fail graduate school and have to drop out. She also revealed she had made two additional suicide attempts in high school, by overdosing on aspirin and by slashing her wrists. She made another attempt three years before our first meeting by overdosing on aspirin while in the process of divorcing her first husband, who had beaten her. A year after the divorce, she saw a psychiatrist for depression and for support while starting a new and demanding job. However, she stopped seeing this psychiatrist after he told her that she should never have children, because she would ruin them in the same way that her mother had ruined her.[3] She married her current husband shortly thereafter, five years prior to our meeting.

One month into her therapy with me, Sharon talked very positively about a holiday she recently had had with her husband and her family (mother, father, and only sibling—a younger, adopted sister). She also revealed that she had had an abortion one week before our first session together. I was struck by the fact that she had withheld this distressing information for so long. Sharon's decision to talk about it now indicated increasing trust in our therapeutic relationship. Her growing confidence in therapy also allowed her to report that she had sexual difficulties with her husband (who had recently visited her), and the only way she could have an orgasm was by masturbation. Furthermore, Sharon reported a dream in which she tries to seduce an unrecognizable psychiatrist, and they go to bed together but don't have sex. Upon waking from this dream, she had been very disappointed that she didn't have sex. It was clear that she was beginning to feel intensely about me, suggesting an erotic component to the transference.

At the end of a school term, despite having received all Bs in her graduate courses (in marked contrast to her fear that she would fail everything), Sharon immediately berated herself for not getting all As. She also questioned why she was in analytical psychotherapy and whether it was helping her. She remained in the Bad News phase of her illness and therapy, trying to sort out her personal conflicts and alternately accepting and resisting my help.

Three and a half months into therapy, Sharon gave me a long account of a dream in which she and her husband wanted to use a nuclear bomb to destroy the motel where they have lived for a long time. Together, they plan an intricate escape from the bombsite. She senses that they can get away in their car and be safe.

About this dream, Sharon said, "I'm going to do something to get off dead center." I felt that the dream indicated that her relationship with her husband was going to blow up, which would lead to profound depression and possibly a suicidal state. I have had many patients who have dreamed of nuclear explosions prior to experiencing a suicidal crisis.

Self-Portrait: Flame of Life Emerges Out of Dead Center

Four months into therapy, Sharon's grades began deteriorating, but she got help from her classmates. At this time, she dreamed that her husband and father were intruding on her space and making it impossible for her to study. In addition to being severely depressed with insomnia, she had lost weight due to her anorexia, and yet still

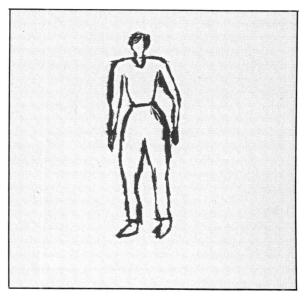

FIGURE 8-1
(Sharon's) First Self-portrait

considered herself to be overweight. I suggested that she draw a self-portrait and she did so (see Figure 8-1).

It is noteworthy that this self-portrait has no facial features or secondary sexual characteristics, although it looks more like a man than a woman. The head is also quite small; in fact, she called this drawing "Pinhead on a Pear." A face with no features suggests an identity problem—Sharon is cut off from her true self. The left part of her body (the feminine side) is deformed, her hand and foot are not well developed, and her foot is turned inward. In contrast, the right side of her body (the masculine side) is overdeveloped and much more strongly drawn. In discussing the weight problem that the pearlike figure suggested, she said that the problem was tied to trying to out-control her mother, who had trouble keeping her weight down.

Four and a half months into her therapy, Sharon reported an extremely distressing dream in which she finds her husband decapitated with his legs cut off at the knees. She needed to rid herself of her negative father complex that had been transferred onto her husband. Discussing this dream, she identified herself with the terrible mother and witch motif, and assumed responsibility for the decapitation and amputations.[4] Since the dream depicted a killing of part of her psyche, she was foreshadowing egocide.

The day after Sharon told me about this decapitation dream, she called to say that she was wrestling with the desire to slash her wrists in order to kill herself. My response was to help her focus on what part of her psyche had to die (i.e., to be talked and analyzed to death). I surmised that her negative persona and ego, in collusion with her shadow, was thinking of cutting into herself. Symbolically, the unnatural desire to cut into oneself is related to the transformative blood mysteries: menstruation, pregnancy, birth, and breast-feeding (in which life blood = milk).[4]

Five months into therapy, Sharon was still feeling suicidal, but had no specific plans. I introduced her to the term *egocide*. She grasped the concept immediately, and agreed that the negative ego parts identified with her mother and father must be symbolically killed, if she were to be her own person and proceed with her life and her own process of individuation. Then she suddenly recalled a recent dream in which her mother telephones her and says that she will not be around much longer. Thus, well ahead of her conscious mind, her psyche had given her a message that her negative mother introject is about to die.

Seven months into therapy, Sharon started to have difficulty recalling her dreams, so I suggested art therapy, which would put her back in touch with her unconscious. I asked her to paint her feelings spontaneously, without intentional craft. I explained that she needed to put herself in the frame of mind of a three- to five-year-old child and to paint how she felt without censoring her active imagination.

Sharon called her first painting "Suspension Between Two States" (Plate II). One state is melancholia, represented by a black cloud and blue rain; the other state is directed energy, showing a masculine tree growing in the left bottom corner but covered by a blue mood. Sharon described herself as the tree, but it actually looks more like a sunflower, which could be interpreted as a combination of masculine (sun) and feminine (flower). However, there is only an insignificant stem or body, and the head is overdeveloped. She saw a green container in the bottom right hand corner as the reproductive end of a fallopian tube with yellow pollenlike seed coming out of it, so the feminine potential is clearly expressed. The day she painted this composition she had felt "empty and hollow inside," as if "something were missing." She was not in contact with her feminine side, either physically or psychically; consequently, she was depressed—in effect, she had lost her soul.[5]

Sharon's second painting (Plate VIII), entitled "My Depression," features a male figure named Djinn (root word for genie). The expression on the face could be either fierce or frightened; she has powerful mixed emotions underlying her depression, rage, and terror. She associated this angry, glowing, red-and-purple demon with her parents, primarily her father. To me, the combination of unconscious rage (red) and guilt (purple), linked with her real-life attachment to her father, implied a profound psychological incest problem, and the strong right arm and fist could symbolize overidentification with the father (right being the masculine side), the ill-formed left hand (feminine side) symbolizing weak identification with her mother.

The painting that followed (Plate IX), represented another step toward egocide and transformation. Sharon created a vision of herself going up in flames while immersed in a sea, an image of transformation and purification in the universal womb *(prima materia)*. An arch of lilacs protects her (she noted that her mother grew lilacs). It is as if her flame of life emerges out of dead center. In the bottom of the sea there is a movement of five small, black figures from right to left, that is, from the mother quadrant of the painting to the unconscious quadrant. Five is the number of the human being, forming a pentagon, with outstretched arms and legs. It also represents the sacred marriage, for it combines the feminine (the even number two) and the masculine (the odd number three). With this therapeutic art, Sharon closed out her first academic year. She had let go of some negative aspects of her male dominated ego-image and regressed in the service of positive ego, which is characteristic of Stage I.

During the summer, Sharon lived with her husband at their ranch in the Rocky Mountains, where she kept horses that she liked very much. She could relax in this setting. When she learned that she had done well on all her final examinations, she realized that she was, in fact, a bright and capable human being. She came back into therapy liking herself more and feeling that she was intelligent and more resourceful. This experience was exactly what was necessary to strengthen her ego and sense of self before going deeper into the process of analytical therapy. Her husband was now staying with her, having arranged to take a year's sabbatical, but she no longer felt so dependent on him. Another sign of her increased autonomy (as well as shame and doubt) was that she had recorded no dreams and made no therapeutic artwork over the summer despite being asked to do so.

Sharon did two paintings (not illustrated here) to mark her entry into her second year of therapy. The first indicated that she was starting to feel depressed again. It shows a blue house with a red window in the attic. A figure with a boyish, adolescent appearance (representing herself) is looking out of a window on the ground floor. There is a closed yellow front door. Sharon felt trapped in a rigid, depressed, mother structure, but she identified with her father (her negative animus figure). The red in the attic window represented anger and rage, which she could feel in her head and which she blamed for her chronic headaches. The yellow door (as well as a yellow sun in the painting) seemed to her to symbolize hope. Nevertheless, Sharon admitted feeling suicidal. I reframed this feeling as egocidal, and we discussed how the adolescent boy part of her ego-identity still needed to die. Death of this part of her psyche was

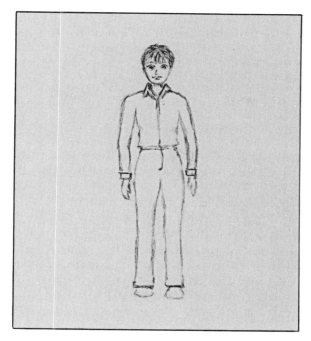

FIGURE 8-2
(Sharon's) Second-self-portrait

represented in the second painting. It contained an image which she described as "a bloody tear." This image contained another one: a counterclockwise spiral pointing into the unconscious. Spirals indicate depression, and a counterclockwise spiral suggests that something sinister is possible. The bloody tear only rendered this interpretation all the more ominous.

Revisioning the Self: Egocide and Transcendence

After a long holiday vacation with her husband, parents, and sister, Sharon returned looking different: softer and more womanly. She reported that her relationships with her mother and her sister were better: She could communicate more effectively with them, and felt more connected to them. This change is reflected in her second self-portrait (Figure 8-2; cf. Figure 8-1). In this drawing, she has discernibly feminine facial features and secondary sexual characteristics, including breasts. However, her right side (masculine) still seems somewhat stronger than her left side (feminine); for example, the right arm is longer and better developed.

Shortly after Sharon drew this self-portrait, her mother stopped calling her. It's significant that she had had the following dream that foretold this outcome.

> DREAM: *Her mother is killed in a plane crash. Her father returns and sorts through all their possessions and gives Sharon one of his mother's (her grandmother's) antique dresses with a jeweled bodice. Then the father leaves to go on an airplane. Sharon knows it is destined to crash, and so does her father; but both of them think it is for the best.*

This dream indicated that Sharon was nearing the end of Stage I of her illness and therapy. It depicted her negative parental complexes as dead or dying, and it contained an image of her receiving a gift from her father and, indirectly, his mother. The father's mothering of Sharon had caused her to develop a certain amount of her feminine identity through her father's anima (which would relate to *his* mother).

Sharon again felt suicidal, wanting to jump from her sixth-story apartment window. We began to meet more frequently. I talked more about egocide; referring to her dreams. For example, in the dream I just recounted, the parents are on vacation when the plane crash occurs; then the father returns for closure before his impending death. I reminded her that her original suicide attempt at age eight took place while her parents were on vacation. However, now she was not acting it out, but rather acting it in through a dream. I was helping her construct a symbolic logic for the painful thoughts and emotions she was experiencing, so that she would respond to them in a symbolic way, that is, by committing egocide instead of suicide.

Sharon's marriage seemed to oscillate between a healthy, egalitarian one and a conflict-ridden one, embedded in a father-daughter complex symbolically incestuous with resultant bitter fights. When Sharon was caught in the complex, she now responded like a teenager wanting to leave home to establish her own independence. In this context, Sharon talked about a trial separation. There were also other moments and even weeks of closeness and healing amity.

Death-Rebirth: Regression in the Service of the Self

After eighteen months of therapy, Sharon regressed into a period of melancholia and anger that she transferred onto me. She was upset and hostile because she saw no progress—or hope—in analytical treatment. Once again, she was visited with hideous thoughts of committing suicide by jumping out her apartment window. As before, I kept bringing her mind back to the concept of egocide, and we talked in depth about what had to die. In time, she gave a small and ambivalent yes to continuing the analytical process.

According to Jung, to snap out of such a Draconian depressive episode, a patient needs a vision of transcendence arising from the union of conscious and unconscious contents.[6] In her following painting, Sharon produced such an image in the form of a maternal uroboros (see Plate III). According to Neumann:

> The uroboros is the "Great Round," in which positive and negative, male and female, elements of consciousness, elements hostile to consciousness, and unconscious elements are intermingled. In this sense, the uroboros is also a symbol of a state in which chaos, the unconscious, and the psyche as a whole were undifferentiated—and which is experienced by the ego as a borderline state.[7]

The subtle gradations of light in this painting give the composition as a whole a luminous quality in keeping with the portentous image of the uroboros. A bright halo surrounding the uroboros dimly illuminates the darkness in which it is suspended; Sharon referred to this halo as spirit. Inside the uroboros is what Sharon described as a womb, with an embryo representing her in the very center (barely visible as a dark spot in the middle of brightness). She went on to say that the embryo is feeding on bloody rage, the very color of the blood-rich placenta. Sharon summed up this powerful, compelling painting by saying, "I'm giving birth to myself." It symbolized a new ego-Self being born out of a healing, maternal matrix. I thought the uroboros was clearly what Neumann calls the *Great Mother*. It represented a few forward steps back to the future in Sharon's therapy, involving her once again in the analytical process identified as "regression in the service of the Self."

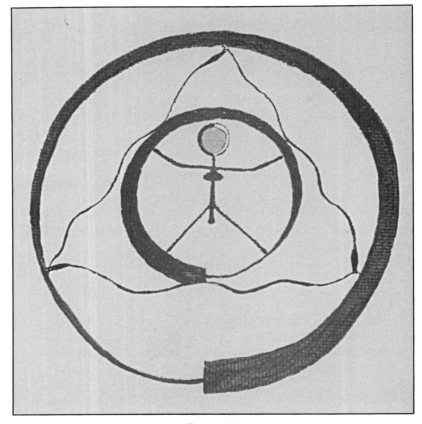

FIGURE 8-3
Hermaphrodite

Sharon's next painting, equally meaningful (Figure 8-3), depicts a classic androgynous or hermaphroditic figure with stylized breasts and penis, which is a key symbol of psychological integration. In addition, all three primary colors are incorporated into the design of the painting: The head of the figure is yellow (a color that Sharon associated with love and clarity); the outer uroboros-like circle is blue (feminine); and the inner uroboros-like circle is red (masculine). As a final, unifying touch, the triangle between the two circles represents synthesis. The *transcendent* function of this artistic product of Sharon's active imagination was remarkably reflected in her night life at the time. Before painting the picture, Sharon dreamed that she bit off the penis of a man who looked like a Greek god. However, as the dream continued, she sewed the penis back on. Then it healed, suggesting that she did, in fact, want union with this god (and reminding me of the story of Isis restoring the lost penis of Osiris and then mating with him). After painting the picture, she had orgasm for the first time with her husband.

Yet, the process of analytical therapy is uneven. At nineteen months into her therapy, Sharon said, "I feel empty, like a two-year-old." She then recalled her mother saying, "It was hell until you learned to talk." Sharon added that she was raised on rage and characterized her mother as cold, verbal, and rocklike. She then painted (not included here) what it felt like when beheld by such a stony figure.[8] "The Eye of the Great Mother" shows a spiral running counterclockwise (i.e., into the unconscious, as in one of her previous paintings, "a bloody tear").[9] Adding to the negative tone of the painting was her comment about it; namely, that a strong toddler was in the process of killing the mother's evil eye (which can be taken as a homonym for negative I or ego in Latin). In other words, the painting involved her negative mother complex, which Sharon called "Medusa." She added, "Her head has to be to cut off." The two-year-old in the painting was wielding an axe and raising it above Medusa's neck. In Greek legend, when Medusa was beheaded, Pegasus (the horse of creativity) and Chrysalor (he of the golden sword) sprang from her severed neck.

One month later, Sharon took a decided turn for the worse. She began drinking alcohol more than usual, her depression deepened, and she began to think that life was pointless. She failed an exam, which was unusual for her, causing her to feel more like a failure. In symbolic terms, it felt to Sharon as if her negative shadow were taking over her conscious ego identity. To add to her insecurity, her husband's sabbatical year was coming to an end, and his departure was imminent. It was clear to me that the impending loss of her husband's presence and support (although it was ambivalent) was creating tremendous anxiety within her and fueling her depression. Her reaction was more than the sadness related to a spouse leaving. It seemed related to a larger and more profound loss (her negative father complex) that was also occurring at the same time.

Witch of Death Vies with Madonna and Divine Child

After Sharon's husband left, she painted "Russian Dolls" (not shown). Her father's mother had possessed a set of antique Russian dolls, which are nested with usually three or four smaller dolls inside. Sharon's mother had wanted a similar set but had never found one. In Sharon's painting, the outer doll has a serene, passive, sleeping quality. Its arms are crossed, which makes it appear closed off and protected, and also evokes the Egyptian symbol of death and the underworld. Inside this doll (actually beside it in the painting, as if the outer doll has already been opened) is another, smaller doll that can be taken as representing Sharon's negative mother complex.

The smaller doll is a witchlike figure killing a snake. Sharon told me that initially she drew the witch killing a baby. This led her to talk about three induced abortions and three spontaneous miscarriages she had undergone; she began crying about the six sacrificed babies. Corresponding to the number six, there was also a hexagram, or six-lined character, in the painting, which means adapting, although she did not know it. She went on to say that her first revision of the witch figure had changed the baby to a skull, a symbol of death. Very significantly, she had first painted a baby (life symbol), then a skull (death symbol), and finally a snake (symbol of death and rebirth as well as healing). Sharon felt that the inner witch, or the negative mother complex, must die. We discussed egocide again, and the idea that this aspect of her ego identity needed to be symbolically killed.

Unfortunately my vacation occurred at this time, which only added to her sense of rejection. However, I was encouraged by Sharon's willingness at the time to verbalize her anger toward me and about the process of therapy. I had suspected that she harbored such feelings, and I was glad that she ventilated them before I left for my vacation.

When I returned, Sharon made it clear that she had felt abandoned while I was away. She talked about suicide, either by cutting herself with a knife or by crashing her car. It was obvious that she had regressed—once again—to a Stage I state of mind. Despite looking healthy and more feminine, she complained about chronic headaches and nausea. Paradoxically, however, she had used her time away from therapy fairly well by enrolling in ballet and aerobics classes:

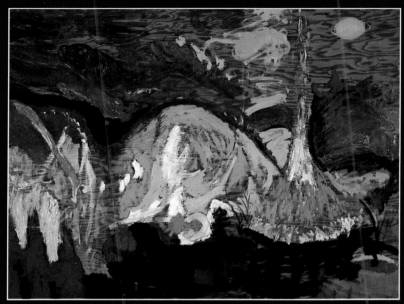

PLATE I Healing Emotional Landscape

PLATE II
"Suspension Between
Two States"

PLATE III
"Giving Birth to Myself"

PLATE IV
Dragon

PLATE V
Lost Anima

PLATE VI
Cosmic Rape

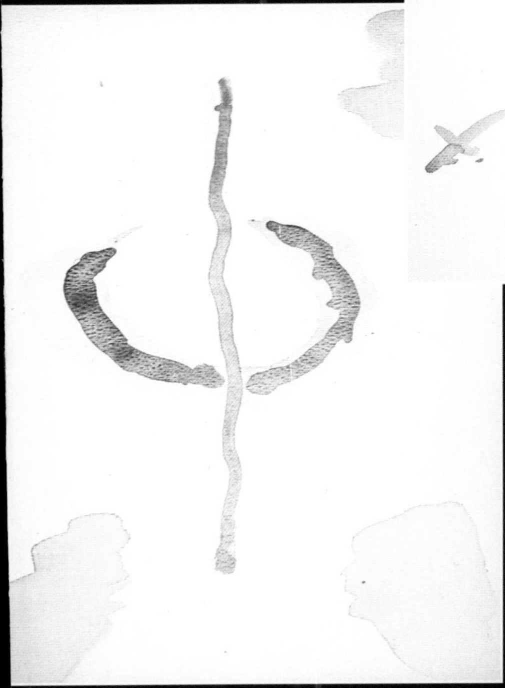

PLATE VII
Toward Wholeness

PLATE VIII
"My Depression"

PLATE IX
Purification

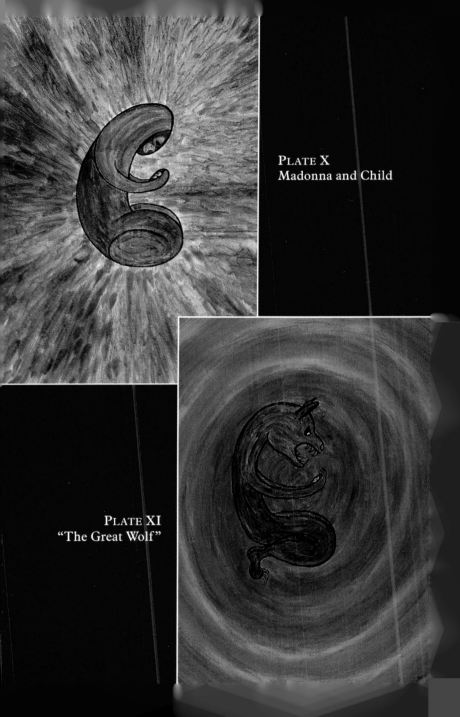

PLATE X
Madonna and Child

PLATE XI
"The Great Wolf"

PLATE XII
"Sunflower/Moonflower"

PLATE XIII
Image of Wholeness

PLATE XIV
Self-Acceptance

PLATE XV
Healing Symbols

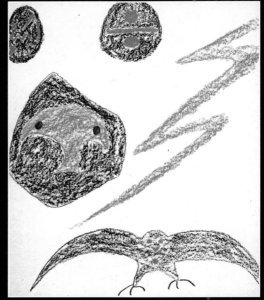

PLATE XVI
Giving Birth to
"Dead Shit"

PLATE XVII
"Anima"

a good means of redirecting her destructive energy toward constructive ends.

Soon, Sharon presented me with two active imagination paintings. The first of these shows a small figure representing herself riding a huge, powerful, black horse (Figure 8-4), as if she were trying to take control of her strong instinctual energy. The black horse is often associated symbolically with death. Sharon described the horse as female, and Jung characterized it as a symbol of the mother within us, which he associated with intuition understanding.[10]

The adjoining painting, entitled "My Garden," features the menacing image of, in Sharon's words, a female blood lily (Figure 8-5). On top of the cliff to the right of this lily are two figures with golden rings representing the union of masculine and feminine; so I could discern a conflict in her psyche between a negative female identity and an identity that had a better balance of male and female elements.

Sharon continued to have problems in school and she began to withdraw from others and drink more; she was involved in self-harmful and self-defeating behaviors. In this context came her next

FIGURE 8-4
Riding a Black Horse

painting, of a woman being raped (Figure 8-6). Through it, Sharon was expressing an image of a symbolic act of psychic violence against herself, which also contains some inescapable transformative elements. In the painting, a black female figure, whom Sharon characterized as an American Indian, is lying on her back and being, in Sharon's words, "screwed at both ends." This is the negative part of the rape: an extreme feeling of helplessness, hopelessness, and suffering. However, hanging over her are three breasts and a penis (a sort of phallic breast), which offer different forms of succor. Milk is coming out of the first breast onto her forehead; Sharon said that she felt nurtured and animated by this love fluid, that it was freeing, and that she felt it was the kind of touch that would alleviate her headaches. Blood is coming out of the second breast, and she is compelled to drink it by the way in which she is being held down by her rapists. Blood symbolizes the primary rejuvenating force; and so the fact that she is drinking blood has a healing value. The third breast drips purple milk on her abdomen, which indicates that her birthing center is in the process of grieving constructively for the loss

FIGURE 8-5
"My Garden"

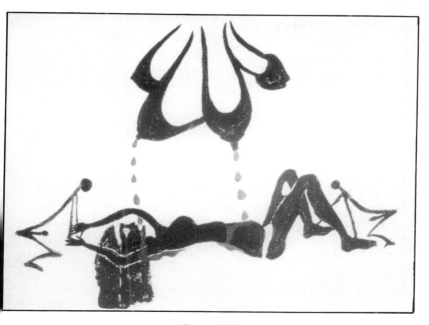

FIGURE 8-6
"Screwed at Both Ends"

of her six unborn fetuses. Out of the penis-breast comes a yellowish, semenlike fluid, which lands on her genitals: a life-stirring solution from her positive animus. This image also constellates the rape fantasy which on a symbolic level can promote individuation.[11]

Sharon's next painting (Figure 8-7) focused on her father, a logical progression from the previous rape painting assuming Sharon had a psychological incest problem. It depicts a crouching figure that she said started out as a fox and then turned into her father. It has a red head, a body half-white and half-black, and an umbilical cord attached to a small amniotic sac. Little red demons are trying to pull the amniotic sac apart. Sharon expressed concern that if the demons succeeded, she would crack up, that is, lose her protective shell, her masculine persona and identification with her father. She also experienced such angry feelings toward her father that she started to cry. Given Sharon's reaction, I concluded that she was confronting her false self, or negative ego-image and persona, in this painting.

As if working toward a rebirth of accepting herself as a woman,

FIGURE 8-7
Father Fox

her succeeding painting (Plate X) is a warm and affirming Madonna-
and-child composition. The brown numinous Madonna figure
represents a holy Earth Mother. The divine child points to transformation, as does the fact that the light and dark tones in the painting
are so luminous [cf. her painting of the maternal uroboros (see Plate
III)]. Sharon obviously was beginning to see herself as a reborn
woman—the mother of her true self.

Sharon's next painting, entitled "The Great Wolf" (Plate XI), is
an equally strong painting but totally opposite in tone, indicating
that she was hovering near the brink of egocide: a dramatic life-death
conflict. She interpreted the obviously fierce and aggressive wolf
image as representative of her negative animus, negative shadow,
and the devouring mother archetype; she realized that she must get

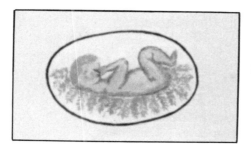

FIGURE 8-8
Baby Girl

this great wolf energy turned around in her favor, because she sensed that the wolf wanted and needed to be loved.

Soon after completing this work, Sharon talked once more about wanting to commit suicide; and again, I got her to recast suicide as egocide. I stressed her positive qualities: She was a bright and capable individual, and I suggested that she meditate on the painting she had recently done of the Madonna and child (cf. Plate X). At the end of the session, I embraced her—something I rarely do, but under the circumstances I felt it would be restorative. Symbolically, it demonstrated that she was being held in the maternal container of therapy.

Sharon's subsequent painting (Figure 8-8) reaffirmed a movement toward rebirth. It shows a newborn baby girl sleeping on green pine boughs (a meaningful symbol associated with the tree of life—pine boughs enabled the legendary hero Aeneas to pass through the underworld and survive). Encasing both the baby and the boughs is a blue structure like an egg or amniotic sac. There seemed to be a special synchronicity between this tender and beautiful image and the soft and refined self-portrait (cf. Figure 8-2) she'd done nine months earlier, the human gestation period.

The very next painting (Figure 8-9) represents a complete reversal in tone, continuing this patient's borderline pre-egocidal state of abrupt turn-abouts. It depicts a sinister woman in black standing next to a black-shrouded catafalque. To Sharon, the figure was the inner witch; she had killed the baby with the dagger in her left hand and holds three dead pine boughs in her right hand. During the session in which we talked about this painting, she felt very sad and despondent. In addition to grieving related to her own wounds at the hands of her mother, Sharon also seemed to be lamenting the loss of her own six babies.

Out of the death of the inner witch comes the rebirth of the

FIGURE 8-9
"Killer Witch"

creative self, as suggested in her next painting (Plate XII). "Sun-flower/Moonflower" is in marked contrast to Sharon's first sun-flower (cf. Plate II). This painting shows a union of opposites: solar (masculine) and lunar (feminine). Sharon said that the blackness of the border, continued in the blackness of the stem, represented growth out of the darkness of death, despair, and sorrow. The purple in the stem symbolizes both mourning and power (specifically, roy-alty). There are two large concentric circles around the flower itself: the silver outer one, associated by Sharon with the moon and the feminine; and the yellow inner one, associated by Sharon with the sun and the masculine. Thus the painting goes beyond depicting growth out of darkness to depicting the growth of light out of darkness. At the very center of the circles and the painting itself is a red form that Sharon associated with both a hand and a heart, connecting with the flower itself, which she thought of as a bird of paradise. The hand signifies power and strength and the heart love and charity. As for the painting as a whole, Sharon felt that it symbolized "purpose, function, and creativity." At the end of the session, she said that she loved herself—a very moving (and atypical) declaration.

Sharon was actually doing well in several areas of her life. She had some good friends, including one especially close friendship with a woman, which was a first for her. She ended up doing well in her second year of school; and after completing her thesis, Sharon received a Master's degree—a real accomplishment. She also felt better as a wife, although as she changed from a dependent daughter to an independent and assertive marital partner, her husband (not in therapy himself) began to talk about his desire for a separation.

Sharon then reported a dream, which contained the same sentiment.

> DREAM: *She is at a country inn and sees a blue butterfly turn into a green butterfly. Then, she and I engage in a long, slow, lovemaking session, ranging from tender to passionate. Describing this scene, she noted, significantly, that we were equal figures and that she didn't feel bad about her body. She was upset in the dream that I wanted to stop before orgasm because I didn't want to get her pregnant.*

Associating with the dream images, Sharon said that she liked the country inn (even referring to it as a chrysalis!), and that she thought of the blue butterfly as the unconscious feminine and the green butterfly as the conscious feminine. The part about loving me she associated to feeling good about me and with loving her own positive animus and inner healer. I felt encouraged by this dream and the symbol of the butterfly. It was as if Sharon could now see—or envision—her soul. Psyche means both soul and butterfly in Greek; additionally, the butterfly is a classic symbol of spiritual transformation. Just as she was leaving this session she recalled a subsequent dream in which she gave birth to a little boy—a symbol of the psychic rebirth of a new, positive animus. After this session she telephoned her husband and told him she wanted a permanent separation.

Immediately after telephoning her husband, Sharon created a painting entitled "Me as a Woman" (Figure 8-10). It is a painting of a woman crouched under a black cloud in a state of oppression, grief, and prayerful obeisance. She said that it showed her worshipping the goddess of womanhood; while she talked to me about this painting, she cried. Although she had experienced near-egocide before, it was at this juncture in therapy that she actually committed egocide and went through Symbolic Death. The persona roles, ego-images, and ego identities associated with being a graduate student and wife to a father-figure all were disintegrating, and she had reached a completely disorganized state of confusion. She had to take an official leave of absence from her studies.

FIGURE 8-10
"Me as a Woman"

Egocide, Psychic Crucifixion, and Near Suicide

Sharon's egocide at this point represented a full transition from Stage I to Stage II of her illness and analytical psychotherapy. Typically, a patient during this transitional period feels dread, agony, and a sense of being out of control. It is a very critical and potentially dangerous time for severely depressed and suicidal individuals; and so they have a strong need to be contained and held in the *temenos* of their analytical sessions and to be allowed to borrow some positive ego from the therapist. It is not always the most difficult period of therapy; but for Sharon, it was.

It was in this context that Sharon called me and said that she had been in the bath (symbolically, immersed in the waters of life and death) with a knife and that she had scratched her left wrist and the inside of her left elbow. After establishing that she was not acutely suicidal, I asked her to paint her feelings and to see me the next day. She brought in a very scary painting, of herself crucified on a red cross (Figure 8-11). She is bleeding, nailed to the cross at the intersection of her negative father and mother complexes. She reported that, in real life, she was near to harming herself. Although there were no family members in the area, she had some social support from a neighbor and several other friends. I saw her on a daily basis during this difficult period; I also asked her to call me day or night if she felt desperate. Thinking of the sacrifice on the cross as a classic image of ego death heralding a rebirth, I felt somewhat hopeful.

Sharon's next painting was done two days later and is entitled "Two Women" (Figure 8-12). The woman on the left is healthy and serene—representing Sharon's new ego-Self axis—and she offers a heart, which Sharon associated with love and strength, to the woman on the right, who is emaciated and dying. Sharon associated this anorexic, needy, self-destructive figure with that part of herself that wanted to be loved and held but was terrified to do so. It was as if Sharon had surrendered her ego to a higher power, the Self, through the crucifixion and, thus transformed, had created a new image of herself.

But the next night Sharon had an ominous dream.

> DREAM: *She is living in a boarding house crowded with men and women in their early twenties (she has obviously regressed). She has a lover to whom she is quite attached romantically. They are in a large excavation on the first floor of the building. Some old boards lie across one of the exposed pipes, and he yanks the boards away, leaving her stranded over a looming gulf. Everyone there, including her lover, laughs at her and mocks her as she stands trapped above the middle of the black, menacing abyss, leaning on a wall for support knowing that she will soon fall in. Sharon screams for someone to help her and for her lover to replace the boards, but to no avail. It seems that she should be able to walk on the pipe to safety as her lover has done, but she knows that her balance has been terrible lately.*

Sharon woke up frightened. Shortly thereafter, she called my home and said that she had made a superficial scratch on her left arm and that she felt distraught and hopeless. I discussed hospitalization with her. She said no, that she could make it with my being available to her or that, in a very serious crisis, she would go to the psychiatric emergency department on her own.

When I saw her the next day, she said that she sometimes felt like giving up, but continued to hang on to life. I would always reframe her references to suicide in terms of egocide and talk about what part, in fact, needed to die. I again discussed psychiatric hospitalization with her, but she refused to admit herself voluntarily, and I

FIGURE 8-11
Crucifixion

FIGURE 8-12
"Two Women"

chose not to commit her against her will. I reiterated my request that she call me at any time if she felt she could not handle the situation.

Sharon's ensuing painting (not included here), brought in the next day, shows a woman screaming ragefully. Sharon said the idea for the painting came from the last dream in which she was screaming for someone to help her. She also said that the woman was herself. Thinking that it was her false self, my response was, "No, the woman is a part of you." She then became extremely angry and told me that she wanted to quit analytical therapy. (I did not appreciate that this was also an omen about her desire to quit life.) After a lengthy conversation, she agreed to continue in therapy, and we planned to discuss this topic again, the following day.

I now realize that I had erred, and that Sharon was crying out for me to take control. In retrospect, I should have hospitalized her involuntarily. She went home, cut her left arm at the inner convexity of the elbow, and screamed. A neighbor heard her, broke in, and drove her to the emergency room where she received six stitches. In the early evening I was called by one of the doctors in the emergency department, and Sharon was then committed against her will to a psychiatric ward. She did not have enough ego strength and social support in her life at that time, and needed the containment and sanctuary of the hospital.

Prior to hospitalization, Sharon, who had sunk into an undifferentiated unconscious state, had gone through Symbolic Death. Her negative ego identity, the part of her that was needy, starving, and death-oriented, had colluded with the remains of her destructive mother and father complexes and her evil shadow to pull her very nearly into the hellish abyss of suicide.

After being on the psychiatric unit only one day, Sharon signed a voluntary form for admission, as suicidal patients often do after involuntary hospitalization: To be in a safe environment actually facilitates healing. During her eight-day stay in the hospital, I saw her daily. Halfway through the hospitalization she decided to fully commit herself to the analytical process as well as to relate to her husband in an adult manner.

Sharon left the hospital with her husband to go to her parents for Thanksgiving. On her return, she reported an overall positive, but regressive, time in her parents' home. She said they had been supportive, and she characterized the whole experience as like crawling back into the womb—a continuation of her post-egocide recovery period. She had been on a major tranquilizer, Stelazine (trifluopera-zine), while she was in the hospital, and she remained on this after her discharge. Psychological tests done in the hospital revealed that she had a very high IQ (between superior and gifted), was severely depressed, in a borderline state, and a high suicide risk.

The first post-Thanksgiving meeting that Sharon and I had was focused on *to be or not to be*. We talked about the concept of egocide, and she agreed to continue to analyze to death more negative aspects of her psyche, in order to sustain the rebirth of more positive aspects. At this point, she said that she was living on, and for, hope.

Sharon's next painting (Figure 8-13), entitled "Must Bite the Bullet," is a picture of a transitional animal that looks part wolf and part dog or horse, which meant to her that it could be tamed. Overall, this animal is not ferocious in appearance except for its teeth. Around the eyes and the top part of its head it looks rather kind, and the painting itself seems a bit hopeful. I was intrigued by the fact that at this point in her treatment, she compared taming horses, which is something she had done for years, to analytical therapy. She said that they both take patience, and that there is a great deal of repetition in both activities. Sharon decided to quit her

FIGURE 8-13
"Must Bite the Bullet"

negative, male-dominated, competitive Ph.D. program. She felt this part of her ego identity had to die, and through this final act, it did. Her subsequent dreams involved positive animus figures, a growing garden, and feminine figures grounded to the earth and in love with the new animus figures.

Sharon's following painting, completed soon after the last, pointed to a taming process going on in her psyche (Figure 8-14). On the right side is a yellow-gold nude woman whom I took to represent a new, grounded aspect of Sharon: an ego-Self connection. The figure has a light gray shadow (now Sharon is manifesting and accepting her own reasonable—not monstrous—shadow). On the left side of the painting is a dark gray nude woman who looks as if she is trying to embrace the yellow-gold woman. Sharon said that the dark gray

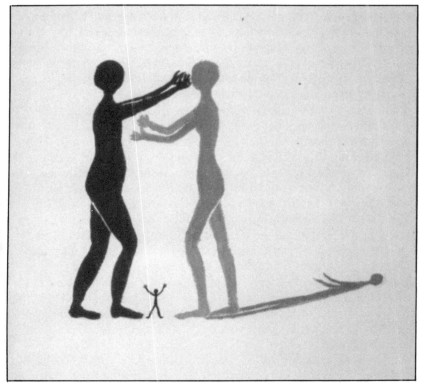

FIGURE 8-14
Taming Process

woman was a witch; however, because the woman is gray and not black, she added, "not a killer witch." According to Sharon, this dark gray woman was heavy and ugly, and she was trying to scratch out the eyes of the yellow-gold woman. In other words, the negative mother was going after her vision (her insight), but she was not succeeding in blinding her. It is most interesting that there is a little, black, negative ego figure in between these two women that Sharon said represented her Ph.D. identity, which is almost gone.

Now two years and three months into analytical therapy, Sharon found herself becoming increasingly grief-stricken and depressed. I need to underscore that she had lost a considerable amount of her previous ego; and even though it was negative ego that she had lost, it was nevertheless a major loss that needed to be mourned. At this point, I chose to treat her with psychological support, analytical therapy, and an antidepressant, Desyrel (trazadone), partly to counteract her increasing depression (causing her to experience very low energy, anorexia, and severe insomnia) and partly to replace her self-treatment of choice, more and more alcohol.

During this period, Sharon had a dream of having sexual intercourse with me, which could be interpreted as having spiritual communion with her positive animus and healer archetype. She was now considering new careers ranging from journalistic or editorial work to a career in one of the mental health professions. When it came time for my vacation, I gave her the number where I would be and asked her to call me if she became despondent and/or desperate.

One night, while I was away, Sharon called sounding drunk and talked about committing suicide. Her husband had just served the divorce papers. Recognizing a pattern developing here similar to the previous suicide attempt, and not wanting to take any further chances, I told her I had to change phones and I would call her right back. In the interim, I telephoned the local police and told them to pick her up. Then I called the hospital and told them to admit her involuntarily unless she agreed to being admitted. I then called her back and, as it turned out, the police had to break down her door to take her to the hospital, where she had to be admitted against her will. It was a repetition of her previous crisis, but not as severe since she had not attempted suicide and she had reached out for help. I called a colleague of mine, who acted as the attending psychiatrist until I returned. As before, Sharon signed a voluntary paper the day after admission. She remained in the hospital for a week, on a regimen of Stelazine and Desyrel. After discharge, she was kept on these medications.

While in the hospital, Sharon did two paintings, one she called "In Prison" (Figure 8-15) and the other called "Angry Rage" (Figure 8-16). "In Prison" shows a woman in a blue cage. It actually looks as if she could easily get through the bars by bending them and slipping out. In "Angry Rage," a woman is surrounded by a red serpent in a clockwise spiral. Sharon called this spiral *healing energy,* which derived from all the destructive fury. In addition to the painting, she talked about wanting to become a psychologist and about a dream that she had been accepted into two Ph.D. programs in Clinical Psychology. Her mother was supportive of Sharon's latest ambition, but her father and husband were not.

Death of the Inner Witch and Birth of the Creative Self

Now two and a half years into analytical treatment, Sharon began to talk about her therapy and her relationship with me in more positive terms.

At this point, Sharon created an active-imagination painting of a golden-yellow woman handing a blue vessel to a black woman (Plate XIII). Above both women is a magenta halo. According to Sharon, the vessel contained bitterness: The black woman had to drink it, but she didn't want to. Sharon associated blue with the feminine and also with melancholia. The black woman she associated with the yin part of the yin/yang principle. This healthy, feminine figure evolved out

FIGURE 8-15
"In Prison"

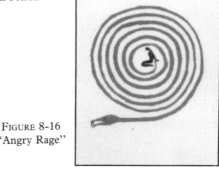

FIGURE 8-16
"Angry Rage"

of several previous black figures that Sharon had painted, including the killer witch-figure, the black American Indian woman who was raped, and the black anorexic woman who needed heart! Sharon felt the magenta halo represented holiness, royalty, wholeness, and an inner marriage of positive and negative (good and evil). To me, the halo symbolized the Self and its transcendent function: in terms of this painting, unifying the black female figure (transformed negative shadow) with the golden-yellow female figure (a new ego-Self identity connected to a goddess-like anima archetype that is the soul).

After this session, Sharon visited her parents, who told her that she seemed more together than ever. Sharon was now in Stage III, with a clear self-Self connection which would manifest by new and creative actions having to do with goals and relationships. At this time, in her parents' home (i.e., from a position of strength), she got her own lawyer to proceed with the divorce. Sharon then dreamed that her husband was dead. She came to realize that it was the negative father complex and negative animus projected onto her husband that had died. Specifically, the projection had been analyzed to death.

Soon afterwards, Sharon had a dream of a demon snake coming out of her husband's penis and she decided to paint a variation of this (Figure 8-17). Here Sharon is dancing with healing energy (represented by the snake).[12] She now has phallic energy of her own and is no longer dependent on her husband's or father's. Sharon is engaged in a dance of psychic transformation.

Sharon then had a dream in which she is with her husband; but it is not her real husband or anyone she knows. She is nine months pregnant. They live in a cramped, dark, converted garage, and she is not happy in this space. Then they move into a new apartment, which is larger and brighter. We interpreted this dream to mean that she had a new, positive animus, and that she was ready to experience a rebirth of her true self. Later she had another dream, in which she is with a man in his late forties who wants to get in touch with his daughter, who is in her mid-twenties. The man was absent during his daughter's childhood and emotionally very distant, and his daughter was hurt by this. Now the man realizes the wrongness of what he did and sincerely wishes to repair the damage. Sharon and I saw this dream as representing an encouraging development in the resolution of her negative father complex and her relationship with her own father.[13]

FIGURE 8-17
Healing Serpent Dance

Afterward, ironically, Sharon received word from her mother that her father had suffered a severe heart attack. Sharon rushed to be at his side. At this point she wanted to stop analytical therapy and to move home so that she could remain close to her father and mother. We talked about this as a regression that would not be in her best interest. She ended up staying at her parents' home for a few weeks and then coming back to her own life after her father miraculously recovered. While with her father, she shared with him the journal entries she had made sometime after her first hospitalization, and he told her, "You are a born writer."

Once we resumed our therapy, Sharon said, "I like you, but I resent you, because you are a life line."[14] In this session, she shared with me one of the journal entries that she had read to her father:

I am conscious of the oceans of my life. My tears, my grief, my aloneness. I listen for the tides, to feel the ebb and flow of them. The water, the feminine, is infinitely patient. It waits for me to come to it, and if I am too long away, it breaks over me in a wave. Subsiding, there is that same misty silence which surrounds me now, in the clear expanse of sand which waits for the writing. I am learning to write my life in the sand, learning to accept that it will once again be washed away, to be written anew. My masculine side is outraged. He wants me to erect a breakwall against the ocean. Memories, like snapshots, are not enough. He wants a monument, freezing in brittle permanence what has gone before. But that way is truly madness and death. I must be deaf to his voice, holding instead to that innate knowing which belongs to being. Like the ocean, the I which I seek is stable in the depths of me, unresisting to the currents of living. I must learn to go with the Tao. It is simply faith which expects the crocus in the snow. And it is faith which must hold me together, especially when, as now, hope is gone. It sits quietly inside me, telling me to bide my time, to wait for the new season. I draw down into myself, as into a chrysalis, and allow the emptiness to wash over me.

Two years and eight months into analytical therapy, Sharon had a dream in which she and a tall, elegant man were in the process of establishing friendly relations with a black tribe. Later, she dreamed of having intercourse with a German shepherd dog who turned into a man. In sum, I felt the dreams were suggesting that she was having communion with her basic instincts. The dog symbolizes healing and fidelity;[15] the dog turning into a man in her dream represented a positive transformation of her loyal animus. Sharon then decided to take a month off and stay with her father while he was recuperating. She noted a change in her relationship with him: He was no longer a God figure. Her mother concurrently saw that Sharon was not as brittle, negative, or angry as before.

On returning, Sharon again talked about wanting to stop analytical therapy with me and expressed a desire to see a woman therapist instead. I supported this development. She then received a call from her mother telling her that her father was back in the hospital and had been there for five days. Her mother had not wanted to bother her earlier; but feeling left out, Sharon said to me, "I could kill her." In the midst of this situation she did her next painting (Figure 8-18).

There is an egg with two women inside, each with an arm reaching out. It is as if the two women are longing for each other. In composition, the egg resembles a uroboros. To Sharon, it seemed to represent incubation and new life and gave her a feeling of hope. The ground within the oval delineates a seahorse; it is the male who has

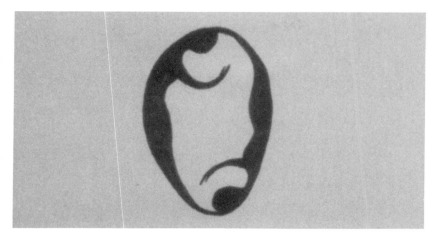

FIGURE 8-18
Seahorse and Incubating Feminine in an Egg

a maternal pouch in which the eggs are laid, and later baby seahorses are hatched! This, of course, parallels Sharon's upbringing and nurturance by her father, which seems like an example of synchronicity.[16] As before, her father recovered, and it turned out that Sharon did not return home as his condition never became life-threatening.

Sharon's last active imagination painting during her therapy with me was done six weeks later (Plate XIV). It shows a radiant child in yellow protected by the Great Mother in blue and standing on a lion.[17] The Divine Child archetype and its transformative nature is evident. A lion represents strength and courage and is also a symbol of combining good and evil, masculine and feminine, solar and lunar.

Sharon finally did contact the female analyst that I recommended and set up an appointment. At the same time, she remembered that her father had been the one who had read to her, had talked with her, and had done things with her when she had been a child. When she had been sick, he had been the one who had held her hand and had sat with her, so essentially he had been a great source of maternal comfort and nurturing. Thus, psychically speaking, she now had a much healthier perspective of her father. Three weeks later, she got a job as a manager trainee in a book store; she also began a new, positive relationship with a man.

Near the end of our work together, Sharon's mother called and reported that her father was in the hospital again and dying of kidney failure. She went home right away, and while there she had a very important dream.

> DREAM: *Her father is dying but he seems rather spry and fit, and everything is going well. They board a hydrofoil boat; and, once they are seated in the cocktail lounge, he begins making a very thin plaster object with a silver mounting on top. She does not understand what the object is and thinks how different from herself and the rest of her family her father has always been. She tells him that the object is very beautiful. He tells her that it is about as strong as crystallized water, and she handles it reverently. She then says that she should get a box for it and contacts a waitress, who eventually brings a box.*

This dream indicated that Sharon's negative father complex had died and that she was developing a positive resolution with her internal father image. In the dream, her father is making something precious for her (a teardrop-shaped silver item that stands for the feminine); and she is accepting this gift and containing it in a box, which is often a symbol for the vagina. Thus, we could see that she was working out a positive psychological union with her father, a union that would serve as a healthy replacement for the negative psychological incest problem she had once had. At the same time that she was resolving her father complex in her dream life, she was also resolving her father complex in her real life by supporting her father while he was so critically ill.

A New Beginning: A Never-ending Healing Journey

Sharon's father rallied again, and slowly but surely made another amazing recovery. After this development, I told her that I would be leaving to take a new position at Texas A&M University, but that we would have several months to talk about it. Her initial reaction to my announcement was shock and sadness; she said it was like finding out that her parents were mortal.

Later, she began experiencing negative emotions from her past,

mainly rage and anger associated with feeling rejected and abandoned. She started taking out her anger and rage on herself. I helped
her focus her rage and anger on me so that she could learn to manage
it more realistically. After the lancing of the boil of my upcoming
departure, healing would endure.

At three years into therapy, Sharon was doing better at her new
job and was no longer thinking of giving up or wanting to die. She
was more assertive, had established a more satisfying rapport with
her sister, and had developed other new relationships with men, one
of them fairly intimate. Regarding this latter change, she said, "My
relationships with men are above board. I am no longer into hiding
things or feelings with you or other men."

Shortly thereafter, Sharon hesitantly told me, "Human to human,
I'll miss you." I shared a similar feeling with her and suggested that
we correspond and that she continue the analytical process with the
woman analyst. Our last session occurred at three years and one
month after the first session. It was a healthy parting, and I had the
sense that I had been on a true healing journey with her. She had
crossed over the water (unconscious) and had successfully transformed negative introjects and shadow aspects of herself, as well as
her own animus. She also had found new and rewarding relationships
with her parents, sister, and, most important, herself, based on her
union with a positive animus. Following her inner marriage, she had
divorced her outer husband, thus freeing herself from a dependency
that had been generated by her negative complexes. As a result, she
felt better about herself. Sharon has transformed her false self into
her true self by finding her lost soul (anima) and contacting the Self.
Her new and positive identity as a woman was based on her new
ego-Self axis (Stage II) as well as self-Self axis (Stage III).

I heard from Sharon several times after she began seeing the
woman analyst. During a year of analytical therapy with this analyst,
Sharon came to terms with her inner wolf (see Plate XI), the devouring aspect of herself that she thought was related to the archetypal
terrible mother. She also found a spiritual teacher—a Native American woman, which was significant, considering Sharon's painting of
the raped American Indian women (see Figure 8-6). With this
teacher, she began to develop her own medicine woman identity,
which coincided with her renewed interest in becoming a healer
herself.

The following summer, Sharon went alone into the Rocky Mountains for two weeks on a spiritual quest.[18] This represents a major change for this patient to have overcome her abandonment issues, so that she could go off by herself without her therapist life line. It suggests that she has discovered an inner supportive figure and healer, so she no longer feels in danger of abandonment. Sharon also no longer wants to abandon herself (suicide). (What a contrast to her initial dream of being dropped off at the Rocky Mountain Chocolate Factory Child Care Center!) Shortly before this sojourn, with the help of her American Indian teacher, she entered a trance state and became a wolf. Later she wrote to me: "The wolf is my totem, my mentor, and my guide." She no longer is in danger of being devoured by the archetypal terrible mother. Hiking and camping on her own was a critical test for her, and in the context of that test, she made a decision based on a vision to continue her own analytical therapy and to pursue formal training to become a healer in the mental health field. Her own words are most telling in regard to her sense of spiritual rebirth:

> The vision of a Mother Earth goddess and a related dream had to do with our undissolvable, inexplicable, unavoidable connection with each other and with all the creatures and with the Earth, and my commitment to be part of the healing of the rifts which have led us to the present, suicidal world state. . . . I pray that in this new age we will find the way back from the cliff's edge. I pray that I may help heal the wounds, and vow to be an instrument in the preservation of this land and its people.

Sharon is currently in training to become a therapist, and she has the potential to become an excellent one, living out the archetype of the wounded healer.

CHAPTER 9

Paul: Egocide and the Buddha

"Suicide is probably always a psychological murder, a killing of a resented parent, an internalized tormenter. The suicidal process is almost always tinctured with elements of the integrative efforts of the ego, and indeed with love and the wish to live and be loved."

—KARL MENNINGER

In Paul's case, we see how egocide allows him to effectively transform morbid depression and a suicide plan into the symbolic killing of the false self and the birth of the true self. This arduous journey is facilitated by Paul's dreams, healing images, and other creative products of active imagination as well as by soul-making. Paul's story reveals that endurance and healing through love are some of our best medicines.

When I first met Paul, he was profoundly depressed. He had been referred to me by an internist worried about his safety. A mental health professional in his late thirties, Paul was acutely suicidal. Thirteen years earlier, he had nearly died after a car accident. He had recovered and had married a year later; a year after marriage, however, he had been in constant psychiatric care. Paul was dissatisfied with the psychiatrist he had been seeing for two years. He also was not being helped by large doses of prescribed tricyclic antidepressants.

Paul felt hopeless and worthless; he found no meaning in life; and he suffered from low energy, insomnia, and a spastic colon. In addition, he had panic attack symptoms from fears of impending doom. For example, when he went shopping, he would run out of the grocery store fearful that he would pass out and die or that the ceiling might collapse. He also had several phobias. He wouldn't eat certain foods, or eat in restaurants, or swim in chlorinated water because he feared being poisoned.

Paul's wife was also in therapy for depression and suicidal impulses. Two years earlier, she had had bilateral mastectomies for breast cancer (electing to have the healthy breast removed for preventive reasons), and her father had killed himself four years before. She and Paul were in marital therapy as well.

Paul desperately wanted to find a solution to his depressive and suicidal state, which he insisted was biological in origin. On the positive side, he was articulate, bright, and a high achiever. He enjoyed computers as a hobby and played computer games for hours on end with great pleasure. On the negative side, he harbored much anger against his parents. He described his father, a rigidly religious and unemotional civil servant, as "Gestapo-like, authoritarian, and sadistic." His father had punished him as a child by locking him in the cellar or the attic, or by making him take cold showers. Paul characterized his mother as "impulsive, smothering, and a self-absorbed dictator." She was a health care professional with a long history of psychiatric problems and suicide attempts.

The First Dream: Entry into Stage I of Therapy

DREAM: *Paul is leading a group of men and women down an incline to some water, women first. There are two men, one of whom is scared and inexperienced at swimming. Nevertheless, everyone swims across a quiet part of the water, then goes into the river channel, which is like a canal with concrete or stone sides. The man who was scared at first becomes comfortable swimming, and the other man who was comfortable at first becomes frightened. Paul leads, and there are moments when they have to get out of the water and jump from rock ledge to rock ledge. Finally, they reach their destination safely. The two men are exhausted, but not Paul. He says to himself, "I must be in better condition than I thought." He also notes that "the women overpowered the men."*

Paul's taking the lead in the dream, and not feeling exhausted at the end, suggest that he had enough ego strength to undertake and complete the analytical process. However, the alternately comfortable and scared men represented shadow aspects of Paul's psyche that indicated problems with his father and his masculine identity. Women overpowering men suggested a negative mother complex, but also a strong anima, again connoting a potentially positive outcome for therapy.

I discontinued Paul's antidepressant Tofranil (imipramine), but because of his severe depression, panic attacks, and phobias, I prescribed Xanax (alprazolam).[1] He experienced some relief, particularly from the panic attacks, but remained very depressed and angry, and had dreams that he was dying. Paul felt as if he were in a prison. He also had a specific fantasy or delusion that he was destined in his late forties to bear witness to the second coming of Christ, suggesting ego inflation and possibly a messianic complex.

During the first few months of therapy, Paul's dreams alternated between cruel unhealthiness, which seemed to reveal some sources of his problems, and a healthy affirmativeness that seemed to point toward resolution of them. These dreams were equally about men and women, indicating inner issues connected with both his father and his mother. He tended to project his problems with his mother onto his wife; during this time, he felt violated by his wife, and their relationship was painful to him. Meanwhile, his wife was distressed that she couldn't be more supportive. At times he associated his wife and mother with being poisoned, invaded, or hurt.

He dreamed his mother arranged for his father to sodomize him as she watched. While this image points to strong conflicts on a personal unconscious level, it also has archetypal significance: In some primitive societies, anal intercourse is an initiation rite for young boys to become men.[2]

Other dreams during this period also commented on sex. He dreamed of a naked couple jumping off a diving board in sexual union and landing in the water, a symbol of Paul having union with his anima. In another dream, he is in a small boat with his wife, lost and afraid of the hazards. It was as if he were confined with his disturbed negative mother introject and sensed danger in going into the unconscious in more depth.

Two months into analysis, Paul had an especially meaningful dream.

> DREAM: *He is with a twin sister [suggesting his anima]. They are plotting to kill his father and they do. Next his mother dies. Then he is in a hospital with his wife, both having been exposed to illness. He writes a good-bye note, wanting to die, but he lives.*

This dream seemed to show that Paul had reached the middle of Stage I, where the negative internalized images of his parents were being analyzed to death. The stage was being set for egocide and transformation.

Egocide, The Buddha, and
Transcendence Over the Gestapo

Three months into the analysis Paul's wife called me, very distraught, because Paul had a suicide plan. I contacted Paul and saw him immediately, and, yes, he had been planning to drive to a lonely place and kill himself by routing exhaust fumes to the inside of the car with a hose. He refused hospitalization. I then introduced him to the term *egocide*, explaining that a negative part of his ego, in collusion with his shadow, was trying to overtake his whole being, and that this abnormal part, not his whole being, had to die. I emphasized that his healthy ego needed to join forces with me in order for him to survive.[3] He readily grasped the concept of egocide, and it helped to decrease his sense of desperation. He promised to call me at *any* time, if he went into crisis.

I saw Paul every day for a week. We walked together near the edge along a narrow path high above the abyss, which is characteristic of the outpatient care of the acutely suicidal patient. By not hospitalizing him, I was taking a chance: assuming that he would call me before attempting suicide. To deal with my self-doubts and concern that I might be making a fatal mistake, I sought professional consultation. I also asked Paul's wife to contact me right away if the situation worsened.

We all made it through this crisis; but afterward, Paul was in agony and completely disorganized. He was unable to work, so I sent a note to his employer stating that he was ill and would be disabled for at least three months. My certifying that he couldn't function finalized his ego death. He had, indeed, committed egocide instead of suicide. I emphasized that it was now essential that he turn his death energy into creative products, and prescribed that he draw his visions, dreams, and feelings at least once a week. At first he resisted, saying that he couldn't draw, but then agreed to do it.

Paul's first active imagination drawing (Figure 9-1) is of a black bird gliding up and down red wind currents. He said that the bird (an ancient symbol of spiritual transcendence linked to the soul) was the life force. Spirals are common in drawings made by depressed and suicidal patients,[4] and he described this red spiral as a "bloody trail—the anger, the hurt part." Based on his early dreams, his

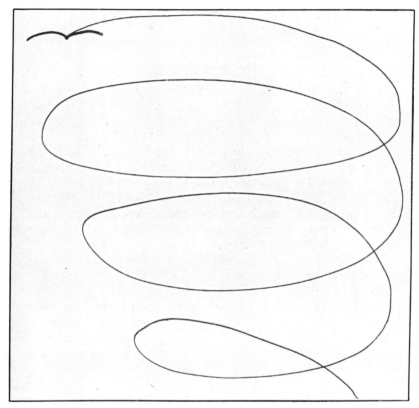

FIGURE 9-1
"Bloody Trail"

progress so far, and this blood-letting drawing, I was encouraged that he was actually going through a cleansing Symbolic Death experience.

Paul's second drawing depicts the same bird being crushed by a purple boot (Figure 9-2). Purple is related to Lent (suffering and the pain of grieving) and to royalty, which is connected to the divine. Paul described the boot as an evil force, the Gestapo, and related it

FIGURE 9-2
"The Gestapo"

to his father, but it also represented the negative archetypal father. With this drawing, Paul opened the floodgates to an inner rage that he didn't know was so strong. I could see that we were now at the beginning of Stage II of his illness and therapy.

In Paul's third drawing, the boot is smiling and frowning—an early sign of a union of opposites taking place in his psyche (Figure 9-3). He called the boot "the vampire sucking my blood and vitals," indicative of his immersion into the collective unconscious.

His fourth drawing (Figure 9-4) shows a spiral charged with spiritual (purple) energy. The bird is reconstituted as a man, and the tip of the boot is metamorphosed into his headdress. Paul saw this figure as a Buddha ("Boot-ah"). This Buddha-like symbol of the Self as soul emerged out of the Gestapo energy of the destructive

FIGURE 9-3
"Vampire"

FIGURE 9-4
Buddha ("Boot-ah")

shadow and was a hopeful image for Paul and his analytical therapy.

In Paul's subsequent drawing (not shown), a bird is hovering over a crushed and bloody human that Paul thought was his wife, or maybe his mother. Paul's wife had decided to leave him, because she couldn't cope with his extreme depression, which was associated with killing off the negative mother within his psyche. Concurrently, he feared that if he vomited he would die. I suggested that he might need to symbolically vomit up the negative mother complex so it could die.

Paul's next drawing of four mountain peaks and four birds (Figure 9-5) illustrated the union of opposites that characterizes the Self. One bird is centered on the top of a purple circle exactly above a black figure representing Paul on the bottom of the circle. The figure and the circle rest on green grass (the first green to appear in his drawings, representing positive growth). The circle itself suggests a mandala, a sacred circle and symbol of wholeness or the Self. The vertical line-up of figure and bird can be taken as Paul's new ego-Self axis, in which the body is joined with the spirit—an important healing image.

FIGURE 9-5
Emergence of the Self

Death-Rebirth Struggle:
Into the Collective Unconscious

Paul then became very upset because a woman colleague hanged herself at the same time that his wife moved out. Significantly, although depressed, Paul was not suicidal.

Paul described his next drawing (this and the next three are not shown) as a face that was almost pornographic in appearance. According to him, the eyes in the drawing are breasts, the chin is formed by buttocks, and the mouth is a vagina full of teeth. He mentioned that he once joked that his wife had teeth in her vagina and remembered that his mother once cautioned him about venereal disease and the dangers of women. Thus, I concluded that this drawing represented the terrible, devouring mother in his psyche. The drawing that followed features a green heart with a bullet hole through it with tears of blood coming out, suggesting that emotional growth, symbolized by the color green, is very painful.

Paul said that his successive drawing of a sea serpent had "a lot of energy and thrust behind it." To me, this picture indicated that he was continuing to reject suicide and, therefore, was feeling stronger as an individual. The serpent, representing his strength, is somewhat phallic in shape but made its home in the sea (feminine and unconscious). The serpent is purple inside, indicating that mourning is taking place. It is moving toward a red star of David, which can be interpreted as both an outer guide (that is, a positive transference, my first name being David) and an inner guide (contact with Self). The sea serpent is helping him to constellate destructive energy and pain into a creative spirit manifested in our healing relationship.

In his next drawing, Paul is shown juggling seven balls. Seven in Genesis represents the number of days it took to produce the world, and it generally symbolizes creativity and illumination. Paul felt that it meant he was juggling too many things at once: He missed his wife, his spastic colon was worse, and he felt more depressed. However, he now had enough new ego strength to go further into the collective unconscious.

After five months of therapy, Paul was coming in two or three times a week for sessions. His ensuing drawing (Figure 9-6) illustrates an incubation, which is central to psychotherapeutic healing.[5] He talked about a mummy person (or archetypal mother) trapped in

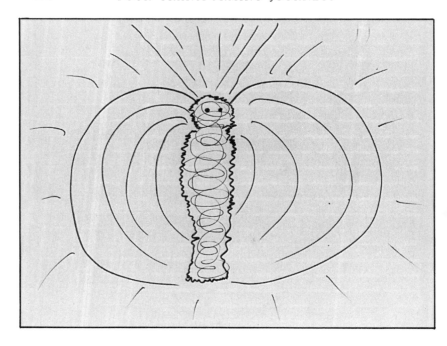

FIGURE 9-6
Radiant Incubation

a cocoon, which suggested that he was not only in Stage II of this therapy but also in Jung's middle stage of human development.[6] He still had to deal with the mother on the collective level, but the drawing shows energy that radiates out—a hopeful sign.

During the period that followed, Paul started thinking of suicide again; but he, and I, knew that suicidal thoughts really meant that more negative parts of his ego and shadow had to die. Every time he would say suicide, I would respond with egocide and shadowcide. Paul's drawing that followed (Figure 9-7) can be related to this struggle as well as to his spastic colon. Sarcastically called "the winner," it depicts a literal disorganization. The male figure (Paul himself) has pulled out his heart, bowels, and genitals, and shit is surrounding him. Paul summed it up: "There you have the boot [i.e., the Gestapo of his earlier drawings] feeling victorious." His subsequent drawing (Figure 9-8) elaborates archetypally on this

FIGURE 9-7
Disorganization

FIGURE 9-8
Devouring Creature

shadow theme. A nightmarish evil creature is smiling victory, spelled out with boots, and devouring what's left of Paul. In his next drawing, he has surrendered to the evil force, spelled out as "the boot!!!" (Figure 9-9). Regarding the caption, "Fuck me 'til I'm dead," Paul recalled the dream of his father sodomizing him. His following drawing completes this psychic minidrama. According to Paul, it shows him being crushed by the "black death force" (Figure 9-10). To me, all four of these drawings revealed that he was in an excruciating transition, mourning several parts of himself that had died, but he was no longer suicidally depressed.

Paul's active imagination drawings then took a slightly new tack. His successive drawing (not shown) reveals the inside of his head as a jail. He said that he was guilt-ridden and obsessed with thoughts of being imprisoned. He felt that he may have literally killed his mother and father. I reassured him that he was not an actual killer and that he did not have to go to a real prison. I explained that in analyzing negative parental complexes to death, he had committed psychic murder. The part of him that was in prison, his true self, representing strength and courage, had to be freed by the death of his negative ego and shadow.

Paul's next drawing (also not shown) shows a candle burning at both ends: a paradoxical but hopeful image. Where there is light, there is hope; and even though a candle burning at both ends is potentially self-destructive, Paul could appreciate that the destruction involved was a means to a good end. He had drawn this picture on the back of a page copied from a book on love; the page was about loving oneself. Was this mere coincidence or a meaningful synchronicity? Paul and I both thought that it was the latter.

Paul needed to analyze to death his own, personal neurotic parental complexes; but to have lasting results, he also had to grapple with similar issues on the collective level. If conflicts are not resolved on a collective level, they will eventually cause conflicts to re-emerge on the personal level. This is why Stages II and III in the analytical process are so critical to healing: The patient must go into deeper levels of the psyche.

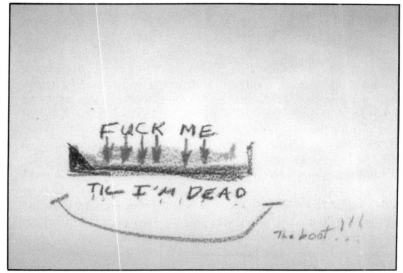

FIGURE 9-9
Surrender to Evil

FIGURE 9-10
"Black Death Force"

Transformation of the Devouring Crab Lady

At this point in his therapy, Paul still feared being poisoned, and he continued to be afraid that if he vomited he would die. In fact, ridding himself of additional negative parts of his psyche would mean going through successive Symbolic Death experiences. Despite his intellectual grasp of the certain results of egocide, he was still experiencing a great deal of anxiety about going deeper into the collective unconscious.

Paul's following drawing (Figure 9-11) depicts what he called a "killer beast" aspect of himself. According to him, the figure is killing itself: head first, then heart, stomach, breasts, testicles, and penis. Paul felt correspondingly disorganized and disintegrated: dead and dying. When we again talked about his vomiting, he recalled for the first time that his mother had once attempted suicide because she was afraid she had been poisoned—a significant memory.

Still in Stage II, Paul struggled for nearly two months to find meaning in his life. He felt partly dead and partly alive. He could now talk with his two brothers, he no longer had panic attacks, and he was down to one milligram of Xanax a day. Paul also began having dreams about a healthy sexual relationship with a new woman, and he obtained a very good consulting job related to his interest in computing. Interestingly during this period when he learned that his mother, who had had twenty or more operations, half elective, was going to have plastic surgery, he became angry. Suddenly Paul's and the beast's removal of multiple organs in Figures 9-7 and 9-11 took on a new dimension, and he was able to see that his mother's problems were hers and not his.

Encouraged by all this progress, Paul wanted to stop therapy, but I was emphatic that this was not the right time to do that. He then had a dream which prompted a drawing (not shown) of, in his words, "a spider-crab creature with the fangs and claws of a woman but the red eyes of a man." To me, this was an image of the collective negative mother with angry animus eyes. There is a vortex in the drawing that can be interpreted as a sinister spider web, made for catching victims.

According to Paul, the subsequent drawing is of a masculine amphibian/reptilian monster injecting something evil into Paul's anus

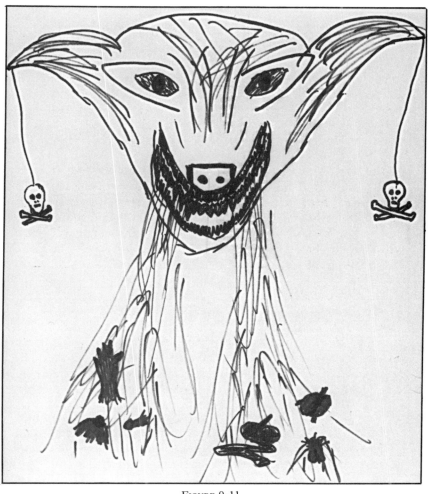

FIGURE 9-11
"Killer Beast"

FIGURE 9-12
Poisoned, Sodomized, and Consumed

(Figure 9-12). At the same time, a froglike crab is cramming something evil down Paul's mouth. These violations are occurring while
Paul is being consumed by "it"—an all-powerful and pervasive evil
energy. Paul is immobilized: "I'm trying to push her [the crab]
away, but I'm failing. I'm paralyzed. I'm suffering. I'm sick, un-
happy, helpless, hopeless." He saw himself as an innocent adolescent
being poisoned by his mother and father; thus the drawing uses
images from the collective unconscious to depict mother and father
complexes on a personal level.

Paul's next drawing (Figure 9-13) discloses a death-rebirth
theme, showing worms eating away at his insides; nevertheless it has
a positive dimension. "They'll die," he said. In fact, the worms do
disappear in the drawing and there is hope, represented by a final
musical note. At this time, he started to play the guitar again, some-

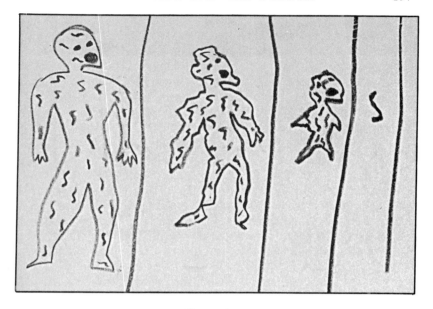

FIGURE 9-13
Death and Rebirth

thing he had not done since high school, and had never mentioned
to me before. Music is an ancient healing method; Chiron taught
Asklepios both medicine and music.

Two weeks later Paul had a nightmare and subsequently he cried
out to God for help. Paul was not a religious person, so he did not
understand what had happened, but he knew it was meaningful. I
felt he was at last beginning to experience the spiritual birth of his
true self. It is noteworthy that this rebirth experience occurred at
nine months into his therapy.

Action and Resolution

As Paul was entering Stage III of his illness and therapy, many
positive changes were taking place in his life. He returned to work,
moved into a new house, and proceeded with his divorce. He also
became interested in the Tao and embarked on a spiritual quest,
suggesting that he had made contact with the Self. He was playing

bridge (symbolically an interesting word) with his mother as his partner for the first time in ten years, and winning regularly. He had no more symptoms of spastic colon. He established a new relationship with a young woman that made him feel more playful and confident. This relationship lasted four months; then he began a second, even more satisfying relationship, with a professional woman. He ate all the food she cooked and had no fear of being poisoned. He also began to relate sexually with this woman.

One year and five months into analytical therapy, after a nine-month hiatus in the art therapy aspect, Paul brought in a drawing, called "The Death of the Patriarch" (Figure 9-14). It's a sad picture representing an active symbolic killing of the repressive, negative personal and collective father. There are three nails in the father's head, a cross and two arrows in his back, and a spear in his chest. He is hanging by a noose as well. At this point, Paul was also writing poetry, something he had not done since college, which was a hopeful sign of New Life.

Paul's subsequent drawing was completed one year and nine months into therapy, and is very interesting (Plate XV). It brings to mind Jung's view that there is an American Indian in every American. It features a large bird that is no longer black (as all the birds were in his previous pictures) but is rather an earthy brown. A similar color scheme is reflected in three dark stones with markings in orange. Orange is a warm color, not like the harsh red that signifies rage. The orange lightning in the drawing represents new energy.

The stones in this drawing are especially indicative of Paul's new-found sense of wholeness. They are earthy and solid, suggesting that he was feeling more solid, joined with Mother Earth. On the largest stone is a double-headed bird, resembling the axlike weapon that in many ancient matriarchal societies was a common symbol of growth. The symbol on the next-largest stone represents a union of opposites: the sun (male) and the moon (female) with a division sign in the middle. The third, oval-shaped stone, represents his anima. This stone contains several important symbols: cross, sun, serpent, arrow, and crescent—standing, respectively, for sacrifice, life force, healing, masculine and feminine.

Two years into his therapy, Paul initiated a relationship with a third woman (his relationship with the second woman had lasted a year). The third woman, a weaver, was exceptionally loving, accept-

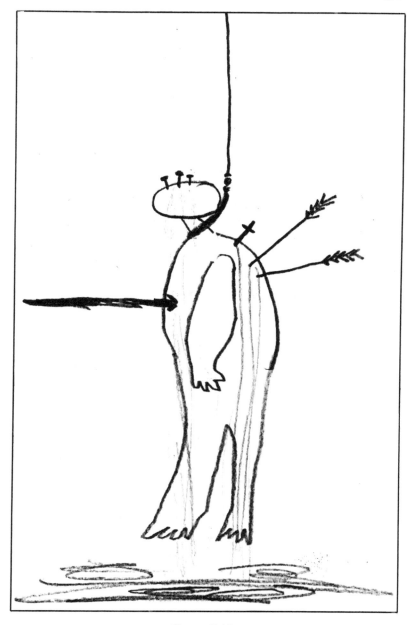

FIGURE 9-14
"Death of the Patriarch"

ing, and creative. He said that this relationship was the best he had ever had with a woman, sexually and nonsexually, and that he had even thought about marrying her and having a family.

On reflection, Paul said he thought that maybe he had found the ideal relationship with a woman. To me, this revealed that he had forged a meaningful inner connection with his anima, because a successful *inner marriage* of this nature often enables patients like Paul to envision a successful *outer marriage*. Paul then recalled a painful memory: When he was fifteen years old, his mother stripped him in front of his younger brothers to see if he had any pubic hairs. Since he had differentiated his anima from his negative mother complex, he could now handle this memory; now he could see it as an example of his mother's pathology, not his.

Things were generally going well for Paul during this period of his therapy. He was exercising, playing baseball (something he hadn't done in many years), and dancing. He made love before coming to one session and told me about it with enthusiasm.

Regression, Soul-Searching, and Overcoming Fear

One of Paul's last active imagination drawings (not included) was completed two years and three months into his therapy. It was a self-portrait, clearly a Christ-like figure, made after he had swum in a pool with his lover, something he had not done for twenty years because of his fear of being poisoned by chlorine. Reflecting on this drawing, Paul said: "All my life, I've suffered and sacrificed for others. I don't think I want to do that anymore." He had seen his spiritual Self in the drawing, in what he termed the cosmic purple in his eyes, a very peaceful part of the composition. There were also mummy (chrysalis) figures in his eyes, suggesting that he was perhaps putting to rest some negative personal and collective mother issues. He maintained that his eyes were crying blood (his lower eyelids were red), because he was seeing and experiencing separation from his mother (thus indicating that the death of the negative mother complex was very painful and upsetting). His mouth was angry red; he related that he had been making nasty comments to his lover and that had distressed him. Regarding why he drew himself as Christ-like, he said that he identified with him and had felt, since the age of thirty, that he would attest to Christ's second coming.

When I implied that this position was ego inflated, he became very angry with me. But at our next meeting, Paul agreed with equanimity that the drawing represented an important, even transcending, symbolic death-rebirth experience.

Paul's self-portrait/Christ-like drawing was made just prior to Christmas, a time he had always found difficult to endure emotionally. However, this year he was able to celebrate Christmas joyfully. He bought his lover a hundred dollars' worth of plants for Christmas, which I thought symbolized continued positive growth in the anima direction, resulting in an even more meaningful outer bond with a woman.

Subsequently, Paul did another drawing (Plate XVI), which features a froglike creature that he said was giving birth to "dead shit" that was yellow, brown, and red (pus, shit, and blood). He described the black part of the creature as his masculine nature and the green part as his feminine nature. Paul felt he was getting something out that he hated. He called it "a mindless, tortured, dead piece of junk."

On a collective level, Paul had joined the two destructive and abusive psychic parts in Figure 9-12 (the masculine reptile monster and the feminine, froglike creature) into a primitive but androgynous whole that was giving birth to something abhorrent that needed to die. This horrific picture is actually a healing image of a death-rebirth experience.

Consequently, Paul had a dream in which he is married to his previous wife and is dying. Either he has killed himself or he has been killed by someone, but only half of him actually dies, making him angry that all of him isn't dead. As the dream goes on, he is killed and revived again and again. When we discussed the dream, he felt that it symbolized that he was on the verge of relinquishing the negative part of his ego associated with his ex-wife and his mother.

Two years and five months into therapy, Paul obtained home movies of his childhood that his parents no longer wanted and were going to throw out! Reviewing these movies turned out to be a very intense and painfully important part of his treatment. It was clear from these films that he had had a very deprived and difficult early childhood. He was not breast-fed but, rather, fed in a detached way, with a propped up bottle and very little human contact. He appeared sad as an infant; at an early age, he was expected to perform for his parents. During his gloomy latency years, he felt that his childhood was over. As a teenager he continued to look depressed.

Two years and six months into his healing journey, Paul felt that he was out of his severe depression and talked about terminating therapy. He felt that watching the home movies and discussing them had helped him enormously, and that he now accepted himself—his wounds and limitations as well as his strengths. He declared that he was a survivor and a creative person and that he was going to challenge the unknown despite his fears. He held on to a mental image of a black dot in the center of a white field, symbolizing that he was on target or at a turning point. He started getting physical massages two or three times a week, and he had a dream that he was taming a male lion that metamorphosed into a female kitten.

At two years and nine months into therapy, Paul decided that he wanted to have a break. I concurred, and we did not meet for three months. During this time, he wrote a computer program for a video game, which involved a woman stripping herself. Paul was letting go of his negative mother as the stripper of his masculine persona and ego/self identity. His own creative anima was able to strip herself (of course with the assistance of Paul's new ego). Following the development of this video game, Paul felt more secure as a man.

Three years into the analytical therapy, I was seeing Paul only once every two to four weeks. He talked about the need to nurture his chrysalis so his butterfly (soul) could emerge. His relationship with his female companion was very affirming. He had a landmark fortieth birthday that he was able to celebrate with her, his favorite brother, and his brother's wife. His lover wanted to get married, and he talked to her about it, but Paul was not yet ready to make such a commitment.

"Soul-Making":
Reunion with Anima and Acceptance of Self

Two months later Paul began to write a number of songs having to do with what he called "soul-making."[7] He wanted to destroy once and for all his lingering negative ego-image and renew contact with his early identity and soul (the true self that, he felt, had died when he was a teenager). The series of soul-making songs Paul wrote were reflections on the traumatic auto accident in his past and on the turbulent years with his first wife. They were sad songs about his being cut off from his internal Self and about losing his soul. He was intrigued by his idea of soul-making as a way to find his soul, and he wanted to stay in therapy to work on separation from mother, which is the essential task of Stage III.

In life, as in therapy, there are ups and downs, and predictably, Paul's depression returned. He developed insomnia, but he was no longer suicidal. He again focused on the idea of his depression being biological; so I referred him to another psychiatrist for a consultation (this colleague was extremely sensitive and an expert in Affective Disorders) to see if there were any antidepressants that might help him. Asendin (amoxapine) in low doses coupled with low-dose Xanax actually did alleviate some of his depressive symptoms. Also during this period, he was informally counselling a depressed and suicidal woman friend, which I interpreted as a strong sign that he himself was recovering.

Three years and five months into his therapy, Paul felt emotionally trapped and remembered an episode from his past when his father trapped him in the cellar. His last active imagination drawing (Plate XVII), entitled "Anima," was completed at this time. Describing it, he said: "It is a woman tied to a pole by biology, the black cesspool of a biochemical depression, struggling to free herself and about to escape." He thought that her blue body represented his feminine and unconscious side, and that his spirit and soul were emerging (from the conch) and would join with the woman when she was free.

At three years and six months into his therapy, Paul was down to one-third of his former daily dosage of Asendin and was feeling much less depressed and more confident. He started to write a short story, he was exercising regularly, and he was working hard to set up professional projects for the autumn. Meanwhile, his relationship with his woman friend was continuing to prosper. During this period, he dreamed that he was a woman and the best at everything: He-as-she was standing in a swimming pool and was slated to marry a man. Paul felt very good about this dream and interpreted it as representing a union of his feminine nature with his masculine nature.

Two months later, Paul brought in the story that he had written. It is about a man (himself) being kidnapped by a vile authority figure who is going to perform homosexual acts on him, including rape.[8]

After escaping, the man accepts and loves himself. Paul felt as if he had been reborn in the process of writing this story, having worked through the death of the malevolent father complex in a creative way.

Four weeks later, Paul was no longer depressed and was talking about getting married and buying a new home. However, during the next two months he became increasingly depressed, experiencing insomnia and thoughts of dying, and asked to be hospitalized, which was a complete turnaround from his attitude during the early months of his therapy with me. The same biologically oriented psychiatric colleague hospitalized Paul and had various tests done to see if a new medication regimen could help him. Synthroid was thus added to his other two medications, Asendin and Xanax. He seemed to do better with this regimen. Paul also decided to stop seeing me, and instead to see this other psychiatrist. I understood and accepted his decision to separate from me, as it was an extension of his desire for separation from mother and his parental complexes, and an act of independence that would make him feel separate from—and in control of—the healing process itself.

Nearly four years after our initial session, in our last face-to-face informal meeting (which I arranged), I shared with Paul that I was moving to Texas. He informed me that although he was still episodically depressed, he felt psychologically stronger than ever and not at all suicidal. He had just finished coauthoring a textbook and loved his work. Paul's relationship with the weaver was closer than ever. He continued to see the other psychiatrist every two weeks, to be gradually decreased to every month or two over the next year. We agreed to stay in touch.

My last contact with Paul was by letter, nine years after our first meeting. He communicated that he was doing extremely well in his work, had just gotten married to the same woman, and was considering having children. His depressive episodes were very infrequent and mild. He had not had any psychiatric treatment in four years and was no longer taking any medication, having stopped the Synthroid prescribed by his internist two years ago. Paul had completely transformed his depression into creative work, living, and loving. Time had proved that his post-egocide metamorphosis into a healthier, happier person was, in fact, durable.

Paul's experience of egocide and transformation enabled him to eventually alter his own identity from psychiatric patient to liberated person. He continues to partake in self-healing and, accordingly, clearly differentiates himself from his parents. The path is open and unencumbered for Paul to have continued success at work, a fulfilling marriage, and a rewarding family life.

With Paul's story, we conclude our in-depth application of the egocide and transformation model for individual analytical therapy. In the next chapter we will explore major crisis points and discuss transforming the resultant bouts of depression.

PART IV

SPIRAL OF CHANGE: SYMBOLIC DEATH AND NEW LIFE

CHAPTER 10

Crisis Points:
How Egocide Can Help

"I find the great thing in this world is not so much
where we stand as in what direction we are moving."

—OLIVER WENDELL HOLMES

T<small>HE</small> spiral seems to be emblematic of the overall nature of the egocide and transformation process. Counterclockwise and descending, it suggests devolution, disintegration, regression, and collectivization. Clockwise and ascending, it suggests evolution, maturation, progression, and individuation. This is my interpretation of the spiral images we've just seen and read about in the four transforming journeys of Rebecca, Gary, Sharon, and Paul.[1] Let us now examine how the spiral may twist and turn in the ordinary course of an individual's life.

Our human life span is like a river with its stagnant places, calmly flowing stretches, periods of rapids, and dangerous whirlpools. These are naturally occurring periods and times of crisis. Although these crisis points are often stressful and full of despair, they are also openings for change and growth. We have seen how egocide allows us to transform depression, and this transpersonal experience gives us hope. Similarly, seeing our lives as part of a larger human journey with its high roads and low roads provides us with another useful viewpoint. Such a point of view involves the human life cycle, which is developmental; one of its chief proponents is Erik Erikson.[2]

How do Erikson's stages of human development benefit us, when we are depressed, hopeless, and suicidal? By offering up hope, which Erikson links to trust and faith in infancy and to wisdom and integrity in old age. A developmental view coupled with a transpersonal one allows us to flow with life, seeing crises also as occasions to transcend and transform.

The human life cycle with its crisis points offers us the chance to experience Symbolic Death and New Life at least three times in our life. These three regularly occurring times are: 1) *early-life crisis,* 2) *mid-life crisis,* and 3) *late-life crisis.* At each of these three developmental points, we have the opportunity to commit egocide and undergo a transformation that will deepen our capacity to feel and bring us closer to our unique nature.

Developmental Crisis Points

In the Jungian view, a baby is a distinct individual who comes out of the substrate of the totality called the Self. Since the fetus is in a state of unconsciousness, the ego—as a potential entity—begins to form at birth. The newborn is then in the realm of consciousness and is confronted by the environment with the need to ensure its own emotional and physical nurturance.

From the moment of birth, the ego drives the self; but both the ego and the self are based on the archetype of the Self, which represents the center and totality of the psyche. As the ego identifies with, and introjects, the parents, a split develops from the Self. Supportive and nurturing parents encourage the development of the child's authentic ego and self—the true self. However, without proper nurturing and support—either through over- or under-parenting—the infant forms a negative mother and father identification and the seeds are sown for the child to develop a false self.[3]

Margaret Mahler and her co-workers maintain that the birth of the psychological self—a sense of self as a separate individual—occurs around the age of two.[4] Positive (healthy) and negative (unhealthy) ego aspects, as well as the true self and false self, respectively, continue to develop as the child matures from age two until adolescence. In Erikson's developmental blueprint,[5] the first stage, trust vs. mistrust (birth to two years), is followed by: autonomy vs. shame and doubt (two to three years); initiative vs. guilt (three to five years); and industry vs. inferiority (six to twelve years).

The first four stages of the life cycle culminate in adolescence (ages 13–19), with the critical psychological issue being to establish one's identity or experience identity diffusion. This is the early-life crisis and the first opportunity for Symbolic Death and New Life. If the young individual does not rebel and break from the parents and their introjected egos (false self) during adolescence, he or she is a likely candidate for emotional disturbance and the development of a divided self. The seeds of the true self are then clearly embedded in the underground psychic soil of anger and guilt, and manifest through the false self as depressive and suicidal states as well as personality disorders. This tragic scenario was evident in the case histories of Rebecca, Gary, Sharon, and Paul. Jung dealt primarily with the mid-life crisis—which is epidemic today; now with the advent of "future shock"[6] and children growing up too fast, we also have to deal with increasing early-life crisis.

Early-life Crisis

Parents, teachers, and counselors know that adolescence is the initial major crisis point in normal psychological development. The ego, which has formed primarily in identification with the parents and the outer collective norms of society, is challenged for the first time to become fully independent. Though the original manifestation of selfhood at age two allowed for partial separation in identity from mother and father, adolescence—with its tumultuous biological, psychological, social, and existential/spiritual changes—is when one's own wholly separated identity emerges.

In characterizing adolescence as the only normal psychosis, Anna Freud was indicating that pubescence is an expectable time period for ego death to occur.[7] However, given the adolescent's angry and rebellious nature, egocide, the killing of the ego, would be a more accurate description. Specifically, the teenager must symbolically kill the dominant introjected parental ego, as well as the persona and ego-image derived from the established collective. Neumann characterizes it this way:

> In the normal life of the individual, the symbolic murder of the parents or its equivalent is a phase of development which cannot be omitted with impunity; often enough, as a large number of cases of [arrested] development have taught us, the advantage of being a "good child" who shrinks from the [symbolic] "murder" of his parents, is purchased at the perilous cost or sacrifice of one's independence in later life.[8]

During this crisis in ego evolution (or more accurately revolution), the adolescent psyche is so fragile that the consequences of any strong emotional experience may be tragic. For example, if an adolescent falls in love, his or her new ego-image can become so wrapped up in the relationship that if it fails, he or she feels completely worthless. This Romeo and Juliet complex is a frequent factor in teen suicide. An adolescent who encounters opposition to his or her choice of life goals can also be driven to severe depression or suicidal hopelessness (as was clearly demonstrated by Sharon's case in Chapter 8). A poignant example is offered in the film *Dead Poet's Society*. The adolescent hero wants to be an actor (true self), but his parents want him to be a medical doctor (false self). Torn by this dilemma, he kills himself, when, in fact, what needs to be killed is the inauthentic (and therefore negative) dominant parental ego. He needed to commit egocide, not suicide.

Teachers, counselors, and parents can apply the egocide and transformation model to help young people weather the shocks and setbacks of adolescence more successfully. For example, young people could be taught to appreciate that if they fail at something, such as a relationship or a school challenge, only a part of their ego, not their total ego, has been wounded. By committing egocide and establishing contact with their own spiritual center or Self, at such times, adolescents can continue on their pathway to self-actualization, rather than taking a permanent detour to self-destruction.

If parents who read this would remain mindful that a breaking away from the parental ego identification is essential for young people in order to develop their own sense of self, both groups would handle conflicts more effectively. Thereby, the prevalence of teenage suicide would hopefully decrease; and, with educational efforts aimed at adolescents and their parents, the prevalence of youth egocide and transformation would, we can hope, increase. This hope is based on the fact that depression can yield creative gifts and does not have to mean actual death but rather Symbolic Death and New Life.

During young adulthood, a sense of ego- and self-identity crystallizes as the individual takes on new roles: for example, developing a career, becoming a spouse, and a parent. In Erikson's schema, during young adulthood one struggles with a sense of intimacy vs. isolation with one's self and others. Then in adulthood there is a period of generativity vs. self-absorption and stagnation, typically involving work and family. When the individual reaches the top of the mountain and the apex in the spiral of ego development, there is a great feeling of achievement (and, often, an inflated ego). Despite this feeling, however, there is usually a sense that something is still lacking. The point at which one cannot go any higher is called the mid-life crisis. This occurs because the ego cannot remain motionless, and now perceives that it can only regress in a downward spiral. It is where Dante begins his *Inferno*, being lost in the middle of one's life, wandering into a dark wood, and descending into a psychological and existential hell.

Mid-life Crisis

The high noon years represent the second principal developmental crisis. For the person who did not resolve most of his or her true self vs. false self issues during adolescence, the mid-life crisis is even more intense. This was apparent in all four transforming journeys (Chapters 6–9). In other words, an individual who has been living according to an inner sense of personal myth based on the true self will have a less severe mid-life crisis. In a mid-life crisis the ultimate danger is that the person will fall or jump off the mountain top and yield to a self-destructive process. The alternative is that the individual will gradually and constructively let go of or symbolically kill his or her negative persona and ego-image (false self) and commit egocide and undergo transformation.

However, if an individual in a mid-life crisis resists a positive (ego-Self) identity change, then the shadow, often through unresolved parental complexes, can form a suicidal complex which manifests as a suicidal self. The result, as in Elvis Presley's case, may be suicide. In contrast, a person who makes a positive identity change, like Betty Ford, will develop integrity rather than despair (Erikson's last developmental stage), and move toward wholeness in his or her social and natural environment.

A developmental perspective encourages you to develop hope through endurance. Erikson's developmental view is an evolutionary process (an ascending and descending spiral) built on a foundation of trust that moves toward development of autonomy, initiative, industry, identity, intimacy, generativity, and integrity. However, in Erikson's, as in Jung's, psychology, all the opposites must be confronted, accepted, and then transcended, which leads to a spiraling double helix psychological model. This is in sharp contrast to a descending spiral built on mistrust and leading to shame and doubt, guilt, inferiority, identity diffusion, isolation, self-absorption and stagnation, disgust and despair, a bleak alternative to individuation. A person involved in an individuation process develops and manifests the following essential strengths (in tandem with associated basic virtues), which are directly related to the eight stages of the life cycle: drive (hope); self-control (will); direction (purpose); method (competence); devotion (fidelity); affiliation (love); production (care); renunciation (wisdom). It is not by accident that Erikson's last essential strength is renunciation; my sense is that he means renunciation of ego and the material world, and the wisdom that he writes about represents the wisdom of soul, spirit, and Self.

Late-life Crisis

As longevity continues to increase, we are experiencing the graying of our country and the world. More and more of us will experience old age and late-life crisis, the third expectable developmental turning point. Egocide and transformation is again a useful model for facing the multiple losses of our sunset years and finding new meaning in our lives. Late-life crisis occurs when we have to renounce the very family and work personas (roles) and ego-images (identities) that we struggled so hard to attain and refine. The children grow up and leave; jobs are lost by failure, disability or retirement; spouses die; we develop various diseases; and finally we face death. In confronting these partings, losses, and endings we can develop a sense of grace manifested by integrity (a sense of spiritual wholeness) and wisdom because we are able to renounce ego for the last time and begin to naturally rejoin the Self. Or, we can develop cynicism, disgust and despair.

The concept of egocide and transformation has particular relevance for the elderly. Older individuals, many of whom are cut off from interpersonal relationships and social support, are very vulnerable to feelings of alienation and impotence, which make them prime candidates for depression. Statistically speaking, the rate of suicide climbs dramatically among older individuals, especially white men. Given this situation, there ought to be concerted efforts through educational campaigns to inform people prior to retirement that their old personas and dominant ego-images must symbolically die before they can go through a healthy transformation to the next phase of their natural lives.

As adults who are not yet elderly, we can learn to provide better-informed (and, therefore, more competent and satisfying) at-home care for our elderly loved ones. By putting them in nursing homes, we are walling ourselves off from our past, and from our future. Each of us is going to be old someday. Unless we know more about the senescent ego issues ahead of time, we won't know how to handle old age on a psychological level when our time comes.

The beginning of life and the end of life parallel the sunrise and the sunset—both are beautiful and remarkable. If we could just keep this comparison in our minds as a transcendent symbol, it might help us to care more compassionately for our youngest and oldest folks. Let's honor birth and death and thereby the cycle of eternal renewal.

Divorce and Death: Opportunities for Rebirth

In addition to the major but expected developmental stages of life, depression is most likely when we face the unexpected loss of a loved one, whether it be through divorce or death, which are, in fact, very similar in their impact on survivors. Both represent painful separations associated with feelings of dissolution, emptiness, and irreversibility. In such an emotional climate, the ego can easily spiral downwards toward severe depression and suicide. Egocide and transformation can help us cope effectively with both of these losses in a healthy and productive manner. Let's first consider the loss associated with divorce and then proceed to consider the loss associated with the death of a loved one.

Divorce: Parting of the Ways

A divorce is, in essence, a mini-death. The persona and ego-image that were intimately involved in the role and identity of being a spouse have ceased, often suddenly, to be viable. Thus, we grieve not only for the person who has been lost, but also for the part of ourselves that was defined in relationship to the lost person. In this lonely and extremely distressing time of *egocide,* it is necessary to reconnect with one's psychic center or Self in order to transform our grief.

For the divorced man who is alone, feeling depressed, and dead to the world, it is his *anima* that serves as a transcendent function, that is, *she* must become the focus and agent of egocide and transformation.[9] After all, the anima is the archetype of his feminine nature—an aspect of his identity that is especially troubled in the wake of a failed marriage. In fact, it is often the projected anima that got him into trouble and the mess of divorce in the first place. Frequently, the anima appears in his life as the woman he has an affair with, or leaves his wife for, or marries next. The anima problem will remain until it is faced internally. The anima appears in a man's dreams as a goddess-like woman who is familiar and yet not a known woman in his life. At times the anima is accompanied by a serpent, an ancient healing symbol. When a divorced man has a dream of union with such an anima figure, he is symbolically loving the feminine side of himself. An inner marriage is taking place: a renewal and healing experience after the ego death. In other words, the man has symbolically killed his outmoded and negative injured spouse ego and has been transformed into a more integrated, Self-oriented individual. His inner marriage provides a better foundation for having a successful outer marriage in the future.

For a divorced woman, the transcendent function would be the *animus* or archetype of the masculine spirit. In a dream, this figure would take the form of a stranger, yet a familiar god-like figure, or *he* could appear with, or as, a serpent or the wind.[10] Following the dissolution and fragmentation of the ego that occurs after a divorce, contact and union with the animus leads to a new axis with the Self and thus creates a new ego-identity for the woman that equips her to live an independent life with open possibilities for new and constructive love relationships.

Assuming it is not a mutual decision to divorce, the spouse who initiates the divorce puts himself or herself in the role of a banisher; therefore he or she tends to feel guilt that can lead to depression. Alternatively, the banished partner tends to feel rejected and worthless, which can also lead to depression. At any rate, both parties need a period of hibernation or incubation. Depression in this context can be a facilitator of growth. Isolation and solitude allow the depressed individual to go through a time of gestation in his or her own darkness or *nigredo*, according to the alchemical studies of Jung.[11] Out of this immersion in darkness comes the guiding light of the soul, the inspiring feminine force within the man, or the revitalizing masculine spirit force within the woman. This inner transformation is a fundamental step in self-actualization or individuation, as seen in the four healing journeys (Chapters 6–9).

Death: The Ultimate Loss

What makes the experience of losing a loved one by death uniquely painful is that it is so final. Unlike a divorce of two living individuals, with each continuing his or her life and possibly even maintaining contact, death represents an irrevocable loss of presence. Death leaves a survivor especially vulnerable to feelings—and memories—of being abandoned and absolutely alone in the world.

After the death itself, the surviving party goes through a prolonged period (three to eighteen months) of withdrawal and grieving; and often tends to identify with the departed loved one in order to maintain a symbolic contact. Sometimes this can lead to an introjection of the lost loved one and to an ego-identity that is in part (and, at times, almost totally) connected to the deceased. If a person goes through this introjection as a child, he or she may create a false self that lingers and leads to depression during the adult years. When losing a loved one, such an individual frequently has to go through egocide in order to let go of the false identity. Otherwise, the person may actually commit suicide to join the deceased. The sad story of the poet Sylvia Plath, who finally succeeded in killing herself after several attempts, illustrates this desire for a mystical reunion through suicide. Her first attempt at suicide was to bury herself under dirt in her basement—symbolic of returning to Mother Earth—so that her spirit could be with her father, who died when she was a preadolescent girl.[12]

When we lose a loved one by death, we have to release ourselves from this person at some point, or we will be so identified with the deceased that it will cripple our own development. It is with this delicate disengagement process that egocide and transformation can be especially helpful. A symbolic killing and letting go of the inner presence of the deceased loved one (for example, by talking it through to the end) allows us to transcend such a profound loss and to go on living out our own personal myth.

Jung says that an individual becomes wounded and submerged in a state of withdrawal following such a major loss; this dark sea of introversion, he notes, is "between annihilation and new life."[13] The individual's ego goes through a symbiotic and Symbolic Death experience, identifying with the lost loved one. There is a regression into the sea of the unconscious (the *prima materia* or the collective—archetypal—womb of the mother) that is the prerequisite for rebirth based on establishing a new relationship between the ego and the Self. This leads to a transfiguration in which the ego is subordinate to the Self, and the individuation process may then advance.

Resolving the Issue of Global Death

The personal issue of suicide is inextricably linked to collective or global death. Since the explosion of the atomic bomb at the close of World War II, mass or world suicide, what I term *omnicide,* has become a real possibility at any moment (see Table 10-1). As Jung prophetically stated sixty years ago:[14]

> Let [people—nations] accumulate sufficient engines of destruction and the devil within [them] will soon be unable to resist putting them to their fated use. It is well known that fire-arms go off of themselves if only enough of them are together.

Even if nuclear disarmament succeeds, the knowledge of how to make weapons of mass destruction will never disappear, and terrorists are more than likely to use the technology. Jung emphasized that the issue of self-destruction, on a personal or world scale, begins and ends with the individual because "we are at war with ourselves." The President of the United States, the head of the People's Republic of China, the ruler of Iraq, and a terrorist are solitary persons who, in some twisted suicidal plan, could destroy the planet and kill everyone else as well. As Nazi Germany demonstrated, nations are capable of following a crazed leader and taking a suicidal course that could threaten the survival of the species. Hence, *to be or not to be* is both a personal and collective issue; and the struggle with persona and ego-image plagues nations (i.e., the nation's role in the world community and its nation-image) and the world as well as individual citizens.

The Whole Human Family on earth (with all of its animals, plants, seas, and minerals) is the collective equivalent of the Self, our center and our totality. Individuals as well as nations must undergo the equivalent of egocide (nationcide) and transformation in order for the human race to fulfill its creative potential. Serving such a higher

TABLE 10-1
PREVENTING OMNICIDE

Stages	Cultural and Human Family Therapy
I	Resistance by nations and negative projections (evil empire) Apocalypse now Loss, sense of failure, and suffering (defeats in Vietnam and Afghanistan) Threat of nuclear annihilation (mass suicide or omnicide) Building trust and positive international relations Withdrawal of negative projections Regression in the service of culture *(true nation)* Death of the evil empire *(false nation)* nationcide
II	Strong mutually interdependent alliances Archetypal positive and negative projections (death-rebirth struggle) Regression in the service of the Whole Human Family culture (nation)-Whole Human Family axis (United Nations)
III	Regression in the service of the earth (world) See earth realistically as seen from space (death-rebirth experience) See all cultures as valuable and interdependent earth (world)-Whole Human Family axis Rebirth of world community/mother earth Sense of wholeness, universal purpose, and meaning

principle means, for example, that we need to rise above selfishness and stop polluting the earth's biosphere with toxic smoke, chemicals, garbage, and weapons of destruction. Instead of killing ourselves and our earth literally, we need to go through a symbolic death-rebirth experience.[15]

Benjamin Wolman offers an interpretation of the egoistic problems suffered by human beings as a whole. He attributes these to the growth of technology, the rise in importance attached to material possessions, and the increasing incidence and prevalence of interpersonal violence and family break-ups. In his description of "the anticulture of suicide," he refers to internal poisons like alcohol and drug abuse, as well as external poisons like industrial pollutants and nuclear weapons.[16] He states:

When the anthropologist Claude Levi-Strauss was asked what he thought of contemporary humanity, he compared [modern] human beings to maggots in a sack of flour. With the increase of the maggot population, maggots become somehow conscious of one another even before they experience any tactile contact, and they secrete toxins which kill at a distance. They poison the flour they inhabit, and eventually they all die. Something similar, Dr. Strauss said, is happening in our time.

Others express more concern over the increasing alienation among individuals caused by today's rapid sociological and technological change as Durkheim forewarned us.[17] The elderly, who tend to be rigidly set in their ways, and adolescents, who are just beginning to form their ways, are most vulnerable to this kind of alienation. But all segments of society are affected. Wolman states:

The estrangement inherent in our way of life; the decline of family ties; the depersonalization in human relationships; and the loss of the individual in mass society are probably the main, or at least the important, reasons why so many people tend to hurt one another and to hurt themselves.[18]

What can we as individuals do toward resolving these kinds of overwhelming problems in human society? We must first become more aware of what is going on within ourselves. If we can commit egocide and thus transcend the self-destructive complexes within ourselves, then we can begin to help make a positive difference on a collective level. If enough people (and nations) go through the symbolic death-rebirth experience of egocide (and nationcide) and transformation, then there is hope for humanity as a whole.

For the Individual and the World:
A Paradigm Shift Offering Hope

The paradigm shift required for an individual to transcend self-destruction is for the ego to sacrifice itself to a higher principle. This kind of paradigm shift is a direct challenge to behavioral and ego psychologists, to biomedically oriented psychiatrists, and to individualists who think that looking out for number one is the ideal. For these people, the process I am advocating represents a truly revolutionary change that they are predisposed to resist. Nevertheless, it is a change that must—and, I believe, will—be made by an increasing number of people, until the whole species is affected.

For a new paradigm to survive, there must be enough supportive people at the time of its origin to make sure that it is not dismissed before it has time to be scientifically investigated and confirmed. Afterwards, the theory needs even more time to evolve to the point where it can replace previous, entrenched theories. Self psychology, a modern theory originated by Jung and nurtured by Rogers, Maslow, and Kohut, is still in the process of gaining ascendance over other theories such as those of Freud and post-Freudian ego psychologists. However, it is destined to cause a paradigm shift in psychology, whereby a higher, more spiritual principle, i.e., the Self—*not* the ego—will be considered the proper center of the psyche.

There are striking parallels between the egocide and transformation paradigm and the process of developing psychic wholeness that is described in the 1200-year-old Chinese work, *The Secret of the Golden Flower*.[19] The existence of this remarkable book reminds us that the human quest to transform inner space has a long history. According to the text, the development of the golden flower, or immortal spirit-body, is dependent on holding to the way of the Tao (the middle path) and to the unity of opposites (yin and yang: the dark feminine soul and the light masculine spirit)—a discipline which separates the ego from oppositional conflicts so that it can again become part of the Tao, the undivided great one. The notion that the ego is part of the Tao is almost identical to Jung's concept of the ego as secondary to and part of the Self. The development of the golden flower actually mirrors the human life cycle and the attainment of integrity and wisdom: the ego emerges out of the unity of opposites—the Self (light and dark, masculine and feminine); then there is a Symbolic Death of the ego (egocide); finally, a return to unity—the Self.

Thus, whether we look at ancient philosophy or modern analytical psychology, we see the same message that the egocide and transformation paradigm communicates: A negative state of mind doesn't have to lead to a self-inflicted death that ends life altogether; but, rather, it can lead to a Symbolic Death that clears the way for a New

Life. From this vantage point depression is an opportunity for hope, growth, and metamorphosis, and suicide is a tragic mistake.

The answer to transforming our depressions and sufferings, to finding meaning in our individual lives and as members of one human family is both simple and difficult, but within our grasp: egocide and transformation.

EPILOGUE

"Suffering ceases to be suffering in
some way the moment it finds a meaning."

—Viktor Frankl

THE egocide and transformation paradigm first deserves your personal philosophical attention. You must look deep within yourself to understand how you value your own life and the lives of other human beings, even if you and they are severely depressed and suicidal.

Above all, egocide and transformation is based on the belief that each and every life has a meaning. This belief is beautifully articulated by Viktor Frankl, who transcended immense suffering in Nazi death camps by retaining his sense of "spiritual freedom—which cannot be taken away—that makes life meaningful and purposeful."[1] One of the most remarkable parts of Frankl's experience as a camp inmate was in preventing suicides. Utilizing Nietzsche's maxim, "He who has a *why* to live for can bear almost any *how*," Frankl would zero in on a specific reason for the afflicted person to live: for example, to see a loved one or to write a book. He states:

This uniqueness and singleness which distinguishes each individual and gives a meaning to his existence has a bearing on creative work as much as it does on human love. When the impossibility of replacing a person is realized, it allows the responsibility which a man has for his existence and its continuance to appear in all its magnitude. A man who becomes conscious of the responsibility he bears toward a human being who affectionately waits for him, or to an unfinished work, will never be able to throw away his life. He knows the "why" for his existence, and will be able to bear almost any "how."

Sometimes the fact that there is a why for each life is affirmed by a revelation that meaning pervades the universe. A recent experience from my own clinical practice illustrates such a revelation. Beth, a young woman and university student, came to see me after being discharged from a psychiatric hospital, where she had been admitted for severe depression and suicidal ideation. Her depression was relentless and seemed to be unending. The negative aspects of her ego-identity included a negative father complex (and cruel animus), various disaffirming shadow figures, and a negative mother complex.

At about nine months into analytical therapy, Beth plummeted into a psychic black hole associated with difficulty in functioning and the feeling that she was dead. It was in this context that she walked into my office for a session one day and reported that she had just seen a yellow butterfly outside her window. I was struck by this observation because it was winter, when there usually weren't any butterflies around. Much to our mutual amazement, at the precise moment when she was telling me about the butterfly (which she interpreted as a hopeful sign), a yellow butterfly appeared outside my office window, and then another yellow butterfly joined the first, and then they danced together, almost as if in a mating ritual. After a long silent period spent staring in awe at the two butterflies, Beth asked, "How do I pull myself out of this well of depression?" In response to her question I asked, "How does the butterfly get out of its cocoon?"

This incident and exchange turned out to be transformative for Beth. Following this session, she was no longer psychologically paralyzed by depression. A positive animus figure showed up in her dreams for the first time, and she began having affirming relationships with men. She had somehow found her lost soul: The butterfly, an ancient goddess symbol of transformation and rebirth, was its outer manifestation.

To me, the appearance of the butterfly was an example of synchronicity revealing that meaning pervades the entire span of existence. Martin Buber once said, "There is meaning in what for long was meaningless. Everything depends on the inner change; when this has taken place, and only then, does the world change."[2]

Now let's return to Frankl, who told his troubled comrades in Auschwitz "that human life, under any circumstances, never ceases to have meaning" and that they must not lose hope but should keep their courage in the certainty that the hopelessness of their struggle and sacrifice did not detract from its dignity and its meaning. Frankl models for all of us what Paul Tillich calls the "courage to be," which necessitates "spiritual self-affirmation" in the face of nonbeing.[3] The process of egocide and transformation is a means of giving depressed and suicidal individuals the courage, the affirmation, as well as the creative and healing response to life that they so desperately need.

Finally, my depressions have been doorways leading to New Life. Egocide has involved sacrifices—Symbolic Deaths of destructive parts of myself and creative processes (like the writing of this book)—which have led to transformations. My life now has purpose and meaning. I have found my holy ground and you, too, can find yours.

> "Darkness within darkness. The gateway to all understanding."
>
> —LAO TZU

> "Darkness gives birth to light."
>
> —C.G. JUNG

> "And we must extinguish the candle, put out the light and relight it;
> Forever must quench, forever relight the flame."
>
> —T.S. ELIOT

NOTES

(See Bibliography for complete information on all references.)

PROLOGUE

1. Kast (1988), 123–145.
2. After Sam died a book of his poems was published. See Weishaus (1974), preface by William Staple, introduction by D. H. Rosen, and postnote by Gary Snyder.
3. Maslow (1980).
4. Wilber (1980).
5. I mean surrender in the Buddhist sense of surrendering one's ego, which leads to transformation. See Wilber (1980) and Jung (1968a), 23–25.
6. I had already started investigating the problem of suicide while I was still in medical school. See Rosen (1970 and 1976a).
7. This estimate was arrived at by calculating the supposed number of suicides from a 1:100 ratio of survivors to suicides. As of 1990 there had been 20 known survivors of leaps off the Golden Gate Bridge; the actual number of survivors or suicides is not known.
8. This quote and the other quotes from this study are taken from Rosen (1975).
9. Rosen (1976b).
10. For a more comprehensive discussion of my philosophy on healing, see Rosen (1973, 1977, 1989, and 1992) and Reiser and Rosen (1985).
11. Regarding this statement, Joel Weishaus made this insightful comment: "The 'conscious ego act' is done with the ego not believing in its own demise. Thus suicide, as opposed to egocide, is not a sincere act, but the ego in its trickster mode."
12. Jung has even stated, "The shadow corresponds to a negative ego-

personality and includes all those qualities we find painful or regrettable." See Jung (1968b), 177.

13. Goldman (1990).

14. Ford and Chase (1988).

CHAPTER 1

1. For more details and discussion about this and much of the historical information in this chapter, see Menninger, Mayman, and Pruyser (1967) and Jackson (1986).

2. Jung (1963), 146–199.

3. Schmale (1973).

4. Engel (1962).

5. Gut (1989).

6. Storr (1989).

7. Regier, Hirschfeld, Goodwin, et al. (1988). These authors indicate that major (psychotic) depression was found in 3 percent of the U.S. population in a 6-month period and almost doubled to 5.8 percent for the period of a lifetime. They maintain that the annual cost to the nation of major depression is more than $16 billion. Dysthymia (minor or neurotic depression) was found in 3.3 percent of the population for the lifetime period. Bipolar disorder (manic-depressive illness) accounted for 1.2 percent of the population. When combining these three disorders, they found the six-month prevalence rate was 5.8 percent or around 10 million people, and the lifetime rate was 8.3 percent or about fourteen million Americans with a lifetime history of depression. In other words, clinical depression is one of our chief public health problems.

8. Frank (1963), 314–315 and Frank (1974).

9. von Bertalanffy (1968).

10. The three main monoamine neurotransmitters are: the catecholamines *norepinephrine* and *dopamine,* and the indoleamine *serotonin.* A growing body of evidence supports the notion that different forms of depression are indeed linked to low levels of each of these biochemical compounds. See Schildkraut, Green, and Mooney (1989). However, several studies have found increased catecholamine output and decreased neuroreceptor activity in depressed patients, which could result in a functional deficiency of neurotransmitters regardless of their actual concentrations. See Rush (1990).

11. Schildkraut, Green, and Mooney (1989).

12. Ader (1981).

13. This study, conducted by Fawzy Fawzy and collaborators including Norman Cousins, is reported in Cousins (1989), 250–263.

14. Cousins (1975).

15. Gershon, Berrettini, and Goldin (1989); Gershon, Hamovit, Guroff, et al. (1982); and Weissman, Kidd, and Prusoff (1982).
16. Abraham (1927).
17. Freud (1959).
18. Kohut (1977).
19. Quotes from Jung in this section are taken from Jung (1967a), 169–170, 293, 404, 408, and 435.
20. Odajnyk (1983).
21. Steinberg (1984).
22. Steinberg (1989).
23. Jarrett and Rush (1985).
24. Ferster (1973).
25. Beck (1972).
26. Arieti and Bemporad (1978).
27. Bowlby (1969 and 1973).
28. Paykel, Myers, Dienelt, et al. (1969).
29. Hirschfeld and Cross (1982).
30. For an argument in favor of this theory, see Bart (1974).
31. Engel (1977).
32. Rosen (1989).
33. The quotes in this section are from Frankl (1984).
34. Jung (1967b), 346 and Jung (1969), 486–487.
35. Maslow (1968).
36. Fulghum (1988).
37. Rosen (1987).
38. Rosen (1989).
39. Kast (1991) and Bloch (1959).

CHAPTER 2
1. Noyes (1968).
2. Alvarez (1972), Jaffe (1978).
3. Studies relating to African tribal attitudes toward suicide as well as general historical information about legal issues relating to suicide appear in Kiev (1972) and Stengel (1973).
4. Ellis (1923).
5. Durkheim (1951).
6. The statistics in this section are taken from two sources: Mishara, Baker, and Mishara (1976) and Peck, Farberow and Litman (1985).
7. Chivian, Robinson, Tudge, et al. (1988).
8. Louise Mahdi brought this to my attention.
9. Goethe (1957).
10. Phillips (1974).
11. Phillips and Caratensen (1986).

12. Gould and Shaffer (1986).
13. Freud (1959).
14. Menninger (1938).
15. Winnicott (1986), 173–182. Also Winnicott (1958, 1965, and 1971).
16. McAfee (1983).
17. Jung (1973), 434 and Jung (1975), 25 and 278–279.
18. Klopfer (1961).
19. Wheelwright (1987).
20. Hillman (1973).
21. French (1982).
22. Menninger, Mayman, and Pruyser (1963). The study cited is: Dorpat and Ripley (1960).
23. Beck and Kovacs (1975) and Beck, Brown, Berchick, et al. (1990).
24. Maltsberger and Buie (1974).
25. Kast (1990).
26. Humphry (1991).
27. Schur (1972).
28. Gibbs (1990).
29. Quill (1991).
30. Perhaps these taboos are changing—could the epidemics of youth suicide and incest be interrelated? It seems we need more scientific research studies and additional efforts to raise our consciousness regarding these painful and tragic predicaments.
31. von Franz (1978), 1.
32. Tabachnick (1973).
33. Stephen (1972).
34. Styron (1990).
35. After experiencing religious devotion and the love of his wife, most likely Styron found that his *anima* (his inner feminine) loved him and his true self (based on an ego-Self connection) loved her (his anima and his wife). He had found his soul and was animated again!

CHAPTER 3
1. Beebe (1992).
2. Morris and Beck (1976).
3. For a summary of recent placebo research, see Cousins (1989), 125–153, 231, and 328–336. Cousins quotes Dr. Henry Beecher as saying, "The greater the pain or anxiety, the more effective the placebo." Cousins himself concludes from all the placebo research that belief affects biology. He also suggests the placebo-like effect of treating pain through laughter therapy and suggests that the body produces its own biochemical agents, endorphins, which promote self-analgesia and self-anaesthesia.

4. Frank (1975).
5. Engel (1961). According to Engel, the normal grief process typically has three phases: (1) shock and disbelief; (2) developing awareness of the loss and the experience of sadness, anger, guilt, depression, helplessness, and hopelessness; (3) prolonged recovery phase during which time the final work of mourning is carried out, the painful loss is overcome, and a state of well-being is re-established.
6. For details of this and other major diagnostic classifications of depression, which inform most professionals, see the *Diagnostic and Statistical Manual of Mental Disorders* (4th edition), *DSM-IV (1994)*.
7. *DSM-IV,* 317–366.
8. Jackson (1986).
9. Psychiatry classifies SAD by using a Seasonal Pattern Specifier code. See *DSM-IV,* 389-390. Also see Wehr and Rosenthal (1989).
10. Schuckit and Montiero (1988); Motto (1975); and Alcoholics Anonymous (1987), which makes the same point as Motto.
11. Jung (1975), 623–625. Roland's story, told to Bill Wilson by a mutual friend, Ebby, was one of the key factors in the creation of Alcoholics Anonymous.
12. The risk schema was formulated by Robert Litman, M.D., but originally in terms of rates used routinely for suicide figures (general rate, risk = 10 per 100,000, low risk = 100 per 100,000 and so forth).
13. Beck and Kovacs (1975) and Beck, Brown, Berchick, et al. (1990).
14. Reiser and Rosen (1985), 91–111.
15. Stern, Mulley and Thibault (1984). Table 3-1 is adapted from this article.
16. Murphy (1975). There is also a high prevalence of alcoholism (23–29 percent) and affective or mood disorders (58–75 percent) in studies of completed suicides. See Rosen (1976a). Also see Murphy and Robins (1967).
17. Mendel (1975), 148.
18. Menninger, Mayman, and Pruyser (1963).
19. Mintz (1971). He cites Gould and his article, "The Phases of Adult Life," for coming up with this creative idea.
20. For information about ECT, I am indebted to Abrams (1988). The common use of mild anesthesia, muscle relaxants, and oxygen therapy allay the feeling of impending doom that is often experienced by patients having ECT, and ensure that the patient will not hurt himself or herself during a convulsion. Another recent innovation is unilateral administration of ECT, that is, applying electrical current to the non-dominant hemisphere of the brain, thus minimizing post-convulsion confusion and temporary memory loss. Although much research has been done, the mechanics of how ECT works are still not completely

understood. One theory holds that the ECT increases neurotransmitter activity, not by increasing neurotransmitter concentrations centrally (which is a competing theory), but by enhancing the sensitivity of the neuroreceptors. Also see Grahame-Smith, Green, and Costain (1978). Whatever specific mechanism accounts for the antidepressant effects produced by ECT, it is clear that often many of the crippling symptoms of major depression are quickly and dramatically reversed.

21. Because ECT has a faster onset time than antidepressant medications, sometimes it is used as an initial treatment for acutely suicidal patients with life-threatening depression.

22. Rush (1990); Feighner (1986); and Feighner, Aden, Fabe, et al. (1983).

One of the newest antidepressants, Zoloft (sertraline), a serotonin reuptake inhibitor related to Prozac (fluoxetine), is a mild stimulant and usually only needs to be taken once in the morning. Zoloft has similar but fewer side effects than Prozac. Zoloft also has a short half-life measured in a few days rather than Prozac's few weeks. Hence it cannot build up to toxic levels in the tissues as Prozac can. Finally, it does not have the controversial association of being linked to suicide that plagues Prozac. Zoloft appears to be a relatively safe antidepressant, i.e., it would be difficult to overdose with this medication, but time will tell. This is also the case with the newest serotonin reuptake inhibitor Paxil (paroxetine).

23. For rapid cyclers, a subgroup of bipolars (about 12 percent) that have four or more episodes of mood disturbances per year, treatment with anticonvulsants, such as Tegretol (carbamazepine), seems to be more effective than treatment with lithium carbonate alone.

24. Rosenthal and Blake (1989).

25. Christensen and Burrows (1990), and Krietsch, Christensen, and White (1988).

26. Frank (1963).

27. Rehm (1981).

28. Beck (1976) has proposed that depression is a result of distorted negative thinking. Cognitive therapy is brief (approximately 12 sessions) and promotes change in the patient through the following mechanisms: recognizing negative thought patterns through self-monitoring; changing patterns of thinking through evaluation and empirical testing of automatic thoughts and silent assumptions; and mastering techniques learned in therapy through the use of homework and everyday practice. Medication is used only as a last resort. Cognitive therapy alone has been found to reduce depression more than Tofranil (imipramine), to have a significant impact on enhancing a patient's self-concept, and to result in a marked reduction of hopelessness. See Rush, Beck, Kovacs, et al. (1982).

29. According to IPT, there are three component processes of depression: (1) symptom formation, (2) social and interpersonal relationships, and (3) personality. Because it is a short-term therapy (typically 12 to 16 sessions), it does not attempt to alter the individual's personality. Instead, its two goals are: (1) to relieve depressive symptoms and increase self-esteem, and (2) to help the patient develop more effective strategies for dealing with social and interpersonal problems. See Arieti and Bemporad (1978); and Klerman, Weissman, Rounsaville, and Chevron (1984).

30. Based on the psychodynamic theories of Freud (1959) and others such as Abraham (1927) and Kohut (1977), short-term analytic psychotherapy (like classical psychoanalysis) operates on the following principles:

    1. Depression represents a problem coping with past and present interpersonal relationships.
    2. Early negative childhood experiences, particularly losses, predispose an individual to depression.
    3. Depression is a result of damaged self-esteem and/or conflict between the ego, superego, and ego ideal, in which rage from childhood conflicts is directed inward toward the self.

Psychoanalytic theory, short-term or long-term, operates on the assumption that patients will use the same coping mechanisms in therapy that they have used in their outside lives, and that, since such mechanisms were learned in significant personal relationships, they are best treated in an interpersonal context. See Strupp, Sandell, Waterhouse, et al. (1982) and Zaiden (1982).

31. Maladjusted people may develop inflated or socially unacceptable objectives of control, resulting from false conclusions about themselves, their experiences, and significant facts in their lives. They may even use means to try to attain their goals that are detrimental to themselves and others. If they should succeed in reaching their goals, which is unlikely, they enjoy only a transient relief at best from their ongoing sense of helplessness. When a conflict arises between themselves and others as a result of these patterns, it often expresses itself in the form of depression. Therapeutically speaking, importance is placed on the belief that the patient's actions have an interpersonal and social meaning and that the patient's maladjustment results from being unable to utilize his or her interpersonal or social experience in an effective manner. See Nikelly (1971).

32. Shneidman (1985).

33. Richman (1986) holds that these two goals may be best accomplished within the framework of the family, "where disturbances in psycholog-

ical integration and social adhesion can best be made up." Family therapy does not necessarily follow any set theory or technique; the procedures used depend upon the therapist and are derived from a wide variety of psychological and sociological schools of thought. They do have the common goal of assisting the identified patient to resolve his or her depression and suicidal intent within the context of the family.

34. These outpatient groups were not restricted to any one therapeutic approach; therefore, they tended to utilize an integrative systems model. These groups tended to be supportive, expressive, analytical (insight-oriented), cognitive, interpersonal, psychoeducational, and they emphasized self-control. The group members had to be in individual psychotherapy and on medication if necessary. One-fifth of the patients had a history of ECT. Using co-therapists as leaders was important because they provided mutual support for this challenging but potentially draining work. See Billings et al. (1974).

35. AA and NA require each member to conform to the same treatment program, which is clearly the major disadvantage of this approach. It is assumed that every member of the group has basically the same problem, so all treatment is directed toward a common goal: immediate and permanent abstinence. It is also directed toward a common plan: the *twelve steps to recovery*. See Alcoholics Anonymous (1987) and Peynot (1985).

36. Unlike other schools of psychotherapy, existential therapy does not try to change a person, nor does it assume that a person is in need of, or even capable of, change. Rather, the aim is to help a person find insight, direction, and meaning in life, as well as methods for dealing with life's difficulties more effectively. See van Deurzen-Smith (1988). Also see Yalom (1980).

37. Frankl (1984).

38. This account is taken from a presentation I made entitled "The Human Side of AIDS," as part of Medical Students Teaching Day, AIDS: Preparing for the 21st Century, University of Rochester School of Medicine, March 19, 1986.

39. Toolery (1978).

40. Koestler (1987).

CHAPTER 4

1. Basler (1953).
2. Menninger, Mayman, and Pruyser (1963).
3. Mill (1960).
4. Cameron (1942).
5. James (1958).

6. Rosen (1975 and 1976b).
7. For quotes in this section, see Jung (1968a), 3–4 and 8–10.
8. Hall (1986), 14–15.
9. Sandner (1987); Sandner and Beebe (1984).
10. Quotes are from Neumann (1969), 137, 138, and 143, respectively.
11. Jung (1968a), 31. To avoid the patriarchal connotations of *Imago Dei*, I prefer the expression Supreme Being.
12. Jung (1969b), 259.
13. Jung (1963), 196–197.
14. Neumann (1959); Edinger (1973).
15. Quotes in this section are from Hall (1983), 28, 39 and Hall (1986), 39.
16. Winnicott (1965).
17. Jung (1968a), 16.
18. Jung (1969a), 309. Early in life the *soul-complex* is part of the child's identity (i.e., manifesting as the innocent child based on the divine child archetype); later the person can become cut off from his or her soul and be depressed and suicidal.
19. Woodman (1982).
20. Jung (1967a), 328.
21. Singer (1973), 333–343.
22. Neumann (1969), 104–105.
23. Kast (1988), 53–67.
24. Neeld (1990).
25. Grof (1972 and 1973).
26. Henderson and Oakes (1971).
27. The survivors of jumps off the Golden Gate Bridge (which can represent both a transformative gate and a bridge connecting two realms—heaven and earth, sky and water) all leaped inward, into the San Francisco Bay, which can be symbolically considered as jumping into the arms of mother. Gold or golden, by the way, symbolizes illumination, harmony, wholeness, and immortality. See Cooper (1982), 74.
28. Maltsberger and Buie (1974).
29. Kris (1952).
30. After utilizing this phrase, I came across a reference to it in Henderson (1984), 16.
31. I am indebted to Sally Parks (1980) for two phrases: "regression in the service of the self" (associated with one's own personal being) and "self-Self axis" (associated with a Supreme Being).
32. Jung (1971), 448–450.
33. Rogers (1977) also used the term self-actualization to express the same concept.
34. Maslow (1970).
35. Woodman (1980).

36. Woodman (1982).
37. Among 200 participants in this type of therapy over 46 months, there were only 10 suicide attempts and one actual suicide, an impressive record for such extremely high-risk persons. Billings, et al. (1974) and Rosen, et al. (1974).
38. Bauer (1982), 72.
39. As shown in Chapters 6 through 9, long-term, in-depth psychotherapy with a chronically depressed or suicidal person focuses on identifying the negative and self-destructive aspects of the ego and the shadow. Only by analyzing these aspects to death can an individual transcend and transform them. No matter how carefully this analytical process is conducted, however, it is never without risk. When a person is committing egocide, he or she is in a precarious and confused state, and there may be risk of suicide.
40. Hillman (1973).
41. Szasz (1963 and 1970).
42. A psychotic patient can go through actual egocide and transformation; there are many successful accounts of this process. For only one of many examples, see Perry (1953).
43. Jung characterizes this as "the regressive restoration of the persona." See Jung (1966a), 163–168.
44. Whitmont (1969), 306–309.
45. Mudd (1990).

CHAPTER 5
1. Neumann (1971).
2. Jung (1966b), 181.
3. Jung (1969a), 134.
4. The best known work in this area was done by Konrad Lorenz, in which goslings during a *critical period* imprinted to Lorenz as if he were the mother goose. See Lorenz (1969).
5. Bowlby (1969 and 1973).
6. Jung (1967a), 328.
7. Lao-tzu (1985), 29.
8. Jung (1971), 425, 460.
9. Jung (1970), 449.
10. Hall (1986), 39.
11. Neumann (1971).
12. Singer (1973).
13. Jung (1969c), 49.
14. Storr (1980), 24–25 and 52.
15. Rosen (1992).
16. Jung (1971), 425–426.

17. James (1958).
18. In addition to the cross and snake, the Archetypal Symbol Inventory (ASI) includes the butterfly (soul) which can also represent psychic transformation as well as the fish, which literally means transformation. Regarding the ASI and discussion of related research, see Rosen, et al. (1991).
19. Henderson and Oakes (1971), 37.
20. Kerenyi (1959).
21. Jung (1968b), 144. Most likely, Jung saw the development of Kundalini yoga as so significant because through discipline the individual was able to control, transcend, and transform shatki (energy and power symbolized as a serpent), which if not confronted and channeled was associated with evil and destructive acts. By way of Kundalini yoga, the individual could allow such energy (and power) to evolve through seven levels from the lowest base levels (which include the sexual and aggressive) to the highest divine level. The white light of the Supreme Being inside and outside the individual is equal at this transpersonal seventh level.
22. For my symbolic interpretations here and throughout the book, see Cirlot (1971); Cooper (1982); and Matthews (1986).
23. Jung (1967b), 282.
24. Henderson and Oakes (1971), 37.
25. Campbell (1968).
26. Miller (1941).
27. Miller (1960).
28. I know it is an almost unbelievable process, but it is true (for example, see Plate I). I suggest that the reader carry out an experiment: Engage in active imagination and see for yourself. First, put yourself in the frame of mind of a three- to five-year-old child. Next, allow yourself to be in a state of reverie, that is, wander in the woods of meditation until you come to the abode of your daydreams, then open the door and paint how you are feeling—letting your creative muse facilitate the process.
29. Despite the fact that the four quadrant picture interpretation method is taught at the C.G. Jung Institute in Zurich, its validity was not found in a recent empirical study, "Picture Interpretation and Jungian Typology," by D.P. Bergeron, D.H. Rosen, R.C. Arnau, and N. Mascaro, *Journal of Analytical Psychology* (2002). Hence, it ought to be used with caution and only in conjunction with other methods. See Furth, G.M. (1988), *The Secret World of Drawings* (Boston: Sigo), and Schavieren, J. (1980), *The Revealing Image* (New York: Routledge).
30. Neumann (1963), 18–23.
31. Beebe (1992).

CHAPTER 6

1. Jacobi (1967), 34.
2. Maduro (1987).
3. For an excellent discussion of the highly unethical and damaging nature of sexual contact between doctor and patient, see Rutter (1989).
4. Young-Eisendrath and Wiedemann (1987).
5. For more discussion of clockwise and counterclockwise spirals, see Cirlot (1971).
6. Jung (1967a), 316; Jung (1969c), 187; Leach (1984), 124–128; and Shepard and Sanders (1985), 56–77, 102–105.
7. Joel Weishaus offered the following thought: Because Rebecca wanted to go into the ministry, the sponge might represent the one Christ was given on the Cross, which, containing vinegar, was a cruel hoax.
8. This statement made me think of what Shengold (1989) describes as "soul murder."
9. Kane (1989).
10. Monick (1987).

CHAPTER 7

1. von Franz (1981).
2. To me Heisenberg's principle of uncertainty means that as you observe something, you change it. Fred Alan Wolf interprets it this way: "To observe is to disturb." See Wolf (1981), 117.
3. Woloy (1990).
4. Years later, Gary related to me in a letter that accepting, embracing, and loving himself was a central issue. As he put it, "Until therapy, I never felt as if a core existed who was 'me' deep down. Before . . . I felt unconnected . . . alien. Loving myself meant a core of me existed and was worthy of loving."
5. This archetype and theme is discussed in two classic works, one older and one newer: see Neumann (1963) and Welldon (1992).
6. Alfred Adler viewed the hermaphrodite as a transformative symbol of psychic development. As cited by Hillman (1983), 100–102.
7. Jung (1968b), 144.
8. de Waal (1989).

CHAPTER 8

1. The essential feature of borderline personality disorder is a pervasive pattern of instability of self-image, interpersonal relationships, and mood, beginning by early adulthood and present in a variety of contexts. These people often have inappropriately intense anger or lack of control of their anger, and they tend to be impulsive, particularly in activities that are potentially self-damaging. Recurrent suicidal threats,

gestures, or behavior and other self-mutilating behavior are common in more severe forms of the disorder. Characteristics of this condition also include marked and persistent identity disturbance, chronic feeling of emptiness, and frantic efforts to avoid real or imagined abandonment. See *DSM-IV*, 650–654.

2. Woodman (1982).
3. This is an example of how a therapist's problem (countertransference) can lead to a sadistic comment that can hurt and even cause a patient to leave therapy.
4. Neumann (1963), 31–32 and 147–208.
5. In contrast to Jung and classical Jungians, I and other Post-Jungians maintain that a woman has an anima or soul. See de Castillejo (1974), 165–182 and Kast (1986), 87–98.
6. Jung (1969a), 69.
7. Neumann (1963), 18.
8. Some theorists claim that Borderline Personality Disorder is strongly associated with gelid maternal rejection. See Ludolyn, Westin, Mosle, et al. (1990).
9. Wadeson (1980) maintains that spirals drawn by patients indicate suicidal states. However, she does not differentiate between destructive (counterclockwise) and constructive (clockwise) spirals, as does Cirlot (1971). I believe this distinction is important and relevant to the egocide and transformation process. In reviewing the drawings in Wadeson's book, the spirals of suicidal patients are, in fact, predominantly counterclockwise.
10. Jung (1967a), 207, 251.
11. Te Paske (1982), 70–100.
12. The serpent is associated with transformation, androgyny, creativity, generativity, and wisdom, as well as healing.
13. Of course, this has transference implications as well. Sharon has the opportunity to work through past conflicts that are projected on to me. For example, Sharon can resolve her father-daughter complex in therapy by gradually withdrawing the father projection off me, which then promotes an egalitarian relationship.
14. I interpreted this to mean that she detested being dependent on me, and like an adolescent she wanted to sever the life line and sink or swim on her own. This comment also foretells her termination with me and her desire to see a woman therapist (the projected identification outside of the healthy woman inside, her true self).
15. Woloy (1990).
16. Synchronicity is a meaningful coincidence. See Jung (1969a), 417–519.
17. Subsequently, I came across a picture of Ishtar (Mesopotamian goddess of fertility and love, also a warrior goddess, circa 2000 B.C.) standing

on the back of a lion, as if celebrating her return from the descent to the land of no return. See Cavendish (1984), 89.

18. It was Sharon's healing destiny to run with the wolves and most surely that is why Clarissa Estés's book strikes a familiar chord with so many, especially women. See Estés (1992).

CHAPTER 9

1. Today I would try one of the new serotonin reuptake inhibitor antidepressants, such as Zoloft or Paxil.

2. Te Paske (1982), 111–115.

3. Illustrated in Table 4-2 as "regression in the service of the positive ego," it is actually "regression in the service of the ego."

4. Wadeson (1980), 49–50 and 98–101.

5. Meier (1989).

6. Jung (1961), 117.

7. It is interesting that Paul himself came up with this term, which is a term that James Hillman uses for similar kinds of activities. See Hillman (1983), 49.

8. Given the repeating theme of homosexual acts, specifically anal intercourse (or here as rape), I wondered if Paul had been sexually abused as a boy. If not physical incest, then for sure psychological.

CHAPTER 10

1. As noted before, my interpretation of the spiral differs from that of Harriet Wadeson, who associates it with suicide, and resembles that of Jung, who associates it with the psyche's innate activity. Andrew Samuels, in a concept compatible to mine, visualizes the spiral as a living symbol for psychological development: "In the spiral, the same elements interact with each other but at a different place with each repetition in the ascent [or descent]. . . . The spiral also illustrates the way in which components of the psyche are operated upon by environmental demands." Samuels (1985), 115. Also see Wadeson (1980), 49–50 and 98–101; Jung (1968b), 28, 179–180, and 217.

2. Erikson (1982).

3. Winnicott (1965).

4. Mahler, Pine and Bergman (1975).

5. Erikson (1959 and 1982).

6. Toffler (1971).

7. In psychosis the person's ego is not functioning; therefore he or she loses contact with reality. By maintaining that adolescence is a normal psychosis, Anna Freud is suggesting that during this time ego death is developmentally the norm.

8. Neumann (1969), 104–105.

9. Jung (1967a), 266 and 437.
10. Jung provides numerous examples of the animus as, or with, the wind, which is a fertilizing and generating agent. See Jung (1967a), 225.
11. Jung (1967b), 331.
12. Alvarez (1972), 3–41.
13. Jung (1967a), 293.
14. Jung (1970), 82.
15. That is why the 1992 Earth Summit in Rio de Janeiro was such an important event, if we think of it as a form of multicultural group therapy and Whole Human Family therapy. It will take a long time for all the world's countries to surrender to the eminent goal of saving ourselves and mother earth. Nevertheless, it is hopeful that even as this book was being written, the process was under way!
16. Wolman (1976), 77–94.
17. Durkheim (1951) and Meštrović (1992).
18. Wolman, loc. cit.
19. Wilhelm (1962).

EPILOGUE
1. Frankl (1984), 84, 87–88, 90–91.
2. Buber (1953), 5.
3. Tillich (1952), 46.

BIBLIOGRAPHY

Abraham, K. 1927. Notes on the Psycho-Analytic Investigation and Treatment of Manic-Depressive Insanity and Allied Conditions. *Selected Papers on Psycho-Analysis*. London: Hogarth Press.

Abrams, R. 1988. *Electroconvulsive Therapy*. Oxford: Oxford University Press.

Ader, R., ed. 1981. *Psychoneuroimmunology*. New York: Academic Press.

Alcoholics Anonymous. 1987. *The Twelve Steps of Alcoholics Anonymous*. New York: Harper/Hazelden.

Alvarez, A. 1972. *The Savage God: A Study of Suicide*. New York: Random House.

Arieti, S., and J. Bemporad. 1978. *Severe and Mild Depression*. New York: Basic Books.

Bart, P. 1974. *Depression: A Sociological Theory*. In Roman and Trice (1974).

Basler, R. P., ed. 1953. *The Collected Works of Abraham Lincoln*, Vol. 1. New Brunswick, NJ: Rutgers University Press.

Bauer, J. 1982. *Alcoholism and Women: The Background and the Psychology*. Toronto: Inner City Books.

Beck, A.T. 1972. *Depression: Causes and Treatment*. Philadelphia: University of Pennsylvania Press.

———. 1976. *Cognitive Therapy and Emotional Disorders*. New York: International Universities Press.

Beck, A.T. and M. Kovacs. 1975. Hopelessness and Suicidal Behavior: An Overview. *Journal of the American Medical Association* 234: 1146–1150.

Beck, A.T., G. Brown, R.J. Berchick, et al. 1990. Relationship Between Hopelessness and Ultimate Suicide: A Replication with Psychiatric Outpatients. *American Journal of Psychiatry* 147: 190–195.

Beebe, J. 1992. *Integrity in Depth*. College Station, TX: Texas A&M University Press.

Billings, J.H., D.H. Rosen, C. Asimos, and J. Motto. 1974. Observations on Long-term Group Therapy with Suicidal and Depressed Persons. *Life-Threatening Behavior* 4: 160–170.

Bloch, E. 1959. *Das Prinzip Hoffnung*. Frankfurt: Suhrkamp.

Bonjean, C.M. and D.J. Foss, eds. 1990. *Mental Health Research in Texas; Retrospect and Prospect*. Austin, TX: Hogg Foundation.

Bowlby, J. 1969. *Attachment and Loss: Attachment*. Vol. I. New York: Basic Books.

———. 1973. *Attachment and Loss: Separation*. Vol. II. New York: Basic Books.

Buber, M. 1953. *Good and Evil*. New York: Charles Scribner's Sons.

Cameron, N. 1942. *William James*. Madison: University of Wisconsin Press.

Cavendish, R. 1984. *An Illustrated Encyclopedia of Mythology*. New York: Crescent Books.

Cavener, J.O., ed. 1985. *Psychiatry*, Vol. 1. Philadelphia: J.B. Lippincott.

Chivian, M.O., J.P. Robinson, J.R.H. Tudge, et al. 1988. American and Soviet Teenagers' Concerns About Nuclear War and the Future. *New England Journal of Medicine* 319: 407–413.

Christensen, L. and R. Burrows. 1990. Dietary Treatment of Depression. *Behavior Therapy* 21: 183–189.

Cirlot, J.E. 1971. *A Dictionary of Symbols*. New York: Philosophical Library.

Cooper, J.C. 1982. *An Illustrated Encyclopedia of Traditional Symbols*. London: Thames and Hudson.

Cousins, N. 1975. *Anatomy of an Illness*. New York: W.W. Norton.

———. 1989. *Head First: The Biology of Hope*. New York: E. P. Dutton.

de Castillejo, I.C. 1974. *Knowing Woman: A Feminine Psychology*. New York: Harper Colophon Books.

de Waal, F. 1989. *Peacemaking Among Primates*. Cambridge, MA: Harvard University Press.

Diagnostic and Statistical Manual of Mental Disorders 1994, 4th edition (*DSM-IV*). Washington, D.C.: American Psychiatric Association.

Dorpat, T.L. and H.S. Ripley. 1960. A Study of Suicide in the Seattle Area. *Comprehensive Psychiatry* 1: 349–359.

Durkheim, E. 1951, (2nd edition, 1930), trans. J.A. Spaulding and G. Simpson. *Suicide*. Glencoe, IL: Free Press.

Edinger, E.F. 1973. *Ego and Archetype: Individuation and the Religious Function of the Psyche*. Baltimore: Penguin Books.

Ellis, H. 1923. *The Dance of Life*. Boston: Houghton Mifflin.

Engel, G.L. 1961. Is Grief a Disease?: Challenge for Medical Research. *Psychosomatic Medicine* 23: 18–22.

————. 1962. Anxiety and Depression—Withdrawal: The Primary Affects of Unpleasure. *International Journal of Psycho-Analysis* 43: 89–97.

————. 1977. The Need for a New Medical Model: A Challenge for Biomedicine. *Science* 196, 129–136.

Erikson, E. 1959. *Identity and the Life Cycle*. Psychological Issues Monograph. Vol. I. New York: International Universities Press.

————. 1982. *The Life Cycle Completed: A Review*. New York: W. W. Norton.

Estés, C.P. 1992. *Women Who Run With the Wolves*. New York: Ballantine Books.

Farberow, N.L. and E.S. Shneidman, eds. 1961. *The Cry for Help*. New York: McGraw-Hill.

Feighner, J.P. 1986. The New Generation of Antidepressants. In Rush and Altshuler (1986), 205–225.

Feighner, J.P., C.G. Aden, L.F. Fabe, et al. 1983. Comparison of Alprazolam, Imipramine and Placebo in the Treatment of Depression. *Journal of the American Medical Association* 249: 3057–3064.

Ferster, C.B. 1973. A Functional Analysis of Depression. *American Psychologist* 16: 857–870.

Flach, F.F. and S.C. Drghi, eds. 1975. *The Nature and Treatment of Depression*. New York: John Wiley & Sons.

Ford, B. and C. Chase. 1988. *Betty: A Glad Awakening*. New York: Jove Books.

Frank, J.D. 1963. *Persuasion and Healing: A Comparative Study of Psychotherapy*. New York: Schocken Books.

————. 1974. The Restoration of Morale. *American Journal of Psychiatry* 131: 271–274.

————. 1975. The Faith That Heals. *Johns Hopkins Medical Journal* 137: 127–131.

Frankl, V.E. 1984, 3rd edition. *Man's Search for Meaning*. New York: Simon & Schuster.

French, T.M. 1952. *The Integration of Behavior*. Chicago: University of Chicago Press.

Freud, S. 1959. Mourning and Melancholia. *Collected Papers*, Vol. 4. New York: Basic Books.

Fulgham, R. 1988. *All I Really Need to Know I Learned in Kindergarten*. New York: Ballantine Books.

Gershon, E.S., W.H. Berrettini, and L.R. Goldin. 1989. Mood Disorders: Genetic Aspects. In Kaplan and Sadock (1989), 879–887.

Gershon, E.S., J. Hamovit, J.J. Guroff, et al. 1982. A Family Study of Schizoaffective, Bipolar I, Bipolar II, Unipolar, and Normal Control Probands. *Archives of General Psychiatry* 39: 1157–1167.

Gibbs, N. 1990. Dr. Death's Suicide Machine. *Time,* June 18, 69–70.

Gilbert, P. 1984. *Depression: From Psychology to Brain State.* London: Lawrence Erlbaum.

Goethe, J.W., trans. B.Q. Morgan. 1957. *The Sufferings of Young Werther.* New York: Frederick Ungar.

Goldman, A. 1990. Thirteen Years After the Death of Elvis Presley New Evidence Points to an Inescapable Conclusion: Suicide. *Life* (cover story), June, 95–104.

Gould, M.S. and D. Shaffer. 1986. The Impact of Suicide in Television Movies: Evidence of Imitation. *New England Journal of Medicine* 315: 690–694.

Grahame-Smith, D.G., A.R. Green, and D.W. Costain. 1978. Mechanism of the Antidepressant Effect of Electroconvulsive Therapy. *Lancet* 1: 254–256.

Grof, S. 1972. Varieties of Transpersonal Experiences: Observations from LSD Psychotherapy. *Journal of Transpersonal Psychology* 4: 45–80.

––––––. 1973. Theoretical and Empirical Basis of Transpersonal Psychology and Psychotherapy: Observations from LSD Research. *Journal of Transpersonal Psychology* 1: 15–53.

Gut, E. 1989. *Productive and Unproductive Depression: Success or Failure of a Vital Process.* New York: Basic Books.

Hall, J.A. 1983. *Jungian Dream Interpretation: A Handbook of Theory and Practice.* Toronto: Inner City Books.

––––––. 1986. *The Jungian Experience: Analysis and Individuation.* Toronto: Inner City Books.

Henderson, J.L. 1984. Reflections on the History and Practice of Jungian Analysis. In Stein (1984).

Henderson, J.L. and M. Oakes. 1971. *The Wisdom of the Serpent: Myths of Death, Rebirth and Resurrection.* New York: Collier Books.

Hillman, J. 1973. *Suicide and the Soul.* New York: Harper Colophon Books.

––––––. 1983. *Healing Fiction.* Barrytown, NY: Station Hill Press.

Hirschfeld, R.M.A. and C.K. Cross. 1982. Epidemiology of Affective Disorders: Psychosocial Risk Factors. *Archives of General Psychiatry* 39: 35–46.

Humphry, D. 1991. *Final Exit: The Practicalities of Self-Deliverance and Assisted Suicide for the Dying.* New York: Carol/Hemlock Society.

Jackson, S.W. 1986. *Melancholia and Depression: From Hippocratic Times to Modern Times.* New Haven: Yale University Press.

Jacobi, J. 1967. *The Way to Individuation.* New York: Harcourt, Brace & World.

Jaffe, A. 1978. *Apparitions: An Archetypal Approach to Death, Dreams, and Ghosts.* Irving, TX: Spring Publications.

James, W. 1958. *The Varieties of Religious Experience*. New York: New American Library (A Mentor Book).

Jarrett, R.B. and A.J. Rush. 1985. Psychotherapeutic Approaches for Depression. In Cavener (1985), 1–35.

Jung, C.G. 1961. *Freud and Psychoanalysis. Collected Works [CW]*. Vol. 4. Eds. Read, H., M. Fordham, G. Adler, and W. McGuire, Trans. R.F.C. Hull. Princeton, NJ: Princeton University Press (Jung's publisher unless otherwise stated).

———. 1963. Ed. Jaffe, A. *Memories, Dreams, Reflections*. New York: Pantheon.

———. 1966a. *Two Essays on Analytical Psychology. CW*. Vol. 7.

———. 1966b. *The Practice of Psychotherapy. CW*. Vol. 16.

———. 1967a. *Symbols of Transformation. CW*. Vol. 5.

———. 1967b. *Alchemical Studies. CW*. Vol. 13.

———. 1968a. *Aion: Researches into the Phenomenology of the Self. CW*. Vol. 9,II.

———. 1968b. *Psychology and Alchemy. CW*. Vol. 12.

———. 1969a. *The Structure and Dynamics of the Psyche. CW*. Vol. 8.

———. 1969b. *Psychology and Religion: East and West. CW*. Vol. 11.

———. 1969c. *The Archetypes and the Collective Unconscious. CW*. Vol. 9I.

———. 1970. *Civilization in Transition. CW*. Vol. 10.

———. 1971. *Psychological Types. CW*. Vol. 6.

———. 1973. *C.G. Jung Letters*. Vol. I. Eds. Hull, R.F.C., H.G. Adler, and A. Jaffe.

———. 1975. *C.G. Jung Letters*. Vol. II. eds. (same as above).

Kane, E. 1989. *Recovering from Incest: Imagination and the Healing Process*. Boston: Sigo Press.

Kaplan, H.I. and B.J. Sadock, eds. 1989. *Comprehensive Textbook of Psychiatry*. Baltimore: Williams & Wilkins.

Kast, V. 1986. Trans. B. Matthews. *The Nature of Loving: Patterns of Human Relationship*. Wilmette, IL: Chiron Publications.

———. 1988. Trans. D. Dachler and F. Cairns. *A Time to Mourn: Growing Through the Grief Process*. Einsiedeln, Switzerland: Daimon Verlag.

———. 1990. Trans. D. Whitcher. The Threat of Suicide. *The Creative Leap*. Wilmette, IL: Chiron Publications, 31–49.

———. 1991. Trans. D. Whitcher. *Joy, Inspiration and Hope*. College Station, TX: Texas A&M University Press.

Kerenyi, C. 1959. *Asklepios: Archetypal Image of the Physician's Existence*. New York: Pantheon.

Kiev, A. 1972. *Transcultural Psychiatry*. Harmondsworth, England: Penguin Books.

Klein, D.F. and R.G. Gittelman-Klein, eds. 1976. *Progress in Psychiatric Drug Treatment*. Vol. 2. New York: Brunner/Mazel.

Klerman, G.L., M.M. Weissman, B.J. Rounsaville, and R.S. Chevron, eds. 1984. *Interpersonal Psychotherapy of Depression*. New York: Basic Books.

Klopfer, B. 1961. Suicide: The Jungian Point of View. In Farberow and Shneidman (1961), 193–210.

Koestler, A. 1987. *The Act of Creation: A Study of the Conscious and Unconscious in Science and Art*. New York: Dell.

Kohon, G., ed. 1986. *The British School of Psychoanalysis: The Independent Tradition*. New Haven: Yale University Press.

Kohut, H. 1977. *The Restoration of the Self*. New York: International Universities Press.

Kovacs, M. and A.T. Beck. 1978. Maladaptive Cognitive Structures in Depression. *American Journal of Psychiatry* 135: 525–533.

Krietsch, K., L. Christensen, and B. White. 1988. Prevalence, Presenting Symptoms, and Psychological Characteristics of Individuals Experiencing Diet-Related Mood Disturbance. *Behavior Therapy* 19: 593–604.

Kris, E. 1952. *Psychoanalytic Explorations in Art*. New York: International Universities Press.

Lao-tzu, 1985. *Tao Te Ching: The Book of Meaning and Life*. London: Arkana.

Leach, M., ed. 1984. *Funk and Wagnall's Standard Dictionary of Folklore, Mythology, Legend*. San Francisco: Harper & Row.

Lommel, A. 1967. *Shamanism: The Beginnings of Art*. New York: McGraw-Hill.

Lorenz, K.Z. 1969. Innate Basis of Learning. In Pribram (1969), 12–93.

Ludolyn, P.S., D. Westin, B. Mosle, et al. 1990. The Borderline Diagnosis in Adolescents; Symptoms and Developmental History. *American Journal of Psychiatry* 147: 470–475.

Maduro, R.J. 1987. The Initial Dream and Analyzability in Beginning Analysis. *Journal of Analytical Psychology* 32: 199–226.

Mahdi, L., S. Foster, and M.L. Little, eds. 1987. *Betwixt and Between: Patterns of Masculine and Feminine Initiation*. La Salle, IL: Open Court.

Mahler, M., F. Pine, and A. Bergman. 1975. *The Psychological Birth of the Human Infant: Symbiosis and Individuation*. New York: Basic Books.

Maltsberger, M.T. and D.H. Buie. 1974. Countertransference Hate in the Treatment of Suicidal Patients. *Archives of General Psychiatry* 30: 625–633.

Maslow, A. 1968, 2nd edition. *Toward a Psychology of Being*. New York: Van Nostrand Reinhold.

———. 1970. *Motivation and Personality*. New York: Harper & Row.

————. 1980. A Theory of Metamotivation: The Biological Rooting of the Value-Life. In Walsh and Vaughan (1980), 121–131.

Matthews, B., trans. 1986. *The Herder Symbol Dictionary: Symbols from Art, Archaeology, Mythology, Literature and Religion*. Wilmette, IL: Chiron Publications.

McAfee, J. 1983. Suicide and the False Self. In *Cave of the Mirror*. Unpublished thesis. C.G. Jung Institute (Zurich).

Meier, C.A. 1989. *Ancient Incubation and Modern Psychotherapy*. Einsiedeln, Switzerland: Daimon Verlag.

Mendel, W.M. 1975. *Supportive Care: Theory and Technique*. Los Angeles: Mara Books.

Menninger, K. 1938. *Man Against Himself*. New York: Harcourt, Brace, & World.

Menninger, K., M. Mayman, and P. Pruyser. 1967. *The Vital Balance: The Life Process in Mental Health and Illness*. New York: The Viking Press.

Meštrović, S.G. 1992. *Durkheim and Postmodern Culture*. Hawthorne, NY: Aldine de Gruyter.

Mill, J.S. 1960. *Autobiography*. New York: Columbia University Press.

Miller, H. 1941. *The Colossus of Maroussi*. New York: New Directions.

————. 1960. *To Paint Is to Love Again*. Alhambra, CA: Cambria Books.

Mintz, R.S. 1971. Basic Considerations in the Psychotherapy of the Depressed Suicidal Patient. *American Journal of Psychotherapy* 25: 56–73.

Mishara, B.L., D.H. Baker, and T.T. Mishara. 1976. The Frequency of Suicide Attempts: A Retrospective Approach Applied to College Students. *American Journal of Psychiatry* 133: 841–844.

Monick, E. 1987. *Phallos: Sacred Image of the Masculine*. Toronto: Inner City Books.

Morris, J.B. and A.T. Beck. 1976. The Efficacy of Antidepressant Drugs. In Klein and Gittelman-Klein (1976).

Motto, J. 1975. The Recognition and Management of the Suicidal Patient. In Flach and Drghi, eds. (1975), 229–255.

Mudd, P. 1990. The Dark Self: Death as a Transferential Factor. *Journal of Analytical Psychology* 35: 125–141.

Murphy, G.E. 1975. The Physician's Responsibility for Suicide. Parts I and II. *Annals of Internal Medicine* 82: 301–309.

Murphy, G.E. and E. Robins. 1967. Social Factors in Suicide. *Journal of the American Medical Association* 199: 303–308.

Neeld, E.H. 1990. *Seven Choices: Taking the Steps to New Life After Losing Someone You Love*. New York: Clarkson N. Potter.

Neumann, E. 1959. The Significance of the Genetic Aspect for Analytical Psychology. *Journal of Analytical Psychology* 4: 125–138.

————. 1963. *The Great Mother: An Analysis of the Archetype*. Princeton, NJ: Princeton University Press.

————. 1969. Trans. E. Rolfe. *Depth Psychology and a New Ethic*. New York: G. P. Putnam's Sons.

————. 1971. *Art and the Creative Unconscious*. Princeton, NJ: Princeton University Press.

Nikelly, A.G. 1971. *Techniques in Behavioral Change: Application of Adlerian Theory*. Springfield, IL: Charles C. Thomas, 21–32.

Noyes, R. 1968. The Taboo of Suicide. *Psychiatry* 31: 173–183.

Odajnyk, V.W. 1983. Jung's Contribution to the Understanding of the Meaning of Depression. *Quadrant* 16: 45–61.

Parks, S. 1980. *The Puer Aeternus and the Narcissistic Personality—Kindred Spirits*. Unpublished thesis. The Inter-Regional Society of Jungian Analysts.

Paykel, E.S., J.K. Myers, M.M. Dienelt, et al. 1969. Life Events and Depression: A Controlled Study. *Archives of General Psychiatry* 21: 753–760.

Peck, M.L., N.L. Farberow, and R.E. Litman. 1985. *Youth Suicide*. New York: Springer.

Peynot, M. 1985. Narcotics Anonymous: Its History, Structure and Approach. *International Journal of Addiction* 26: 1509–1523.

Perry, J.W. 1953. *The Self in the Psychotic Process*. Berkeley: University of California Press.

Phillips, D.P. 1974. The Influence of Suggestion on Suicide: Substantive and Theoretical Applications of the Werther Effect. *American Sociological Review* 39: 340–354.

Phillips, D.P. and L.L. Caratensen. 1986. Clustering of Teenage Suicides After Television News Stories About Suicide. *New England Journal of Medicine* 315: 685–689.

Pribram, K.H., ed. 1969. *On the Biology of Learning*. New York: Harcourt, Brace & World.

Quill, T.E. 1991. Death and Dignity: A Case of Individualized Decision Making. *New England Journal of Medicine* 324: 691–694.

Regier, D.A., R.M.A. Hirschfeld, F.K. Goodwin, et al. 1988. The NIMH Depression Awareness, Recognition, and Treatment Program: Structure, Aims, and Scientific Basis. *American Journal of Psychiatry* 145: 1351–1359.

Rehm, L.P. 1981. *Behavior Therapy for Depression*. New York: Academic Press.

Reiser, D.E. and D.H. Rosen. 1985. *Medicine as a Human Experience*. Rockville, MD: Aspen Publishers.

Richman, J. 1986. *Family Therapy for Suicidal People*. New York: Springer.

Roman, P. and H. Trice, eds. 1974. *Explorations in Psychiatric Sociology*. Philadelphia: F.A. Davis.

Rogers, C.R. 1961. *On Becoming a Person*. Boston: Houghton Mifflin.

————. 1977. *Carl Rogers on Personal Power.* New York: Delacorte.

Rosen, D.H. 1970. The Serious Suicide Attempt: Epidemiological and Follow-up Study of 886 Patients. *American Journal of Psychiatry* 127: 764–770.

————. 1973. Physician, Heal Thyself. *Clinical Medicine* 80: 25–27.

————. 1975. Suicide Survivors: A Follow-up Study of Persons Who Survived Jumping from the Golden Gate and San Francisco–Oakland Bay Bridges. *Western Journal of Medicine* 122: 289–294.

————. 1976a. The Serious Suicide Attempt: Five Year Follow-up Study of 886 Patients. *Journal of the American Medical Association* 235: 2105–2109.

————. 1976b. Suicide Survivors: Psychotherapeutic Implications of Egocide. *Suicide and Life-Threatening Behavior* 6: 209–215.

————. 1977. The Pursuit of One's Own Healing. *American Journal of Psychoanalysis* 37: 37–41.

————. 1987. Casualties of the Health Care System: Patients Depressed by Medicine's "Moral Dilemmas." *Pharos* 50: 19–20.

————. 1989. Modern Medicine and the Nature of the Healing Process. *Humane Medicine: A Journal of the Art and Science of Medicine* 5: 18–23.

————. 1992. Inborn Basis for the Healing Doctor-Patient Relationship. *Pharos* 55: 17–21.

Rosen, D.H., C. Asimos, J.A. Motto, and J.H. Billings. 1974. Group Psychotherapy with a Homogenous Group of Suicidal Persons. In Uchtenhagen, Battegay, and Friedman (1974), 201–212.

Rosen, D.H., S. M. Smith, H.L. Huston, and G. Gonzalez. 1991. Empirical Study of Associations Between Symbols and Their Meanings: Evidence of Collective Unconscious (Archetypal) Memory. *Journal of Analytical Psychology* 36: 211–228.

Rosenthal, E. and M.C. Blake, eds. 1989. *Seasonal Affective Disorders and Phototherapy.* New York: Guilford Press.

Rush, A.J., ed. 1982. *Short-term Psychotherapies for Depression.* New York: Guilford Press.

————. 1990. Recent Advances in Mood Disorders Research. In Bonjean and Foss (1990), 61–79.

Rush, A.J. and K. Altshuler, eds. 1986. *Depression: Basic Mechanism, Diagnosis and Treatment.* New York: Guilford Press.

Rush, A.J., A.T. Beck, M. Kovacs, et al. 1982. Comparison of the Effects of Cognitive Therapy and Pharmacotherapy on Hopelessness and Self-concept. *American Journal of Psychiatry* 139: 862–866.

Rutter, P. 1989. *Sex in the Forbidden Zone.* Los Angeles: J.P. Tarcher. (Revised edition in paperback, 1991, New York: Fawcett).

Samuels, A. 1985. *Jung and the Post-Jungians.* London: Routledge.

Sandner, D.F. 1987. The Split Shadow and the Father-Son Relationship. In Mahdi, Foster, and Little (1987), 175–188.

Sandner. D.F. and J.A. Beebe. 1984. Psychopathology and Analysis. In Stein (1984), 294–334.

Schildkraut, J.J., A.I. Green, and J.J. Mooney. 1989. Mood Disorders: Biochemical Aspects. In Kaplan and Sadock (1989), 868–879.

Schmale, A.H. 1973. Adaptive Role of Depression in Health and Disease. In Scott and Senay (1973), 187–214.

Schuckit, M.A. and M.G. Montiero. 1988. Alcoholism, Anxiety and Depression. *British Journal of Addiction* 83: 1373–1380.

Schur, M. 1972. *Freud: Living and Dying.* New York: International Universities Press, 528–529.

Scott, J.P. and E.C. Senay, eds. 1973. *Separation and Depression: Clinical and Research Aspects.* Washington, D.C.: American Association for the Advancement of Science.

Shengold, L. 1989. *Soul Murder: The Effects of Childhood Abuse and Deprivation.* New Haven: Yale University Press.

Shepard, P. and B. Sanders. 1985. *The Sacred Paw: The Bear in Nature, Myth, and Literature.* New York: Viking.

Shneidman, E.S. 1985. *Definition of Suicide.* New York: John Wiley & Sons.

Singer, J. 1973. *Boundaries of the Soul: The Practice of Jung's Psychology.* New York: Doubleday.

Stein, M., ed. 1984. *Jungian Analysis.* Boston: Shambhala.

Steinberg, W. 1984. Depression: Some Clinical and Theoretical Observations. *Quadrant* 17: 7–22.

————. 1989. Depression: A Discussion of Jung's Ideas. *Journal of Analytical Psychology* 34: 339–352.

Stengel, E. 1973. *Suicide and Attempted Suicide.* Harmondsworth, England.

Stephen, B. 1972. Alvarez: Life Is the Only Argument Against Suicide. *San Francisco Chronicle,* May 22, p. 18.

Stern, T., A.G. Mulley, and G.E. Thibault. 1984. Life-threatening Drug Overdose: Precipitants and Prognosis. *Journal of the American Medical Association* 251: 1983–1988.

Stevens, A. 1983. *Archetypes: A Natural History of the Self.* New York: Quill.

————. 1993. *The Two Million-Year-Old Self.* College Station, TX: Texas A&M University Press.

Storr, A. 1980. *The Art of Psychotherapy.* New York: Methuen.

————. 1989. *Solitude: A Return to Self.* New York: Ballantine Books.

Strupp, H.H., J.A. Sandell, G.J. Waterhouse, et al. 1982. Psychodynamic Therapy: Theory and Research. In Rush (1982), 215–250.

Styron, W. 1990. *Darkness Visible.* New York: Random House.

Szasz, T.S. 1963. *Law, Liberty, and Psychiatry: An Inquiry into the Social Uses of Mental Health Practices.* New York: MacMillan.

———. 1970. *The Manufacture of Madness: A Comparative Study of the Inquisition and the Mental Health Movement.* New York: Dell.

Tabachnick, N. 1973. Creative Suicidal Crises. *Archives of General Psychiatry* 29: 258–263.

Te Paske, B.A. 1982. *Rape and Ritual: A Psychological Study.* Toronto: Inner City Books.

Tillich, P. 1952. *The Courage To Be.* New Haven: Yale University Press.

Toffler, A. 1971. *Future Shock.* New York: Bantam Books.

Toolery, K.M. 1978. The Remembrance of Things Past: On the Collection and Recollection of Ingredients Useful in the Treatment of Disorders Resulting from Unhappiness, Rootlessness, and the Fears of Things to Come. *American Journal of Orthopsychiatry* 48: 174–182.

Uchtenhagen, A., R. Battegay, and A. Friedman, eds. 1974. *Group Therapy and Social Environment.* Bern: Verlag Hans Huber.

van Deurzen-Smith, E. 1988. *Existential Counseling in Practice.* London: Sage Publications.

von Bertalanffy, L. 1968. *General Systems Theory.* New York: George Braziller.

von Franz, M.L. 1978. *Interpretation of Fairy Tales: An Introduction to the Psychology of Fairy Tales.* Irving, TX: Spring Publications.

———. 1981. *Puer Aeternus: A Psychological Study of the Adult Struggle with the Paradise of Childhood.* Santa Monica (now Boston): Sigo Press.

Wadeson, H. 1980. *Art Psychotherapy.* New York: John Wiley & Sons.

Walsh, R.N. and F. Vaughan, eds. 1980. *Beyond Ego: Transpersonal Dimensions in Psychology.* Los Angeles: J.P. Tarcher.

Wehr, T.A. and N.E. Rosenthal. 1989. Seasonality and Affective Illness. *American Journal of Psychiatry* 146: 829–839.

Weishaus, J., ed. 1974. *Bits & Snatches: The Selected Work of Sam Thomas.* Brooklyn: White Rose Press.

Weissman, M.M., K.K. Kidd, and B.A. Prusoff. 1982. Variability in Rates of Affective Disorders in Relatives of Depressed and Normal Probands. *Archives of General Psychiatry* 39: 1397–1403.

Welldon, E.V. 1992. *Mother, Madonna, Whore: Idealization and Denigration of Motherhood.* New York: Guilford Press.

Wheelwright, J.H. 1987. Old Age and Death. In Mahdi, Foster, and Little (1987), 389–411.

Whitmont, E. 1969. *The Symbolic Quest.* New York: G.P. Putnam's Sons.

Wilber, K. 1980. A Developmental Model of Consciousness. In Walsh and Vaughan (1980), 99–114.

Wilhelm, R., trans. and ed. 1962. *The Secret of the Golden Flower: A Chinese Book of Life* (with commentary by C.G. Jung). San Diego: Harcourt, Brace, Jovanovich.

Winnicott, D.W. 1958. *Collected Papers: Through Pediatrics to Psychoanalysis.* New York: Basic Books.

————. 1965. *The Maturational Process and the Facilitating Environment.* New York: International Universities Press.

————. 1971. *Playing and Reality.* London: Tavistock.

————. 1986. Fear of Breakdown. In Kohon (1986), 173–182.

Wolman, B.B. 1976. The Anticulture of Suicide. In Wolman (1976), 77–94.

————. ed. 1976. *Between Survival and Suicide.* New York: Gardner Press.

Woodman, M. 1980. *The Owl Was a Baker's Daughter: Obesity, Anorexia Nervosa and the Depressed Feminine.* Toronto: Inner City Books.

————. 1982. *Addiction to Perfection: The Still Unravished Bride.* Toronto: Inner City Books.

————. 1985. *The Pregnant Virgin: A Process of Psychological Transformation.* Toronto: Inner City Books.

Wolf, F.A. 1981. *Taking the Quantum Leap.* San Francisco: Harper & Row.

Woloy, E.M. 1990. *The Symbol of the Dog in the Human Psyche.* Wilmette, IL: Chiron Publications.

Yalom, I.D. 1980. *Existential Psychotherapy.* New York: Basic Books.

Young-Eisendrath, P. and F. Wiedemann. 1987. *Female Authority: Empowering Women Through Psychotherapy.* New York: Guilford Press.

Zaiden, J. 1982. Psychodynamic Therapy: Clinical Application. In Rush (1982), 251–310.

Index

Photo by Diane Walsh

DAVID H. ROSEN, M.D. is a psychiatrist and Jungian analyst who holds the only American full professorship in Jungian psychology at Texas A&M University, where he is also professor of psychiatry and behavioral science and professor of humanities in medicine. David Rosen is the author of several books, including *The Tao of Jung: The Way of Integrity, Medicine as a Human Experience* (with David Reiser), *Evolution of the Psyche* (with Michael Luebbert) and *The Tao of Elvis*. He conducts lectures and workshops and lives in College Station, Texas. Readers may contact the author at dhr@psych.tamu.edu.